# "The Murderers" and "The Hydra"

## TWO CLASSIC ADVENTURES OF

### by Walter B. Gibson
### writing as Maxwell Grant

**Foreword by Gahan Wilson**

with New Historical Essays by
Anthony Tollin and Will Murray

**Published by Sanctum Productions for**
## NOSTALGIA VENTURES, INC.
P.O. Box 231183; Encinitas, CA 92023-1183

Copyright © 1938, 1942 by Street & Smith Publications, Inc.
Copyright © renewed 1965, 1969 by The Condé Nast Publications, Inc.
All rights reserved.

*The Shadow Volume 4* copyright © 2007 by Sanctum Productions/ Nostalgia Ventures, Inc.

The Shadow copyright © 2007 Advance Magazine Publishers Inc./The Condé Nast Publications. "The Shadow" and the phrase "Who knows what evil lurks in the hearts of men?" are registered trademarks of Advance Magazine Publishers Inc. d/b/a The Condé Nast Publications. The phrases "The Shadow Knows" and "The weed of crime bears bitter fruit" are trademarks owned by Advance Magazine Publishers Inc. d/b/a The Condé Nast Publications.

"Listening to The Shadow Laugh" copyright © 2007 by Gahan Wilson. Cartoon © 1976 by Gahan Wilson.
"Spotlight on The Shadow: On the Air," "From Out of the Shadows" and "A Tale of Two Cranstons" copyright © 2007 by Anthony Tollin.
"Introducing Margo Lane" copyright © 2007 by Will Murray.

This Nostalgia Ventures edition is an unabridged republication of the text and illustrations of two stories from *The Shadow Magazine,* as originally published by Street & Smith Publications, Inc., N.Y.: *The Murder Master* from the February 15, 1938 issue, and *The Hydra* from the December 1, 1942 issue. Typographical errors have been tacitly corrected in this edition.

International Standard Book Numbers:
ISBN 1-932806-25-3    13 DIGIT 978-1-932806-25-0

Series editor: Anthony Tollin
P.O. Box 761474
San Antonio, TX 78245-1474
sanctumotr@earthlink.net

Consulting editor: Will Murray

Copy editor: Joseph Wrzos

The editor gratefully acknowledges the assistance of Dennis Lien and Karl D. Schadow.

Nostalgia Ventures, Inc.
P.O. Box 231183; Encinitas, CA 92023-1183

Visit The Shadow at www.shadowsanctum.com
and www.nostalgiatown.com

# Volume 4

The entire contents of this book are protected by copyright, and must not be reprinted without the publisher's permission.

## CONTENTS

*Two Complete Novels From The Shadow's Private Annals As told to Maxwell Grant*

### Thrilling Tales and Features

**Foreword: LISTENING TO THE SHADOW LAUGH**
by Gahan Wilson ......................................................... 4

**THE MURDER MASTER** by Walter B. Gibson
(writing as "Maxwell Grant") ..................................... 6

**SPOTLIGHT ON THE SHADOW: ON THE AIR**
by Anthony Tollin ...................................................... 62

**THE POWER TO CLOUD MEN'S MINDS** ..................... 68

**THE HYDRA** by Walter B. Gibson
(writing as "Maxwell Grant") ..................................... 70

**INTRODUCING MARGO LANE** by Will Murray ......... 127

**A TALE OF TWO CRANSTONS** ................................... 128

**Cover art by George Rozen**
**Interior illustrations by Edd Cartier and Paul Orban**

# LISTENING TO THE SHADOW LAUGH by Gahan Wilson

I'm very glad to be doing the introduction to what might be called the "radio edition" of *The Shadow* because, the truth be told, the first time I encountered and was frightened by and became addicted to both this profoundly sinister crime-fighter and his insanely evil enemies was during my early teens in the final years of his radio show which then starred Bret Morrison of the smooth voice and jaunty manner but genuinely intimidating air.

I have no exact recollection of how I came across *The Shadow*. I was probably just trolling through the radio stations on a rainy weekend afternoon and I would like to think that my young fingers froze upon the dial control knob (this was an essentially pre-push button era) when the machine's speaker trembled with the richly weird vibrations of The Shadow's trademark chortle.

The broadcasts were a genuine work of folk art, a lovely final honing of what had become a real urban legend. They were the product of years of affectionate shaping and gentle polishing passed down through the hands of all kinds of skilled actors and writers and other skilled creators and producers—including one as wise in spookiness as Orson Welles—until it had achieved an almost cozy air of menace.

Though it was entirely based on the character Walter B. Gibson created and wrote about in the magazine adventures, the radio Shadow differed in many important ways from the Shadow of the pulps, most obviously in that he was a far more fantastic creature. The pulp's Shadow was far more bound to day to day reality and had to execute a lot of canny sneaking and ducking in order to avoid being spotted by his opponents who, though often colorful in the extreme and arch villains for certain, were mostly nitty-gritty flesh and blood crooks of varying talent, imagination and intelligence trying to make a buck.

The Shadow of the radio shows was a smooth magician with weird occult powers who could glide into invisibility at will and was able to toy with the minds of his opponents who tended to be on the extremely bizarre side: spectacularly mad scientists abounded as did hideously-distorted monsters and borderline supernatural entities gently lifted from the gaudier kinds of horror movies and comic books.

Another great difference between the two versions of this weird enemy of evil was that the complicated Shadow of the pulps had been lovingly produced by a slight of hand expert who had been ghostwriter for and close personal chum of fellow magician Harry Houdini. Dear old Walter Gibson was always the sly trickster ever eager to conjure up yet another new way of adding another secret panel or hidden trapdoor to the character of his weird, black-caped hero in order to make him as incomprehensible and mysterious as possible, whereas the radio Shadow, though very genuinely sinister in a likable sort of way, was really quite a simple and clear-cut kind of fellow once you got to know him.

For one thing, and very importantly, there was never any doubt in the radio scripts that he actually was Lamont Cranston. Furthermore, and a very big furthermore it was, there was also no doubt that Lamont Cranston actually was Lamont Cranston, "wealthy young man about town" and not just a stand-in for Kent Allard, a mysterious aviator who might—one never knew with Gibson—just might be a stand-in for somebody else who in turn might in turn be a stand-in not only for a somebody but maybe even a something else. Given a little more time Gibson could very well have got around to that last notion.

Bret Morrison, as I have learned for the first time from Anthony Tollin's article in this issue, was an all-round theatrical trooper, even a reasonably popular ballad belter (likely singing under a slowly rotating mirrored ball) and I've no doubt this had a great deal to do with the elaborately droll tone he managed to infuse into Cranston's voice—an excellently handled sort of showbizzy above-it-all drawling delivery which struck me—a wide-eyed innocent youth of Evanston, Illinois, as being amazingly sophisticated.

I only realized fairly recently that there was one ordinary-seeming element of the radio broadcast which gave it—for me, at least—an added subtle spookiness. It doesn't sound like all that much at first, but then it kind of sneaks up on you as it snuck up on me—the sponsor of The Shadow was Blue Coal!

Try to think about it the way I thought about it way back then, sometimes consciously, sometimes in dreams: blue coal is ancient stuff dug up at great danger to the diggers from the bowels of the Earth. It is the residue of dinosaurs and their offal and the thick, swollen jungles wherein the dinosaurs prowled all squished together into a solid flammable mass which has turned shiny black-blue with the passage of incomprehensible aeons.

And do not the words "Blue Coal" describe the hue of The Shadow's long, billowing cloak? Do they not call to mind the color of the wide brim of his tall hat from which he peers out at you fearsomely with his gleaming hypnotic glare moments before you can't see him anymore at all no matter how hard you squint?

You bet it does!

Or at least it did to me.

# LISTENING TO THE SHADOW LAUGH

"Lamont Cranston? No, there's no Lamont Cranston here."

A Complete Book-length Novel from the Private Annals of The Shadow.

Thousands heard the death-dealing orders of

# The Murder Master

over the air waves! But only The Shadow dared take the one chance to uncover this fiend!

As told to

## Maxwell Grant

### CHAPTER I
### THE MURDER MASTER

STATION WQJ was on the air. Its waves were spreading through the ether, seeking the favor of a vast audience that ignored it. Few radio listeners had ever heard of WQJ. Their dials were tuned for larger and more popular stations; particularly at this hour—eight in the evening—when national networks were parading their best-liked programs.

Those millions who scorned station WQJ were to miss the most sensational radio mystery that had ever been staged. Real tragedy, not the mock variety, was on the air tonight.

One group of listeners was interested in the program from WQJ, although they had not been

forewarned regarding its real significance. That group was gathered in a small, well-furnished office that formed part of an apartment. They were the guests of New York's police commissioner, Ralph Weston.

The commissioner, a brisk man with a military mustache, was still explaining matters to his friends, while a voice from the radio was filling in with a drab announcement of the program. Beside the radio set was a stocky, swarthy man who was trying to hear the announcer over Commissioner Weston's voice. The swarthy man was Joe Cardona, ace inspector of the New York police force.

"It's a new kind of mystery drama," stated Weston. "This letter"—he showed a typewritten sheet—"suggested that we listen in. Apparently, the program has some features that give new slants on crime detection. That ought to interest you, Graham."

The man that Weston addressed was a tall, aristocratic individual, whose high nose supported gold-rimmed spectacles in front of his mild gray eyes. Faultless in attire, Melvin Graham was quite the most distinguished looking person in the group, not excluding the police commissioner. The smile that Graham gave was indulgent, but well-mannered.

"I am interested in crime elimination, commissioner," observed Graham, his voice a modulated baritone. "Once it is accomplished, crime detection will be a secondary matter. Reform, not reprisal, is the way to deal with criminals."

Weston didn't agree; but there was no time to argue it. Cardona motioned that the announcer was about to say something important. Commissioner Weston shrugged his shoulders and turned toward the radio. As his eyes took a last flash at the group, he muttered:

"I wonder why Allard didn't get here."

The commissioner had reference to Kent Allard, a friend of his who had a strong liking for adventure. Weston had called the Cobalt Club, to which they both belonged, to invite Allard to join the group tonight. Allard had not been there, so Weston had left a message for him. With another shrug, Weston decided that the message must have been overlooked or delayed.

At that particular moment, the police commissioner held the opinion that Allard wouldn't be missing anything of consequence. Weston was due to change that impression within the next few minutes.

The announcer's voice had come at last to a dramatic pitch. With a sudden gusto, it declared:

"WQJ presents—the Murder Master!"

There was a blare of music from a tinny orchestra. It took a peculiar discord; faded out. Cardona was thumbing the dials; the program seemed to be cut off. It came back again, but the music had changed.

The orchestra must have added a few members, or changed entirely, for its tone was much improved. So was the theme. There was a grip to the haunting tune that strained from the ether. It brought creeps, even to this group of blasé listeners. The music swelled; finished with a sharp blare that echoed with the crash of cymbals.

A voice took the air. It was cackly, incoherent, like the babble of a self-satisfied maniac. Its words gained a chuckling tone, direct and insidious. That voice from the void was speaking directly to this audience. Its words were addressed specifically to one man present: Commissioner Ralph Weston!

"DO you hear me, commissioner?" The cackle was frenzied. So was the crazed laugh that followed it. "Yes—you hear me. You shall remember me! I am the Murder Master!"

A lull brought gasps from the listening group. Weston looked toward Cardona; the inspector's poker face was grim. Beside the commissioner, Melvin Graham gripped the arms of his chair. There was horror in the pale eyes that peered through the reformer's gold-rimmed spectacles.

"I am the Murder Master!" The chuckle from the radio was a forced monotone. "I decree death! It shall strike within five minutes. The victim—a lawyer. His name"—the pause was the space of a long-drawn breath—"his name is Richard Hyvran!"

Weston had heard that name; he couldn't place it for the moment. He looked toward Graham, who nodded. He, also, had a recollection of a man named Richard Hyvran. It was hard to place thoughts, though, under that strain, for the Murder Master had resumed his insidious chortle and was holding it prolonged.

It was Joe Cardona who had the right idea. He was grabbing telephone directories from atop the radio cabinet. He shoved the Manhattan book to Weston; tossed another, at random, to Graham. With a third book for himself, Cardona thumbed the pages to find the letter "H." Weston and Graham started the same process.

It was Cardona who found the name of Richard Hyvran; it was in the Queens directory, which the inspector had chanced to keep. Pouncing for the telephone, Cardona began to dial the lawyer's number. By odd coincidence, the Murder Master's voice spoke fitting words from the radio.

"Efforts to save Hyvran will fail," gloated the voice. "He is marked to die! Marked!" The words rose shrill. "Marked, I tell you! It is I who have marked him—I, the Murder Master!"

Cardona received an answer to his phone call. There was only a faint crackle of static from the radio. Everyone in the room was intent upon Cardona. His end of the conversation told everything.

"Hello..." Joe was gruff, but rapid. "I want to talk to Richard Hyvran. I'm Inspector Cardona, of the New York police... Yes, it's very urgent... Still time to reach him? Good... Yes, summon him at once..."

The inspector's grim face relaxed into a smile. Holding the telephone away from his ear, Cardona faced the group. He gestured toward the radio, where the subdued half-chuckle of the Murder Master had resumed.

"We'll soon have a line on that hoax," expressed Cardona. "I just talked to Hyvran's butler. Just in time to catch Hyvran before he left. He's started out to the garage to get his car. The butler is calling him—"

A sound interrupted. It didn't come from the radio; instead, the telephone produced it: a splitting crackle that vibrated the instrument in Cardona's hand. Faint echoes rattled from the receiver. They were audible to every person in that room. Cardona, with the telephone in his own fist, showed a look that told he recognized the sound. He shouted into the mouthpiece.

The Murder Master had resumed his cackle. Again, it was that crazed incoherence; but the babble was toned with satisfaction. The words took sense, but the listeners scarcely noticed them. Cardona was getting an answer from the telephone.

The inspector's features froze. Stolidly, Cardona replaced the telephone on the desk. He turned to the anxious group.

"The butler didn't get to the garage," Cardona told them, solemnly. "That sound we heard was an explosion. The butler says the blast wrecked the garage. All that he saw in the flash were chunks of an automobile, flying everywhere."

"And Richard Hyvran?"

It was Weston who shot the question. Cardona slowly shook his head. He answered:

"The butler says there's only one place that Hyvran could have been. That was in the automobile!"

NEWS of grim tragedy awed the listeners. There was to be no rest, though, for their jarred nerves. A voice was rising in that very room—the chortle of the Murder Master gloating its satisfaction over the air.

"Five minutes have ended!" The glee was high-pitched. "My prediction of death has been fulfilled! Richard Hyvran was doomed, as I declared!" A chuckle; then the question: "Do you hear me, commissioner? Do you believe me? You do! Very, very good!"

The frenzied laugh descended the scale, a full octave. Dryly, the voice resumed its words, at lower pitch. It repeated its reminder of accomplished murder, and in its harsh cackle the tone earned the ominous impression that it intended another prophecy.

"Five minutes have marked the death of Richard Hyvran." The gloat was ugly; contemptuous in its satisfaction. "Five minutes is but a fraction of our program. Shall we have another murder? Why not? I am the Murder Master!"

The voice scaled its chortle upward, shrilling to its former frenzy. It shrieked with new prediction:

"Another five minutes! Within that time, another murder! One that you cannot prevent, commissioner, though I shall name the man—likewise, the place where he shall die!"

Static crackled with the glee that furied from the radio. Slumped men sat helpless; chief among them was Commissioner Ralph Weston. He, the commander of the law's entire force, was most powerless of all.

The proof of the Murder Master's strength had been established. Weston could do no more than listen, until the fiend's new croak pronounced another stroke of doom.

## CHAPTER II
### DEATH IN THE CROWD

BRIEF seconds lingered; the pause was torture for the listeners, especially Joe Cardona. The ace inspector hadn't yet admitted the cause impossible. Cardona thought there would still be time to avert another killing, if the Murder Master would hurry with his promised decree.

Moments were precious, since five minutes were to be the time limit.

The murderous cluck came from the air:

"My second victim is a retired manufacturer! His name is Justin Palbrock! His place of death—" the cackling voice delayed, enjoying a malicious pleasure—"the Pennsylvania Station!"

Justin Palbrock!

All the listeners knew that name. Palbrock was wealthy; he had spent large sums in civic welfare; he had championed the building of low-rental apartments, to replace slummy tenements. Hyvran, perhaps, had made enemies; certainly Palbrock had not.

Those thoughts were striking Commissioner Weston; but Joe Cardona's mind was centered elsewhere. He was thinking of the Pennsylvania Station, a huge haystack in which to find a human needle. It was a place, though, where things could be started in a hurry and finished in short order.

Five minutes! Cardona set his lips as his finger hurried the telephone dial. Maybe it would be time enough.

In less than one minute, Cardona had the railway station on the wire and was talking to the man he needed. All the while, the Murder Master was gloating over the radio.

Weston turned the dial down, so Cardona could talk. But the commissioner didn't turn the program entirely off. There was no telling what gruesome clues might suddenly come from the Murder Master. That killer seemed to think he could spread his cards so everyone could see them, and still win.

"The ball's rolling," assured Cardona, as he finished his phone call. "It won't take them long to locate Palbrock at the Pennsy Station, if he's there."

"There are only five minutes—"

"That's more than enough, commissioner. There'll be a report back before that time is up. Leave it to them; they'll handle it!"

Confident in his statement, Cardona tuned the radio to hear the full tone of the Murder Master's voice. This time—Joe was sure of it—death would be foiled. Justin Palbrock would receive protection that could defeat the murderer's swiftness.

EVENTS at the Pennsylvania Station seemed to be justifying Cardona's belief.

A human voice, amplified dozens of times its normal strength, was calling a stentorian summons over a loudspeaker. That impressive announcement reached every nook of the vast terminal. Hundreds of persons halted, riveted by its call.

"Justin Palbrock!" The name came clear from the loudspeaker. "Justin Palbrock! Wherever you are, declare yourself to the nearest uniformed attendant! Justin Palbrock! This is urgent! Make yourself known at once! To any attendant in the station—"

Cardona had started action at precisely five and a half minutes after eight. The big clocks in the huge terminal showed eight minutes past the hour. Cardona's headwork had clipped into the five minutes that the Murder Master had allowed.

A rangy, gray-haired man was standing at a telegraph booth, while a porter waited, holding a heavy suitcase. The man had just arrived on a train from Washington. He had come directly to the booth to write the telegram.

There were usually pencils at that counter. Tonight, there was a shortage. The rangy man had found a pencil in his own pocket. The lead was hard; he was chewing the end of it, as he paused between the words he wrote.

"Justin Palbrock!"

The rangy man snapped his head upward, as he realized that his own name was issuing from the loudspeaker. The big-throated voice had an impelling tone:

"You are in danger, Justin Palbrock! Declare yourself at once! To a uniformed attendant only. This order comes from police headquarters! Justin Palbrock—"

Mechanically, Palbrock let the telegraph blank flutter. His hand shoved the pencil in his pocket. He stared at the waiting porter; he wondered whether the redcap rated as an attendant. He looked toward the information booth in the center of the concourse. There were several attendants there.

Palbrock hurried toward the booth. He quickened his step as the resonant tone from the loudspeaker began to repeat his name. As he hastened, Palbrock winced. He had to halt; a sudden pain had gripped him at the side of the stomach.

After a momentary waver, Palbrock resumed his course. He stretched his hand toward the information booth. An attendant saw the gesture; sensing something wrong, he beckoned to some passing redcaps. They came on the run.

Palbrock's hands were clutching the edge of the booth's counter. The attendant saw a face that had gone suddenly haggard. Eyes were bulging; lips looked bloated, puffy, as they gasped.

"I'm—I'm Justin Palbrock!"

Hands slipped. The attendant made a futile grab for them. Scrambling redcaps arrived to catch Palbrock's slumping body before it hit the floor. There were three of them, yet the weight was all that they could manage. The man in the booth knew the reason, when Palbrock's head rolled backward.

The haggard face was ashen. Bulging eyes had glazed. Foam flecked those puffed lips. The attendant gulped one word:

"Dead!"

The long hand of a huge terminal clock was marking the ninth minute past the hour.

THIRTY seconds later, Joe Cardona was taking the report by telephone. He turned to Weston, Graham and the others of the gloomy group. They knew from Cardona's expression that new doom had struck.

"They paged Palbrock in the Pennsy Station." Cardona's glum announcement was given to the accompaniment of a tuned-down chuckling from the radio. "Right after that, a man collapsed at the information booth. They don't know for sure yet, but they think it's Palbrock. They say it looks as if he's dead."

There was a trace of vaguely hopeful doubt in Cardona's statement, but there was none in the harsh ripple that rose from the radio. The tenth minute had ended. It was time for the Murder Master to cluck new evil triumph.

Commissioner Weston turned the knob, to bring the mysterious speaker's voice to its full pitch. Much though he hated it, the commissioner could not ignore the Murder Master. With two men mysteriously assassinated, the only clue to the man who ordained death would be the memory of that voice from the ether. Commissioner Weston urged his companions to listen to every peculiarity of tone.

"Five minutes have marked the death of Justin Palbrock!" The evil confidence of the Murder Master dispelled Cardona's last hope to the contrary: "Our time on the air"—the voice was precise—"is not yet ended! For your entertainment, commissioner, I shall decree another death! Again, it shall strike within five minutes!"

Moments seemed endless; yet only a few seconds lapsed before the next pronouncement.

"The victim—a politician!"

Quick looks passed between Weston and Cardona. This might be someone known personally to both of them.

"His name—Frank Denniman!"

They did know Denniman. "Big Frank," a friend to every cop in town. One fellow who had gained his influence through good will. To Frank Denniman, politics was a game, and he always played it square.

"The place—the Metrolite Hotel!" The Murder Master paused; then added another detail. "To be specific, Frank Denniman will lie dead outside the hotel's main entrance. Within five minutes!"

Mumbled laughter followed. Again the Murder Master was filling time while the law sprang to futile effort. Cardona was at the telephone, calling the Metrolite. Joe was assuring the commissioner that he would have doormen, bellboys, house detectives flocking to the space outside the Metrolite before the precious five minutes were half gone.

To Commissioner Weston, that promise meant nothing.

Weston was resigned to the belief that Denniman's death was a certainty. Looking further, the commissioner groaned with the conviction that the Murder Master, himself, was out of reach. The program, Weston remembered, was a fifteen-minute one. That, at least, indicated that the chain of death would soon be finished.

But what of the future? Who could cope with a monstrous fiend like this killer, whose cackled laugh reeked with malicious pride in his own security? That high pitch from the radio was proof that the Murder Master regarded himself immune. If the law could take no steps against him, who else could?

Commissioner Weston was too strained to

think of an answer to his own mental question; but there was one. Already, a friend of justice was taking measures to combat the Murder Master before the superfiend could leave the studio where he issued his decrees of doom.

The Shadow, foe to all who dealt in crime, was nearing a swift-chosen destination.

That goal was the obscure radio station, WQJ.

## CHAPTER III
## THE LAST DECREE

COMMISSIONER WESTON had mentioned his friend, Kent Allard. Though Weston did not know it, Kent Allard was The Shadow. That was something, too, that the Murder Master had not guessed. He would probably have given his broadcast a different twist, had he known that The Shadow had been invited to Weston's apartment to hear the mystery broadcast.

Luck had favored the Murder Master. Weston's message to Allard had been temporarily forgotten by a negligent clerk at the Cobalt Club. The fellow hadn't remembered it until just before eight o'clock. Finding a note that Allard was visiting a friend in New Jersey, the clerk had phoned the message there.

The Shadow's intuition was acute. He had sensed the ominous in the request that Commissioner Weston listen in on the program from WQJ. It couldn't be a publicity stunt; in that case, the commissioner would have been invited to the studio. A hoax was out of the question. WQJ couldn't risk its license with a proposition of that sort.

Something definite lay at stake. That was why Kent Allard had started at once for New York.

Allard's big limousine had reached the Skyway leading to the Holland Tunnel when the program began. While the chauffeur kept the car at the top speed the law allowed, Allard was tuning in on the limousine's radio. His long, hawk-featured face was immobile in the tiny light of the dial. Keen ears heard every tone of the Murder Master's threats.

Allard's eyes, usually quiet in their gaze, had taken on a strange, far-seeing burn.

They were the eyes of The Shadow.

Hyvran was dead. So was Palbrock. The Shadow took those deaths as certainties, when he heard the Murder Master's chuckles. The very confidence of the evil voice proved that those murders had been prearranged, so cunningly that nothing could avert them in the brief periods that the Murder Master allowed.

The limousine was almost through the Holland Tunnel, when The Shadow heard the announcement of Denniman's doom. There wasn't a chance that it could be halted, even by The Shadow. The Murder Master's insidious gloat was still audible, despite the poor reception of the radio while the limousine roared up the incline leading from the river tunnel.

OUTSIDE the Hotel Metrolite, at that very moment, hastily called men were learning that their efforts were too late. They were on the sidewalk, looking anxiously about, one minute after they had received Cardona's call. They saw a taxi swing up to the curb.

Large hands were on the ledge of the door window; a broad face was pressed against the glass, the head above it hatless. Before the driver could reach out to open the rear door, a hotel detective sprang to do it for him. The door whipped open; the bully passenger pitched headlong to the sidewalk.

Eager hands raised the body. A policeman, pressing through the throng, saw the face and gulped:

"It's Big Frank! Big Frank Denniman! Dead!"

The group stood silent, for five stunned seconds. Then a house dick made a sudden dash into the hotel to give the news to Joe Cardona, who was holding the wire open.

The clock above the hotel desk pointed to thirteen minutes after eight.

DOWN near the tip of Manhattan, The Shadow's limousine was making its final spurt along a crosstown street. The passenger was no longer Allard. Every trace of his tuxedoed figure had disappeared. From beneath the seat, The Shadow had pulled out a drawerlike shelf that contained garments of black. He was attired in long cloak, a slouch hat on his head. His hands were gloved.

The limousine slid to a stop beside a dingy, six-story building where lights glowed on the top floor only. To The Shadow, those lights were a beacon. They marked the location of the broadcasting rooms used by station WQJ.

With his left hand, The Shadow cut off the car radio, stopping the chortle of the Murder Master as it rose to the high pitch that predicted a new announcement.

Simultaneously, The Shadow opened the door with his other hand. He was out of the limousine. Swiftly, unseen, he crossed the sidewalk as the big car started away. Reaching the darkened entry to the building, The Shadow glimmered a flashlight on the door of an elevator shaft.

The dial showed that the elevator was at the sixth floor, and The Shadow decided immediately that it must be out of use. Lights were off in this lower entry; that was sufficient proof that something had gone wrong. The Shadow's flashlight showed a stairway—the only available route to the sixth floor.

The Shadow began the long ascent. He had one minute to spare before WQJ went off the air.

BECAUSE of his effort to reach the studio in that last minute, The Shadow was unable to hear the finish of the Murder Master's program. That climax was reserved for the group assembled at Weston's.

Amid the glee of the Murder Master, Joe Cardona was repeating facts that came across the telephone from the Hotel Metrolite. Denniman was dead, like Hyvran and Palbrock. The cab driver was being questioned, but the fellow was too overwhelmed to give any details. It appeared he didn't know what had happened to his passenger.

That seemed proven by the announcement that came suddenly from the Murder Master.

"Five minutes have marked the death of Frank Denniman," croaked the voice. "A third mystery to baffle you, commissioner! Perhaps"—the tone had a bitter ugliness—"you regret, as I do, that this program is finished.

"More time—more deaths! More deaths—more clues!" The laugh went high. "Clues? There will be none, commissioner! Unless, perhaps, a final death will serve! Very well, we shall have one, as a fitting sequel!"

Cardona wasn't listening. For the first time, his own folly had struck him. He'd wasted fifteen minute trying frantically to halt three surefire murders, and, all the while, he'd missed the biggest bet of all. That was the quest of the murderer himself.

Cardona would have given plenty to have that quarter hour back again. He knew what he would do with it. He would head hotfoot for WQJ, to snag the killer in that lair. It wasn't too late to try it, anyway. Cardona was dialing the operator, to get headquarters on the wire, to start police squads on their chase.

The hoarse orders that Cardona shouted were brisk but adequate. Soon, patrol cars would arrive downtown. The law would form a cordon. Maybe the nest would be empty. Cardona would find out for himself, when he reached there.

Slamming the telephone on the desk, the ace inspector grabbed for his hat. He halted before he reached the door.

Cardona had seen the tense expression on the faces of the listeners. They were clustered close about the radio, with Weston and Graham in the center of the group. They were straining to catch the last falsetto pronouncement from the Murder Master. Only fifteen seconds left; that quarter minute was to prove as vital as the quarter hour that had just gone by.

In those fifteen seconds, Joe Cardona was to realize the value of the quick orders that he had just dispatched to headquarters.

"One more death!"

The precise chuckle over the radio repeated the promise that Cardona had failed to hear.

"This time," came the gloat, "I shall name the place first! Murder will occur here, in this very studio!"

A PAUSE, so timed that it had a terrific effect upon the craning listeners. It was almost as if the Murder Master were present, the way he held the attention of the group. This was no aftermath; it was a superclimax. Those tragedies that had gone before were a build-up to this monstrous, sensational finish.

Everyone present knew it; Joe Cardona was so powerfully gripped that he couldn't budge beyond the door until he heard that final sentence. It didn't occur to him that the threat itself made it all the more imperative for him to be on his way. He had to listen to that last pronouncement. Like the others, Cardona was oblivious to all else.

"The scene is set," voiced the Murder Master. "The victim will be—"

A gong struck. That reverberation over the ether indicated a studio signal, announcing that the program's time was up. It seemed that the Murder Master heard it, for he halted. The listeners thought, for the instant, that he would not complete his sentence.

Then came the cackle once again, its tone determined. Despite the signal, the speaker was snatching a last few seconds in which to complete his ominous decree. Defiantly, the Murder Master croaked:

"The victim will be the meddler who calls himself The Shadow!"

The name was uttered with a rising pitch, that broke into a screechy jubilation. The hideous laugh trilled, blended with a sudden crackle of static. Then came the blot of an abrupt silence.

That hush solemnized the Murder Master's decree.

Station WQJ was off the air.

## CHAPTER IV
## LURKERS OF DEATH

SILENCE gripped the sixth floor; with it, darkness. The entire studio was blanketed with a gloom that had occurred within the past few dozen seconds. Two minutes ago, The Shadow had heard the air-cast voice of the Murder Master. He had seen lights in this very studio. The voice had silenced, the lights had faded while The Shadow was on the stairs.

The situation offered no surprise. The Shadow had more or less expected it. It was logical that the Murder Master would have called for lights off the moment that the broadcast was concluded. Unquestionably, the killer chief had aides. Darkness would help their departure. Probably they would take precautions when they fled. That did not trouble The Shadow.

As The Shadow considered it, the odds were all in his favor. He had arrived at the most timely moment, when crooks would think that they had gained security. Darkness had produced the situation that he liked best. Gloom was the favorite shroud in which The Shadow moved to his attacks on crime.

So natural was this sequel that The Shadow failed to sense the trap that it concealed. The subtle Murder Master had called for The Shadow's own element, darkness, to make a perfect lure. In delivering other deaths, the Murder Master had left little to chance. This time, he was risking more; nevertheless, he had provided death that was prearranged.

The murderer had calculated that The Shadow would start for the studio while the broadcast was still in progress. He had estimated The Shadow would arrive near the finish of the program. Where the murderer had seemingly taken a long chance was when he had added that final threat. Had The Shadow still been in his car, had he reached the sixth floor a half minute sooner, he would have been prepared for a direct thrust of doom.

Curiously, the radio broadcast itself bore proof that the Murder Master had not left that detail to chance.

The gong, had the Murder Master wished it, could have meant the cutoff of the program without the addition of The Shadow's name. The reason that it had gone through completely was because The Shadow's big car had been spotted—not from the studio, but by a watcher in a house on the other side of the street.

The Murder Master had foreseen that The Shadow would be the first comer to reach the studio. The time element had suited the watcher, even though he had not spied The Shadow's blackened form. Therefore, the complete threat had been delivered.

Moving through the darkness of the sixth floor, The Shadow heard muffled pounding. He discerned white faces pressing against glass. They were the personnel of the office, locked in an unused broadcasting room.

Easing along the wall, The Shadow found another panel of glass. This was the darkened room he wanted—the one that the Murder Master's crew had taken over for their own insidious program.

THE door opened silently under The Shadow's grip. He came into the stillness of a soundproof room. He blinked his flashlight warily along the floor, keeping its rays well controlled. In his other fist, The Shadow gripped an automatic.

The broadcasting room was empty. No one had left it by the main door. There was only one plausible answer: Exit had been managed through the control room on the other side.

Working in that direction, The Shadow eased past a microphone. His flashlight revealed other equipment among tangled wires. Familiar with methods that he himself had used in broadcasts, The Shadow decided that the Murder Master had not spoken from this room at all. Instead, his voice had been piped in from elsewhere.

That meant that a meeting with the supercrook would have to be postponed. The discovery, however, changed none of The Shadow's determination. The quest was still important, for others must be lurking here. Those tools of the Murder Master would be the persons through whom The Shadow could locate their evil chief.

There was an element in the situation that The Shadow missed.

Proof of the Murder Master's absence made the present quest seem easier. Instinctively, The Shadow increased his progress. He had less need of caution, dealing with hirelings, than if he actually had to encounter a foe so crafty as the Murder Master.

That made the coming trap a surer one.

It was an odd case, this venture of The Shadow's; different from any that he had previously encountered. Though WQJ was an insignificant station, there were a few thousand scattered listeners who had heard the Murder Master's frenzied broadcast.

Every one of those persons—with a single exception—had been horrified by the final utterance. The lone person who had missed that promise of an added murder was the one for whom the death was designed: The Shadow!

The master who hunted down crime was thrusting himself into the snare that the Murder Master had not only provided, but had announced to all the world—except The Shadow!

The door of the control room swung open; its hinges were noiseless. The slight click of the knob was almost inaudible, so trivial that The Shadow thought that no one could have heard it but himself. He thought the same when he closed the door behind him. The latch seemed to muffle the knob's click.

That latch was a giveaway of The Shadow's moves. The socket in which it fitted had been wired. The opening of the door broke a contact, that resumed when the door was closed. Lurkers knew that The Shadow had reached the control room, was ready to move through it. They did as ordered.

A light came on suddenly from a corridor. At the far end of the control room, The Shadow saw an opened door; beyond it, two men huddled and masked. They were trying to shove a large square box into a waiting elevator that would take them down to the ground floor, away from the entry through which The Shadow had come.

Dragging after the box was a long, heavy-insulated wire, coiled so snakily that it looked loose. One man was reaching, as if to gather it. The move deceived The Shadow. He hissed a fierce command, as he took a long surge across the control room. The Shadow wanted to reach that far door, threaten the two masked men into terror before they could enter the elevator.

THREE seconds were all The Shadow needed; that wasn't long enough for the rogues to recover from their startlement in seeing the cloaked avenger looming upon them. It was time enough, though, for one of the crooks to perform an intended move. The fellow snapped a switch on the side of the square box.

At the same instant, The Shadow took a half sprawl, that would have been unlucky on any other occasion. This time, it proved more fortunate than anything else he might have done. The object over which The Shadow stumbled was the rim of a steel plate, invisible on the darkened floor of the control room.

Tripping, The Shadow nearly cleared the steel plate, before he hit it on one hand and the other knee. His body still had momentum when he struck. But it wasn't cold metal on which The Shadow landed. The thug at the elevator had altered that when he pressed the box switch. The wire was connected to the plate.

There was a crackle, a flare of lights, as The Shadow's body took an upward jolt. Quivered by thousands of volts, the cloaked figure jerked upward, did a grotesque backspin in the air. The Shadow had received a shock as powerful as the current used in an electric chair.

Dimming lights in the corridor told how the

★ ★ ★ ★ ★ ★ ★ ★ ★ ★ ★ ★ ★ ★ ★ ★ ★ ★ ★ ★ ★ ★ ★ ★ ★ ★ ★ ★ ★ ★ ★ ★ ★

## *THE SHADOW KNOWS!*

*In crime capitals the world over, criminals gather in secret and smugly plan attacks on the populace at large. Hell's Kitchen in New York—Limehouse in London—under the shadows of the Sacre Coeur in Paris—along the Tiber in Rome—in the back streets of Berlin—beside the Bund in Shanghai—in San Francisco's Chinatown—in cities the globe over, crooks mumble their plans of murder, arson, theft—every crime known to man!*

*But hidden in a sanctum in New York, a being in black ponders beneath a blue light and slyly chuckles to himself as he peruses reports of his agents. For The Shadow knows! Before crime plans have been put into being, word has come from his agents in far-flung corners of the world—and The Shadow has laid plans to thwart the hordes of evil!*

*Earphones on the wall lead to Burbank, contact man—and through him go the Master of Darkness' instructions to his aides. Instructions to Harry Vincent to report on the scene of incipient crime, to lay the groundwork for The Shadow's approach; to Hawkeye and Cliff Marsland, in their underworld guise, the paths* juice had been diverted. Flayed by the voltage, The Shadow was hurled bodily through the door, to end with a fantastic sprawl beside the masked men who had tricked him. Grins spread on ugly lips behind bandanna masks.

"It's The Shadow!" growled the man at the switch. "He fell for it, like the chief said he would. Say, did it hook him? I'll say it did!"

"He oughta have fried longer," objected the other. "We was supposed to let him sizzle a full minute, before we cut off the juice."

"Shove him back on again. We got time."

The crook who had suggested it made a reach for The Shadow's shoulders. He became jittery when he looked at the box. He made a gesture toward the switch.

"Yank that off," he told his pal. "Whatta you want me to do? Burn, too? Say—we can't stall all night!"

The thug at the box threw the switch. He started to help his companion lift The Shadow. Both paused when they heard a faint, distant sound. It wouldn't have been audible in the soundproof control room; but in this outside corridor it could be heard. It worried the two lurkers, because it was the last thing they expected.

The sound was the wail of a police siren.

One tried to laugh it off, saying it was a fire engine. The other shook his head. He thought he could hear another shriek, from a different direction. For the first time, something had gone wrong with the Murder Master's plans.

The master of death had concentrated upon settling The Shadow. He hadn't figured that Joe Cardona would do anything about it until after the broadcast was completed. Cardona, though, had anticipated matters by two minutes or more. That time was just sufficient to save The Shadow from another jolt of electricity.

"He's croaked," assured the first crook, nodding his head at the cloaked form. Then, amending his statement: "He will be, anyway, when we're through with him. Shove him aboard."

THEY rolled the inert figure into the elevator. They yanked the heavy wire from its socket; hauled in the steel plate. The metal was still too hot to handle; the killers kicked the plate aboard the elevator and dragged the box in after them. The door clanged; the elevator rumbled downward.

Crooks were under a strain, but their grins still showed. They had reason for their satisfaction, as they gazed through the slits of their masks. Prone, motionless, The Shadow was dead, to all appearances. As the downward ride continued, the murderous men were becoming more convinced that the powerful shock had finished him.

Nobody could take a jolt like that and still live, one assured the other. His pal agreed. He'd seen a lineman take hold of a high-tension wire, a couple of years back. That fellow had been cooked by the time he hit the ground. The same with The Shadow. Once a guy was knocked stiff, he couldn't come out of it.

★ ★ ★ ★ ★ ★ ★ ★ ★ ★ ★ ★ ★ ★ ★ ★ ★ ★ ★ ★ ★ ★ ★ ★ ★ ★ ★ ★ ★ ★ ★ ★ ★ ★

*they are to follow; to Clyde Burke, reporter for the Classic, the necessary information to be gained through newspaper channels; to Moe Shrevnitz, taxi driver of the first rank, work of transporting the Master Fighter to his field of battle; to Rutledge Mann, hiding behind the "front" of an investment broker, the word to be ready with his invaluable aid; to Jericho, giant African, the standby message to aid, if necessary, with his terrible strength.*

*Agents obey orders—and then from the sanctum glides a being in black—to reach the scene of crime and strike swiftly with blazing automatics. The Shadow against minions of the underworld! One gun against many! But when the triumph laugh peals out under a midnight sky, there has been but one ending: The Shadow has vanquished his foes, and crime for the time being has been stilled.*

*To two persons only is The Shadow's true identity known—that of Kent Allard, internationally famous aviator—and those persons are Xinca Indians, servants picked up by Allard during a stay among their tribe in Central America. A guise often used by The Shadow is that of Lamont Cranston, world-renowned big-game hunter and traveler, when Cranston is away on his travels. This is by the leave of the real Cranston, a man of deep understanding.*

*"Crime must go!"—thus The Shadow's slogan.*

The elevator reached the basement level. The thugs opened the door; they heard new wails of sirens, as a third husky beckoned for them to hurry. Hoisting The Shadow, they chucked him into a darkened car that was parked in the alley. The equipment followed swiftly. The crooks piled aboard.

Lurkers of death were on their way, confident that they were carrying The Shadow's corpse as a trophy for the Murder Master.

## CHAPTER V
## THE LAW'S TURN

THE car that bore The Shadow had scarcely reached the front street before the driver spotted the lights of a police car. With a snarl, the driver changed the sedan's direction. He swung another corner in a hurry. The crook beside him turned around to see if the police were following. They were.

The third thug was crouched above The Shadow, pointing a revolver at the cloaked figure. The man beside the driver sped a quick hand to stop his pal's shot.

"Hold it!" he snapped. "You gone screwy?"

"Whatta you mean?" was the rejoinder. "We're croaking The Shadow, ain't we? I'm making sure of it!"

"With the bulls almost on us? Lay off with that heater! Wait'll we clear, so's they won't hear us shoot."

These crooks weren't the only ones that scented trouble. In the next block, another pair came dashing from a house door, to pile into a coupe. The sedan's driver grunted.

"They're scramming in a hurry" was his comment. "They should 'a' brought the machine along with them. Bad stuff, leaving it up there."

"It don't make no difference," objected the man beside him. "The chief won't care if the cops find out about the record. He said so. Only, he didn't figure they'd be tailing us like this."

"We'll shake 'em!"

The driver didn't keep that promise. He made a bad mistake at the end of the third block, when he turned right instead of left. The coupe went in the other direction; it slipped through the closing cordon. The sedan, though, was almost boxed when it crossed an avenue.

Police cars showed up from both directions. They guessed the sedan was in flight, because of its speed. They took up the chase that the first patrol car had lost.

It was a race through twisty streets—the driver fuming, the man in the back seat anxious to load The Shadow with lead, then open fire on the police. The one cool head was the fellow who sat on the driver's right. He had handled the switch on the electric box; he was showing the same quick thought that he had used in downing The Shadow.

"Keep dodging," he told the driver. Then, to the man in back: "No trigger work! We've got too much to lose!"

"Where's it getting us?" demanded the driver. "They're closing in from everywhere!"

"We're heading for the chief's. You can make it."

The driver shook his head.

"That'd be a giveaway," he declared. "They'll box us there—"

"Sure—while we unload. But when we get started again, we can shoot it out! We won't be carrying anything that we won't want them to find."

Prospects of gun work brought the approval of the man in the rear seat. The plan was won by a vote of two to one—a plan which was to have much bearing on The Shadow's future, though neither he nor his captors recognized it.

THERE was no fakery in The Shadow's motionless condition. Had he possessed one trace of consciousness, he would have shown it during that twisty ride.

Shots were pursuing the sedan. Not one of its occupants offered battle in return. That helped them; for there were times, when they scudded corners, that other police would have marked them, had they shown a spurt of guns.

The driver doubled on his course, shook off pursuers long enough to make a straightaway run. He had reached the numbered streets when he took a quick turn to the left.

The sedan pulled along a narrow street, rolled into a little alley between two blank walls. The driver turned off the motor. He and his pals listened.

They could hear sirens, whistles, that indicated the police were circling this neighborhood. They lost no time with their task. The driver jumped from the car, hauled out the equipment. The other pair carried The Shadow.

They unlocked a door, moved through a passage. They had a key to another, stronger, barrier; beyond it, they reached a darkened room. The pair that lugged The Shadow eased him to the floor. The one who wanted to do the gun work growled that his chance had come. He met with double objection.

"Whatta you want to do?" snapped the self-appointed leader of the trio. "Queer the works? The Shadow's croaked, I tell you! Didn't you feel the weight of him?"

"Yeah. He's heavy, like a stiff. Only some lead would make him weigh more!"

"He don't need it. We don't want nobody hearing us in here. Get busy. Heave some of this junk."

The three moved tables and chairs. They found the center of the floor; lifted a trapdoor. Dank coldness issued from below. At a whispered word, two men assisted the third. They lowered The Shadow's body, then let go.

The thump that followed brought satisfied mumbles from the trio. It had a sound that indicated hard stone below. The trap went back in place; there was another shift of furniture.

The crooks stole out by the route they had used to enter. They reached their car; the driver backed it from the alley. A few minutes later, he was picking a cautious route, still trying to avoid the persistent sounds that told of circling police.

**At a whispered word … they lowered The Shadow's body.**

The sedan covered about a quarter mile before the driver could chance a run along an avenue. He'd hardly gotten under way, when a police whistle blew. The driver snarled that the cops had previously spotted the license number, were now looking for it. The man beside him said that didn't matter. They were through with this bus, anyway.

Whatever usefulness the car possessed was due to be ended with that chase. Police were already in the offing, firing as before. At last, the killers were free to blaze away.

They waged a fast battle as they sped northward. When the going became hot, the driver headed east. He was a block ahead of the pursuers; he saw a subway station. He didn't wait for the approval of his pals. He careened the car around the corner, jammed the brakes as it hit the curb.

The sedan did a half climb on a pair of house steps. Whipping off his mask, the driver sprang from the car and made for the subway. The two other thugs followed his example.

They were lucky in that dash. Not only were they gone when the police arrived; the three reached the subway just as a train pulled in. The change-maker saw them from his booth, but thought they were ordinary passengers trying to catch the train.

It was five minutes before any officers arrived to ask questions. It was too late, then.

handful of thugs. But this was one time—of all times—when Cardona had held a definite hunch that The Shadow would appear. That was why Joe Cardona retraced the whole course of the chase, following back to every spot where the sedan had been reported.

Cardona's car circled through many districts, stopping often, while accompanying detectives alighted to look for traces. That search seemed

UP on the street, a grim man was examining the car that the mobsters had abandoned. Joe Cardona had received reports of the chase and had managed to get into it, although his car had been at the rear of the pursuers. The wrecked sedan showed cracked windows, where police bullets had hit; but there were no signs of bloodstains.

Two things were evident: The occupants had escaped unscathed; they certainly had not time to drag anyone with them. Nevertheless, from all reports, this was the only car that had left the building where station WQJ was located. There had been another machine—a coupe—but it had ducked in later and had ducked out again.

Cardona subtracted one from one, to make nothing.

The Murder Master had promised The Shadow's death, which indicated that he had held The Shadow, helpless, at the radio studio. But The Shadow hadn't been there when Cardona arrived. Joe had supposed, therefore, that he had been carried away in this car. The minus quantity in the case was The Shadow's own absence.

Usually, in a wild chase like this, The Shadow would move in from nowhere, to take his hand in it. Tonight, that hadn't happened. True, there were plenty of chases when The Shadow wasn't about. He didn't show up everytime the law went after a

thorough; but it wasn't. It went bad in the very district where The Shadow had been dropped.

Reports from that sector were erroneous. Cardona's car didn't even go along the street where the fleeing thugs had made their brief halt in an alley. After an hour of futile search, Cardona found himself back at station WQJ.

Cardona had business there; for Commissioner Weston was on hand, quizzing the personnel of the radio station. Gloomily, Cardona went up in the elevator.

By the time he reached the sixth floor, Cardona had brightened. He figured he had seen through a bluff maneuvered by the Murder Master. Somehow, that hidden killer chief must have known that The Shadow was busy elsewhere. Maybe the Murder Master had decoyed The Shadow out of town.

Nobody would take a chance, announcing by radio that he would trap The Shadow, then be so foolish as to attempt it. Subtracting one from one, Cardona decided upon his answer. The zero meant that The Shadow had not been here at all.

That, in turn, gave Cardona the opinion that he would hear from The Shadow, later. Joe was glad that the Murder Master had talked so big, across the air. That sort of stuff was the very type that would bring The Shadow on a criminal's trail.

Confidently, Joe Cardona looked forward to The Shadow's prompt cooperation with the law.

The ace inspector would have lost that confidence—and more, besides—had he even guessed of The Shadow's present plight.

## CHAPTER VI
## BROKEN CLUES

THE next day marked steady investigations by the law. The police were seeking the Murder Master through his crimes; but each retraced trail—like Cardona's hunt for The Shadow—went astray.

In the case of Richard Hyvran, tiny pieces of wire were the threads that enabled the law to reconstruct how the lawyer had died.

Someone had planted a bomb in Hyvran's automobile, wiring it to the motor. When Hyvran had stepped on the starter, the car had instantly gone sky-high. That scheme, concocted by the Murder Master, had been almost certain of success.

Hyvran was the only person who ever used that car. He carried the only set of keys. He drove the car only in the evening, for he lived close to a Long Island Railroad station and commuted to and from the city. As for the fact that Hyvran intended to use that car at eight o'clock, nearly everyone who knew the lawyer could have supplied that information.

Once a week, Hyvran attended the meetings of a club composed of suburban businessmen. The meetings were held at eight-thirty. A man of punctuality, Hyvran always left his home at eight o'clock on those nights. His regularity was such that when he stopped at houses to pick up other friends, they knew almost to the minute when he would arrive.

The Murder Master had simply learned of Hyvran's schedule and had suited it to his own purposes. When the bomb was planted, no one could guess. The range of time ran from eleven o'clock the night before, until just before the explosion—a period of about twenty-one hours. No prowlers had been reported around Hyvran's home. That was no surprise, for the house was well obscured by hedges and the detached garage was never locked.

That, in substance, was all that Inspector Cardona could learn regarding the murder of Richard Hyvran.

The case of Justin Palbrock promised more; but it petered out in the same rapid fashion.

Palbrock had been poisoned. The pencil that he had used to write his telegram was tipped with a most virulent substance, as a chemical examination proved. The circumstances, however, that led up to Palbrock's death were so natural that they afforded no loophole.

Palbrock had made a trip to Washington, to discuss a legislative matter with some New York congressmen. The subject had involved costs of a government project in New York City. Palbrock had left the matter of costs an approximate one, until he talked with the congressmen. Since they had been favorable to the plan, Palbrock had spent most of his return trip working at a table in a Pullman car.

Someone must have filched Palbrock's pencil and planted the poisoned one in its place. Arrived in New York, that same person—or a waiting confederate—had walked off with the pencils at the telegraph booth. The wire that Palbrock was about to send had been a telegram to Washington, giving the complete estimates.

Unfortunately, none of the train personnel remembered any suspicious party watching Palbrock. The clerks at the telegraph booth had not observed the disappearance of the pencils. Both moves had been bold; but therein lay their perfection. Handled by a cool worker, they were the sort of actions that would not be noticed.

As for Palbrock's visit to Washington, it was a publicly known matter. Palbrock had told many persons that he was going to the capital; and that he would go into the matter of detailed figures after he had presented his plan. Since he was due back in New York for a nine-o'clock banquet, it was obvious that he would be on the train that arrived at eight o'clock.

The Murder Master had allowed five minutes for Palbrock to come up from the train and make his stop at the telegraph booth.

THE murder of Frank Denniman introduced a remarkable chain of consequences.

At eight o'clock, Big Frank had been playing pinochle in a political club near Seventy-second Street. That was Denniman's habit, seven nights a week, except when he had special appointments elsewhere.

Somebody had called saying that Big Frank was wanted at the Hotel Metrolite. That was the usual tip that certain political friends of his were having a gabfest. Mention of names was never considered necessary in such cases; in fact, there were times when it was inadvisable.

Big Frank had hurried from the club; he had taken the first cab that he saw. It was the only cab waiting outside the club. Usually, there was none.

The cab was driven by a hackie who worked for a large company. He was one of a few dozen who had been laid off, awaiting a shipment of new cabs. He had received a typewritten postcard telling him that his new taxi was at a Seventy-second Street garage.

He had gone there to get it. He'd hardly arrived there before there was a call on the telephone, ordering him to go to the political club and wait outside for a passenger.

The taxi company disclaimed all knowledge of the cab. The garage was also perplexed. The cab had been stored there, money in advance, late the night before. The attendant on duty hadn't particularly noticed the fellow who handed him the cash, for the cab was driven into a darkened corner of the garage.

The cab, itself, held the secret of Denniman's death.

Its windows were airtight, shatterproof. They could not have been opened with anything less than a crowbar. The inside door handles were dummies, which meant that the cab could be opened only from the outside.

Fitted to the exhaust pipe was a broad plate, with small outlets attached to holes in the floor. Through these had fizzed the full quota of carbon monoxide produced by a spluttery motor that had an ill-regulated carburetor.

Big Frank Denniman had absorbed enough of the deadly gas to finish him at the end of a five-minute ride. There had probably been monoxide in the cab when he stepped aboard it; but the poisonous fumes were odorless.

Those clues looked great to Joe Cardona; but they went awry when he tried to trace the death cab back to its source. It had been shipped by the manufacturer to the company that wanted it, fully a week ago; but it had gone astray. Neither organization had been able to locate it. How and where it had been outfitted with its death device was an absolute mystery.

LATE that afternoon, Cardona arrived at the police commissioner's office, wondering how his superior was going to take these incomplete reports.

When the inspector was ushered in, he found Melvin Graham with the commissioner. That pleased the inspector; for Commissioner Weston seldom cut loose with caustic comments when a visitor was present.

Weston wanted the reports; Cardona gave them. He was surprised when Weston and Graham exchanged smiles.

"You missed something, inspector," chided Weston, mildly. "The link between the three murdered men."

"What link was that?"

"A political one. You should have discerned that, Cardona."

The inspector was puzzled, until Weston mentioned that Richard Hyvran was a State assemblyman, representing the Long Island section where he lived. Cardona knew that, but had seen no connection between the fact and Hyvran's death. Compared with his large law practice, Hyvran's membership in the State legislature seemed of minor importance.

"That links Hyvran with Denniman," reminded Weston, "because Big Frank was a politician. I know what you are thinking, Cardona: the link seems slight. But it will grow in significance when I tell you something else. Justin Palbrock intended to announce his candidacy for the State senate."

That galvanized Cardona. He was quick with his question: "Who told you that commissioner?"

Weston bowed toward Graham. Removing his gold-rimmed spectacles, the distinguished man explained.

"I met friends who were at the banquet where Palbrock was expected," declared Graham. "The word had gone around among them. I was surprised, until I realized that Palbrock had been coming more and more into the public eye, thanks to speeches that he had given. I would say, also, that he was the sort of man who would gain a large support."

Cardona considered. He was well up on politics; enough to see the setup. Hyvran represented a different group than Denniman; but that could have meant a compromise. This news regarding Palbrock made Cardona picture the retired manufacturer as a political candidate seeking double favor. From that, Cardona jumped to a prompt conclusion.

"Maybe the Murder Master is boosting someone for the State senate!" exclaimed Cardona. "He figured his candidate would be out, if Palbrock went after it. The easiest way was to get rid of Palbrock."

"Extreme measures," objected Weston, "with nothing more at stake than a seat in the State senate. What is more, Cardona, we must consider the sentiments of the candidate chosen by the Murder Master. If there is such a man, he would never have sanctioned Palbrock's death."

"Maybe he didn't know about it, commissioner."

Weston shook his head; that idea didn't suit him. Graham had a different suggestion.

"I would class the murderer as a fanatic," he declared. "His whole process indicates it. He must be a man who has some insane aspiration to power, and considers that he has made progress toward it."

The commissioner nodded. This was more like it.

"He naturally chose men in the public eye,"

continued Graham. "He picked each as representative of a group that has much to do with public affairs. Hyvran, a lawyer and member of the State legislature. Palbrock, a champion of civic welfare. Denniman, an out-and-out politician. There is one question, though." Graham seemed suddenly loath to accept his own theory. "Why should he pick men who were largely confined to New York in activity?"

CARDONA had the answer. He had seen soundness in Graham's comments.

"A crazy man would do just that," he asserted. "I've run into plenty of them. They get all hopped up over one idea. It's what those psychopaths call a 'fixture.'"

There were smiles from Weston and Graham.

"You mean what psychoanalysts term a 'fixation,'" corrected the commissioner. "Allowing for your mistaken nomenclature, Cardona, I would say that you are correct. Your conclusion supplements and substantiates the one advanced by Mr. Graham. We have to deal with a fanatic, whose one idea is to murder men whom he considers to be important. How long he will continue quiet is a matter for conjecture."

Weston paused; then added:

"Fancy it! A man so exaggerated in his notions, that he would occupy a radio studio and flaunt his evil deeds over the air!"

Cardona remembered a last-minute report that had come into headquarters.

"The Murder Master wasn't in that studio at all," affirmed Cardona. "We found a big phonograph in a house across the street. It was all wired up to connect with WQJ."

"A transcription!" ejaculated Graham. "Did they find the record, inspector?"

Cardona shook his head.

"That was gone. But it's a bet the Murder Master wasn't the fellow who took it. He wasn't anywhere around."

"Which means," asserted Graham, to Weston, "that the Murder Master may have been away from New York at the time of the broadcast."

"That's an idea, all right," agreed Cardona. "But here's another. Whoever the Murder Master is, he's got thugs working for him. He needed smooth workers to set those traps for his victims; and there was a bunch that blew into WQJ to take over last night's broadcast."

Commissioner Weston nodded solemnly. He asked what results Cardona had gained from the roundup that had been in progress ever since last night.

Cardona was forced to admit that there had been no results. Stool pigeons had brought no worthwhile information. Whoever the Murder Master's workers were, their insidious chief had ways of covering them.

Weston and Graham showed mutual disappointment. There was a light, though, in Graham's gray eyes, as they gazed patiently toward the commissioner. At last, Weston rapped the table. He looked to Graham and voiced a decision.

"You may be right," declared the commissioner. "The measure that you proposed seemed useless, but I am ready to give it a trial. You may send for those men at once."

Graham looked pleased as he picked up the telephone. Cardona was puzzled. What Graham had proposed; who the men might be, were new mysteries to Joe Cardona. He realized, though, that he would soon have the answer.

The law was about to take a drastic step. Melvin Graham had presented it as a sound one, and Commissioner Weston had come to agree with him. With that move, however, were hidden factors so deep that it was only logical that both Graham and Weston should overlook them.

The law was making a play straight into the hands of the Murder Master.

## CHAPTER VII
## THREE STRAIGHT CROOKS

WHILE Graham was on the telephone, Weston undertoned a preliminary explanation to Cardona. It was almost unnecessary, for the inspector was catching the gist of it from Graham's telephone talk. The double conversation had Cardona dizzy, however, so he finally concentrated on what Weston had to say.

"The reform of criminals," the commissioner explained, "is valuable to society. I admit that heartily, although I do not agree with Graham, when he says that it will abolish crime entirely. However, Graham has done fine work, putting ex-crooks straight."

Cardona nodded. Nevertheless, he grumbled something about the State parole board being too lenient with convicts.

"Not when a man like Graham takes charge," argued Weston. "He makes those fellows toe the mark; at the same time, he gains their good will. That puts them on the right path, and we are to witness the proof of it."

"The proof of it?"

"Yes. Graham was approached today by three of the men who have most benefited through his interest in them. All were shocked by the Murder Master's crimes. They are anxious to cooperate in tracking down the murderer."

This news gave Cardona a medley of thoughts.

The idea was new to him; but the more he juggled it, the better he liked it. As a reformer, Melvin Graham had certainly done excellent work in voluntarily aiding the parole board. He had seen to it that convicts, out on probation, were given jobs to which they were suited.

If they were fired from those jobs, Graham looked into it. If he found that they had been treated unfairly because of their past records, he raked the persons responsible. He either saw that the ex-cons got their jobs back, or were put on better ones.

Cardona could remember the old horse-and-wagon days when old ladies waved umbrellas at horse-whipping teamsters, threatening to bring down the wrath of the law. Graham reminded him of that, when the reformer shouted at people who were unfair to paroled convicts.

Joe had been brought into some of Graham's wrangles as a qualified witness. He'd laughed to himself, sometimes, regarding Graham; but in boiling it down, Cardona had to admit that the reformer got results.

His present efforts showed it.

Graham was bringing in the services of reformed crooks, to help the law snare the Murder Master. If he wanted to class them as detectives, that would be fair enough. These fellows would be on their old home ground, when they looked into affairs of crime.

If, instead, they were to be regarded as a flock of stool pigeons, and serve as such, the law would still be benefited. These chaps would certainly be superior to the squealer type of lowbrow crooks that the police managed to enlist as stoolies.

By the time Graham had finished his call, to announce that the men were on their way, Cardona's interest was keen.

THE men, themselves, looked good when they arrived. Graham introduced them one by one, though that was hardly necessary. Joe Cardona had met them before they went to the big house.

The first was "Ace" Curdy, a long, lean, block-faced man with peculiarly deep-set eyes. Ace gained his nickname from his ability with a revolver. Around shooting galleries, he had used a .22 to drill the center of an ace of diamonds without fringing the edges of the red spot. In gun frays, Ace had shown that same uncanny marksmanship. He nicked his foemen, instead of killing them; that was why he had escaped a murder charge.

"Dobie" Kring was the next—a jolly, big-faced fellow who didn't look like a crook. His hands, though, weren't so pudgy as the rest of him. Those fingers had managed lots of things—forged checks, the combinations on safes. Dobie had been a mine worker once; he knew the art of mixing "soup" that would blast a strongbox when skill couldn't open it.

The third man, "Doc" Harstell, had a professional air. He was a graduate of a medical school who had chucked his career, then taken it up again, for illicit profit. Doc was a "sawbones" who had helped out wounded crooks. He'd worked with a lot of gangs; knew every cranny of the underworld. He had finally taken a rap for those services to society's lower crust.

With each introduction, Graham put a single question. He asked each man to tell why he wished to aid the law.

"I wanted a mouthpiece once," declared Ace. "I went to Hyvran, asking if he'd take the job. He wouldn't have it. I told him I put round holes in guys that didn't listen. He said that put us out of the same class, because he shot square.

"I liked the guy. I've been for him ever since. That's why I asked Mr. Graham if I could go after the mugs that got Hyvran. There were some sharpshooters in that car that was chased last night. Maybe I can find out who they are."

Dobie's story was one of a more recent event. Like others under Graham's wing, he had experienced trouble keeping jobs. He had finally wound up as a bank clerk, and again found prejudice against him. But he hadn't needed to go to Graham. It happened that Justin Palbrock was a director of that bank.

Palbrock had taken up Dobie's cause; had kept the job for him. Dobie had been promoted to a teller; and he owed it to Palbrock. Whatever phony work the Murder Master had used in getting rid of Palbrock, Dobie figured he could help in ferreting it out.

Doc Harstell owed a lot to the dead politician, Denniman.

"I've got a job in a dental lab," stated Doc. "Making good money, but there's a lot of fellows trying to coax me back into my old racket. When I haven't listened, they've tried to shake me down. All I had to do was tell Big Frank about it.

"I'm the sort that crooks are always trying to reach. Sooner or later, I can get a line on that Murder Master, through his mob. That's why I came around today and talked to Mr. Graham. I hoped he would consider me useful."

THERE was earnestness in every story. That, plus the qualifications that the men possessed, sold them to the commissioner.

The grudge angle was the one that Cardona liked. He figured these fellows would go the limit to get back at the murderer who had slain their benefactors.

The three were told that work would be arranged for them. Dire necessity called for extreme efforts by the law. Weston shook hands all round; told the trio to keep in touch with Graham, so that whatever they learned would be forwarded to the police.

Graham received Weston's congratulations after the paroled men had gone.

"If we had selected those men ourselves," asserted the commissioner, "we could not have made a better choice. The old saying, 'Set a thief to catch a thief,' should still hold good. Your pardon, Graham"—Weston had noted a disapproving look on the reformer's face—"I recognize that these men must no longer be classed as criminals. I merely had reference to their past."

"The present suits me," put in Cardona. "Those lads know their onions! They'll kid their old pals into thinking they're off the straight and narrow. You'd better keep tabs on them, though, Mr. Graham."

"That has been arranged," assured Graham. "Both my secretary and my chauffeur are in my confidence. They have always kept careful check, without the paroled men suspecting it. Right now, they are delivering them to their respective lodging places."

That met the approval of Weston and Cardona. But they, like Graham, would have been badly jolted had they gained a television flash of Graham's big car at that very moment. Ace, Dobie and Doc were in the back seat, as the limousine rolled through the dusk. In front, the secretary was leaning back to chat. The chauffeur was chuckling with him.

"So you put it over" laughed the secretary. "Say—we'd sure like to have seen it! Who busted the ice?"

"I did," returned Ace. "Just the way the chief wanted it. Why shouldn't they fall for it? Nobody can tell them that I planted the pineapple in Hyvran's car."

"My trip to Washington also passed unnoticed," reminded Dobie. "I suppose I was mistaken for a lobbyist, returning to New York. Even Palbrock didn't know I was looking at him. That pencil switch was a cinch! Palbrock was half asleep when I made it."

"I didn't dwell too long on my mechanical ability," added Doc Harstell, dryly. "No one could connect me with that fixed cab Denniman was in, and those timely phone calls."

Chuckles followed—less hideous than those voiced by the Murder Master, but sufficient to show the delight that these unreformed crooks took in crime. In brief statements, all concurred that their main job was to keep Graham totally deceived. The secretary and the chauffeur assured them there would be no trouble on that score.

Already, the pair had mentioned phony alibis covering Ace, Dobie and Doc at the time of the Murder Master's broadcast. The car kept southward; it neared the street with the alleyway where crooks had carried The Shadow last night. Ace beckoned to the two men beside him.

"Give me the reports," said Ace. "I'll shove them in the door for the chief."

Dobie and Doc passed him envelopes. Ace alighted at a darkened house and thrust the envelopes through a mail chute, adding a report of his own.

"The chief's not back yet," remarked Ace, as they drove away. "It was a smart gag, him being out of town for a couple of days. He pulls that professor stuff swell, I guess. I'd like to hear one of his screwy lectures."

"We ought to hear from him tonight," said Dobie. "Come on down to my place. I got the mixer working swell. We won't miss anything that comes over it."

Only Doc Harstell was silent. Ace nudged him.

"What you thinking about, Doc?"

"I'm thinking about the professor—" Doc caught himself. "I mean the chief. When he goes away, he leaves that fellow Thoyer there."

"Why not? Thoyer's a boob. Makes a good blind."

"But maybe he gets a look at our reports."

"What if he does? They're in the code the chief gave us, ain't they? Forget Thoyer! Say—he wasn't even awake last night when me and the guys with me dumped The Shadow."

Soon, the three criminals were dropped off at the places where they lived. The big car headed back, to pick up Melvin Graham and take him to his apartment. Those lesser tools—chauffeur and secretary—were straightfaced when Graham entered the car, along with Weston.

Graham had invited the commissioner to dine at the Cobalt Club. The men in the front seat were listening intently as they heard their employer chat with Weston. The smiles that were secretly exchanged in the front seat were proof that the pair regarded Graham as the greatest dupe with whom they had to deal.

The real master of the servants that Graham trusted was the same master who ruled the paroled crooks that the reformer had so carefully put along straight paths.

That master was the Murder Master!

## CHAPTER VIII
## THE DOOMING EYE

CROOKS had good cause to praise the Murder Master.

Crafty were the methods of that supercriminal; many were his exploits. Greatest of all, he had accomplished the result long sought by all the underworld.

The Murder Master had conquered The Shadow.

Men of crime believed The Shadow to be dead. Ace Curdy had emphasized that belief in his statement to Dobie Kring and Doc Harstell. If any of those three had been told that The Shadow still lived, they would not have worried.

The Shadow had been placed where he was at the mercy of the Murder Master.

The Shadow, himself, realized that plight when he awakened, a few hours later. His first glimmering sensations gave him an impression of his surroundings. When he revived further, he began to reconstruct the circumstances that had brought him to the depths of a pitch-black cell. He also understood why he still lived.

Recollecting that terrifying shock in the control room of WQJ, The Shadow recognized that it had been intended to do more than stupefy him. The huge voltage was enough to deliver death, under certain conditions. The Murder Master had overlooked one important provision.

Killers had hooked the metal plate to the radio station's current. Like most of the buildings in Manhattan, it used direct current. Long ago—so many years that it had almost been forgotten—experimenters had learned that direct current lacked destructive force. That was why State prisons used alternating current to burn persons sentenced to the electric chair.

Direct current could kill; but if it failed, there was always a chance of the victim's survival. The Shadow had demonstrated that by his present revival. Oddly, he owed his recovery partly to the men who had served the Murder Master.

Rocketed from the floor plate, The Shadow had been alive when his captors carried him away. Not only had they decided that bullets were unwise and unnecessary; they had placed The Shadow in a spot best suited to restore the flicker of life that remained to him.

This cell was damp, its floor streaked with moist, oozy mud that formed a long accumulated sediment. Friends of The Shadow could have chosen no better place for his recuperation than the one which his enemies had so unwittingly selected.

Feeble at first, The Shadow moved more steadily as he began his exploration of the cell. He was utterly unable to calculate the time that he had lain helpless. That, however, seemed of little consequence, compared to the prospect of escape from this pit.

The door was evidently that of an old, abandoned cellar. The Shadow's fingers found crevices between the flagstones, as he crawled about. Those cracks along the ancient floor accounted for the muddy surface. At first, The Shadow held the hope that this was merely some forgotten pit where he had been flung by persons who believed him dead.

That hope faded when The Shadow reached a wall.

There, he encountered a smooth steel surface. Groping along that wall, he came to another, also of metal. A complete tour of the cell proved that it was square, and entirely lined with steel. This chamber was evidently one that the Murder Master had reserved for prisoners who might be capable of escape from ordinary traps.

THE SHADOW'S flashlight was gone, like his automatics. Ace and his pals had found time to take those trophies the night before. Unable to see the ceiling, The Shadow rose in a corner of the cell, stretched his arms high above his head. The ceiling was beyond his reach.

Stone floor—steel walls—such were formidable barriers. Whatever the structure of the ceiling, it would be the logical spot to attack, particularly since it would offer a route above ground. In the blackness of the pit, however, The Shadow could not even see the ceiling, let alone climb to it.

Given a wall with the scantiest crevices, The Shadow could scale it like a human beetle. These steel walls were impossible. Except at the corners, where steel plates joined, they had no cracks.

For smooth walls like these, The Shadow had often used rubber suction cups that gave a powerful hold. He seldom carried them, except on planned expeditions. He lacked the suction cups this night.

The Shadow's only course was to wait, while he learned what might befall him in this trap. The longer he waited, the better; for his strength was below par. As minutes passed, he could feel a distinct recuperation. Perhaps, at the end of hours, he could decide upon some plan of escape.

The Shadow followed the assumption that every trap had a loophole. Past experience had demonstrated that fact to his satisfaction. Unfortunately, there was another quality that many traps possessed. They sometimes became more than pitfalls, turning into death devices under the control of a master hand.

Such was to be the case with this metal-lined pit. At the end of a long, leisurely hour, The Shadow saw symptoms of arriving hazard.

A dull glow began to fill the prison room. It came from the ceiling; there, The Shadow noticed four small glass sockets, their surfaces on the ceiling level. Each contained a bulb that glowed with greenish light that increased with painful slowness. At first the rays were hazy; but as their emerald flicker became stronger, The Shadow could make out the entire cell.

The ceiling, like the walls, was of steel; the rounded glass-surfaced light sockets were too small to be of consequence. There was a larger opening, however, that intrigued The Shadow the moment that he observed it.

That was a circular object, squarely in the ceiling's center. It was metal-bound; fitted with glass, like a large porthole. It was large enough to allow a person's passage.

The difficulty was to reach the porthole.

It was fully nine feet above the stone floor. There was nothing that The Shadow could use as a ladder. Even the walls were useless, should he find a way to scale them, for they were too far from that center opening.

It seemed like a tantalizing bait, that porthole, put there to give mental torture to the prisoner who would find it out of reach. It had a simpler purpose, as well. It was obviously the hole through which The Shadow had been dropped to this steel-lined dungeon.

IT was not until the lights had reached their full glow that The Shadow learned another reason for that metal-rimmed glass.

The glare produced a ghastly green that brought a curious reflection from the glass. Light became vivid on the floor, showing The Shadow fully outlined as he stared upward to the glass-blocked opening. That glass, The Shadow noted, was concave. Staring toward it, he saw a curious blur of color that came from above the entire surface.

The hues were circular; but they wavered and shifted. Sometimes they dimmed; whenever they increased, they did not pass the blurry stage that The Shadow had first observed.

Suddenly, the answer linked.

The concave glass was the lens of a gigantic microscope. The blurred color above it was the outline of a human eye!

The Shadow had become a laboratory specimen for the superkiller who had captured him. The Murder Master, possessed of a new victim, was studying his captive at leisure. Every move The Shadow made was magnified. That curious eye—rendered mammoth by the microscope—was calmly surveying the black-clad fighter that all other foemen feared.

The Shadow became motionless. He was standing near the center of the dungeon, his head tilted slightly upward. His eyes peered past the front edge of his downturned hat brim. The eye of the master murderer was steady, also. In that period of fixation, neither observer learned facts regarding the other.

By the time the Murder Master had focused the microscope, The Shadow had taken his position. His hat brim sheltered his face from his foeman's view. Similarly, the big eye above was too blurred for The Shadow to note features by which he might later identify it.

The situation, though, was not an even break. The Shadow's instinctive interest in the rising glow had caused him to play into the enemy's hands. The Murder Master had come to his laboratory for one primary purpose: to learn if The Shadow still lived. Having discovered the prisoner to be alive, the supercrook was ready for new measures.

The Shadow saw color dwindle. The eye had moved away. The Murder Master was satisfied with the trap; convinced that The Shadow's position was a helpless one. Slowly, the green lights faded; as token that the master killer was through with his brief study of the biological specimen called The Shadow.

As the ghoulish green diminished, The Shadow sensed new danger. He knew that he could expect but one verdict from the Murder Master: that of death. The thrust would come when darkness was again complete; for the present, The Shadow could not surmise what its source would be.

He foresaw only that the Murder Master would choose one of two measures, whichever suited his whim. Either the death method would be swift, almost instantaneous; or it would be agonizing and prolonged. Halfway measures did not belong in the Murder Master's catalogue.

THE prison room was a vague green outline when the move began. From somewhere beyond steel walls The Shadow heard a *thrumm* of muffled machinery, that pounded with a beat of doom.

Straining his eyes toward one wall, The Shadow detected a slow, quivering motion. Before he had time to study the wall further; the lights were totally blotted.

The wall that The Shadow had observed was to his left. The same *thrumm* was coming from the right. It was toward that wall that The Shadow moved. As he spread his gloved hands against it, he could feel the steel's steady pressure. For a dozen seconds, The Shadow held his ground; then he was forced to shift away, or be shoved off balance.

Crossing to the opposite wall, The Shadow met the same incoming power. Each wall was thrusting inward at the rate of a foot a minute. Each minute, therefore, cut down The Shadow's dwelling space by two feet.

It was a dozen feet across the room. Six minutes more, the walls would clamp together. But, to The Shadow, as he now stood, there belonged only a five-minute life span. The sixth minute would not be his.

Those final sixty seconds were the time when crushing walls would shatter bone and pulpify flesh. That minute would bring death that would prove the lone relief from the horror that produced it.

## CHAPTER IX
## MADDENED MINUTES

STEADILY, like living things of doom, the creeping walls loomed closer. Twin Juggernauts, each possessed of a huge crushing force, they were fated to complete their appointed course. Only the Murder Master could have halted them, and he was not the sort to have last-moment regrets.

In the darkness, The Shadow remained motionless. Had there been light, with the Murder Master viewing from above, the supercrook would have supposed that The Shadow was resigned to his fate. Actually, the black clad prisoner was tense.

For one minute only, The Shadow had stood fully helpless. Then the slow closing of the walls had itself given him a plan. This was one trap that had no available loophole. It also filled the qualification of being a death device. It was that double feature that produced its weakness.

The Shadow had not forgotten the mammoth lens that filled the opening above. It could never have served him had the Murder Master let the cell remain as it was. The master fiend, in providing two separate purposes for his dungeon, had outrun his own craftiness.

The Shadow wanted those steel-sheeted walls to close. His arms extended, he was welcoming them—not as jaws of doom, but as the one means that might enable him to effect his own rescue. In a sense, those first minutes were The Shadow's greatest strain. Once they were ended, he could begin the action that would make him forget the menace of the pressing walls.

At the end of three minutes, The Shadow could feel each wall touching an outstretched hand. Still, he remained rigid. Effort would be wasted until they were even closer. Mechanically, The Shadow was counting off the seconds; all the while, his hands were coming closer to his shoulders. He could tell by touch, as well as time, when the right moment had arrived.

That was at the end of four minutes, when the walls were four feet apart. The Shadow's waiting ended. He came to action.

His first move was one of pressure. With all his strength, he forced his hands against the walls. He was like a Samson, thrusting against temple pillars; but these walls were inflexible. Compared to the motors that impelled them, The Shadow's strength was puny.

*Thrumm—thrumm—*

The dooming throbs seemed to mock the victim, as hideously as if the Murder Master had been on hand to add his insidious cackle. Inch by inch, the walls closed unflinchingly. The Shadow's hands were being forced upward under their pressure. From his lips came a whispered laugh.

The trap was working as The Shadow wanted it.

JABBING one foot against a wall, The Shadow utilized an angled pressure with his opposite arm. That gave him a free hand to thrust higher. His opposite foot came up; he shifted pressure. His next crisscross shift was swifter, likewise longer. Swaying back and forth in the darkness, he jockeyed from wall to wall with an eccentric upward course.

The Shadow was scaling four feet to every foot that the walls closed.

He was near the top before the walls had reached his shoulders. In coming closer, those barriers had added ease and speed to The Shadow's progress. At the start, there had been danger of a slip. That was ended when he neared the top.

With outthrust elbows and pressing feet, The Shadow held himself fixed between the walls, and their increasing pressure added to the surety of his position.

Hands upward, The Shadow was clutching at the steel-rimmed porthole. He couldn't break the glass; he was depending on the chance that the rim would loosen. A portion of the rim wabbled upward, taking the glass with it; but The Shadow could not push it clear until he utilized his last resort.

For a few seconds, he rested; then, as the walls pressed his shoulders, he spread his knees and worked his whole body upward. Sidewise pressure was no longer necessary. The walls, with their crushing force, were supporting The Shadow in place.

Head tilted back, The Shadow thrust his arms straight upward in front of his body. His hands bashed the glass hard. With the smaller supporting frame, the lens whipped upward on a hinge, into a large cylindrical space above.

The Shadow could clutch the interior of the upper tube, but he could no longer pull his body upward. The walls had him clamped with torturous pressure that was almost at the bone-breaking stage. Crosswise between those slow-vibrating slabs, The Shadow had scant seconds in which to act. He used them to their limit.

**Inch by inch, the walls closed unflinchingly. The Shadow was like a Samson, thrusting against temple pillars.**

Hands clutching the sides of the uptilted lens frame, The Shadow gave a powerful twist. His shoulders, body, legs—all figured in that wrench. His body did a quarter turn. Instead of being hard clamped, crosswise, he was dangling almost loose, his face to one wall, his back to the other.

There wasn't time for The Shadow to slip downward, even if his hands had released their grip. *Thrumms* from the machinery brought the walls two inches closer together; enough to sandwich their victim between the metal slabs.

As that pressure came, The Shadow's arms pulled upward. His body slithered from the closing walls, bringing him hip-high in the space above the ceiling.

There, with a final heave, The Shadow braced upon an interior ledge. His feet, pushing hard against a moving plate, forced his legs up through the hole. Curling about the inside of the darkened cylinder, The Shadow found the framed lens and slapped it downward. As it thumped into place, he rolled upon it, to lie exhausted.

THE SHADOW had cleared the pressing walls when they were scarcely more than a foot apart. Less than a half minute remained after he had flattened the porthole; yet that time seemed far longer than the maddened minutes that The Shadow had spent in his climb.

The token that told the finish was a clang as the walls came together. The shudder of that metallic meeting brought a tremble to the cylinder where The Shadow rested secure.

The machinery had stopped automatically. There was a *whirr* of a sound; then it went into reverse. The Shadow could hear the slow rumble of the receding walls. They had a grind that reminded him of a grumbling monster, angered at loss of its prey.

The pit below was safe; but The Shadow had no desire to return to it. Rising in the cylinder that formed his present prison, he found another glass just above his head. From its shape, it was probably another lens that served as part of the oversize microscope.

The overhead frame was wedged more tightly than the lower one. When The Shadow finally released it, the glass swung downward on a hinge.

Just above, The Shadow found a trapdoor. He worked it upward; threw it open. He drew himself up into a room above. There, The Shadow's first action was to feel for the upper lens and put it into place, after which he edged the trapdoor into position.

The room in which The Shadow found himself was pitch-black. As he felt his way through the darkness, he encountered tables and other items that were apparently part of a laboratory's equipment. Reaching a wall switch, The Shadow listened intently. The room was definitely deserted. The Shadow turned on the light.

The room proved to be a laboratory—well outfitted but little used, judging by the dust that streaked some of the benches. Moreover, the place was untidy; papers, notebooks, jars and other items were piled hodgepodge on tables. It looked as though the owner had started certain experiments, then discarded them. He was probably an inventive genius as well as a scientist, for a workshop adjoined the lab.

One table, pushed into a corner of the laboratory, was fitted with a large microscope. Examining it closely, The Shadow found that the table had a metal rim which could be removed by loosening corner screws. That allowed a central board to slide out from beneath the microscope.

This table had simply been pushed over the mammoth lens tube below the floor. By adjusting the ordinary microscope, the Murder Master had been able to enlarge his vision to include the prison room. In searching for the switch that controlled the cell-room lights and the moving walls, The Shadow could not find it.

The walls of the room had panels; probably one hid the switches. That was likely, considering the state of the trapdoor through which The Shadow had arrived here.

Instead of showing conspicuously on the floor, the trapdoor was invisible; so closely fitted, that The Shadow had to probe to find it. There was no give when he stepped upon the trap. Its boards extended between those of the solid floor. A person who did not suspect the trapdoor's presence would probably never locate it.

The laboratory had a heavy door that apparently led to the front door; another that looked like an entrance to a side passage. Both doors were locked; before trying to open them, The Shadow decided to inspect the workshop.

There, he made a definite discovery. On a workbench were items of radio equipment. Beneath the bench was a large phonograph, with a stack of big records, the sort used in electrical transcriptions.

The inventor who occupied these premises had all the equipment needed to deliver the Murder Master program. Probably one of those records had been used for the broadcast at WQJ, The Shadow needed the inventor's name; he found it, painted on a box of electrical equipment that had come by express.

The box was addressed to Professor Jerome Quedden, New York.

AT the back of the workshop was a spiral staircase that led upstairs. A further search of the premises promised more important results. A forgotten flashlight, dropped behind a workbench, was all that The Shadow needed. Taking the flash, he extinguished the lights in the laboratory, then picked his way to the spiral stairs.

On the second floor, The Shadow found another laboratory, evidently the one that Quedden used more regularly. It was equipped with chemical appliances; everything was in shipshape order. Under the only door, The Shadow saw a glow that indicated a hallway light. He extinguished the flashlight and tried the door. It was unlocked.

There were several doors opening from the hall. All were closed; they looked like living quarters. There was a curtained passage to the left of the laboratory door, which was at the hallway's end. Spreading the curtain, The Shadow saw a long side hall, with an open room at the end.

Passing one door that stood ajar, The Shadow flicked his flashlight to see a storeroom that had side windows. They were shuttered, like all other windows that he had seen. There was a squatty window, though, at the rear of the storeroom. It was wide, but very low. It was set high in the wall, indicating that it opened on a roof. The wide window had no shutters; simply a drawn shade.

About all that the storeroom contained were old trunks, boxes, and a few articles of furniture. The Shadow passed it, went on to the rear room. It was furnished like an office.

Evidently the office was vital to Professor Quedden, for its shutters were newer and heavier than any others. The room had a desk, a metal filing cabinet, a safe in the corner. There was a curtained doorway opening into a closet; there, The Shadow found a discarded wooden filing cabinet.

Before The Shadow could give closer inspection, his ears caught a distant sound. It gave the faint impression of a clicking door latch, carrying through the passages of the old house.

Edging from the office, The Shadow listened; there were footsteps on the front stairs that came directly to the upper hall.

The logical place to go was the storeroom; but there was no time to reach it. The curtains stirred at the front of the long hall, proving that the person who had entered the house was coming directly to the little office.

Extinguishing his flashlight, The Shadow whisked back into darkness.

He had already picked a good spot in the office itself. Silently, The Shadow reached that place: the curtained closet. He wedged past the old filing cabinet; found the exact space that he required, in back of it.

Thanks to a slight adjustment that he gave the curtain when he passed it, The Shadow had a clear view to the desk. Once the office lights were turned on, he could see whoever sat there, although The Shadow's own lurking space would be unseen.

The Shadow had begun his quest for the Murder Master. As the situation stood, The Shadow seemed due to gain his first view of Professor Jerome Quedden.

## CHAPTER X
## HIDDEN CRIME

THE lights of the little office came on within a half minute after The Shadow had taken to his hiding place. The wall switch was by the office door; that was why The Shadow did not immediately see the man who entered. Instead, he received nothing but audible impressions of Professor Jerome Quedden.

Those were sufficient to form a link with the past. The sounds that Quedden emitted as he fussed about the room were low mumbles—odd clucky sounds that indicated he was in good humor. Though less dramatic than the tones that had come over the air, those mutters were highly reminiscent of the chuckling remarks that the Murder Master had used to fill in time between his announcements of death.

Alone, Quedden could hardly be expected to provide such high-pitched utterances as he had used for that recorded program over WQJ. At moments, his voice was precisely as The Shadow had remembered it. At other times, it dropped to a half whisper that could hardly have registered on the microphone.

By the time Quedden finally decided to approach the desk, The Shadow had formed half a dozen impressions of his possible appearance. The final one was accurate in many details, although The Shadow missed in gauging the professor's height. Jerome Quedden was so short of stature that his hips barely reached the desktop when he passed it.

Undersize, wizened, baldish—those summed the professor as The Shadow first saw him. When Quedden seated himself in the big swivel chair behind his desk, he looked like a dried peanut in its shell. His eyes, though, proved him to be more than a wizened old fossil.

Those eyes were beads that shone with blackish brilliance. Their glow revealed shrewd thoughts that were in the old man's brain. Perhaps the mutters that came from Quedden's dryish lips were maudlin expressions that showed a mental letdown between his keener thoughts. On the contrary, they could have been intended—a pretense to make it seem that he was absentminded.

One fact was positive. Whenever he muttered, Quedden emitted no words that could be understood. Nor did the flashes of his eyes, the odd smiles of his lips, give any clue to his actual thoughts.

Looking about the desk, Quedden stroked his chin. His eyes fixed toward the door; they registered anger, then suspicion. That look turned to a crafty one, with an accompanying smile, as he pressed a button beneath the desk.

Soon, there were footsteps in the hall. A sleepy-faced man entered, wearing slippers, trousers, collarless shirt. He had a dull look on his roundish features; but there was something methodical in his manner, by the time he reached the desk.

That was where The Shadow first saw him. He noted that the man had a weak-chinned profile. The man's tone, too, was a rather weak one, as he asked:

"You rang for me, professor?"

"Use your wits, Thoyer!" snapped Quedden. "Who else could have rung for you? Do you think that I would have visitors at this hour of night?"

"I didn't know, sir."

Quedden shook his head.

"You are an excellent laboratory assistant," he remarked, testily. "For the ability that you show in your work, I would expect you to be intelligent in other matters! However, we can let that pass. What messages came today, Thoyer?"

THE lab assistant fished in his hip pocket. He brought out a long, fat envelope, with a few smaller ones. Quedden leaned far across the desk, snatched the big envelope greedily. He ripped it open, spilled the contents on the desk.

There, The Shadow saw crisp currency: bills of large denomination. There was five thousand dollars in the packet. Quedden counted it several times, to make sure. He finally peered inside the big envelope, then tossed it toward a wastebasket. The envelope fluttered to the floor. Thoyer methodically picked it up and put it in the basket.

"From the Foundation," chuckled Quedden. "They are doing well with my inventions, Thoyer. This time, they have paid me in cash. Last time, it was bonds."

"It's odd, sir," put in Thoyer, as though he for once had an idea, "that they never sent payment by check."

"Not a bit odd," retorted Quedden. "My arrangement was made on a cash basis."

"But bonds are not cash—"

"They are as good as money," cackled Quedden, tilting his head. "I keep all that I gain.

So where is the difference, Thoyer?"

The assistant shook his head. Evidently the whole matter was beyond him. Quedden turned to open the safe and put the money away. While he did, he chuckled some more statements for Thoyer's benefit.

"The Foundation for Inventors is an excellent institution," declared Quedden. "They seem to understand an inventor's problems. After they negotiated with me and learned my wants, they equipped this house in precisely the fashion that I desired. When I first came here, I was amazed at the thorough preparations that they had made! They even provided you, Thoyer!"

Quedden swung around from the safe in time to hear Thoyer offer an objection.

"I never heard of the Foundation, sir."

"You told me that before, Thoyer," interjected Quedden. "They had heard of you, though. That is why you were recommended. The fact that I communicated with you, and actually hired you, does not lessen your obligation to the Foundation."

Thoyer was prompt to say that he was grateful to the Foundation for Inventors. That appeased the old professor. He waved his hand in dismissal, with the remark:

"You had better get to bed, Thoyer. If you don't get up early, you will never find time to put the lower laboratory in order. I am going to need it, soon; and the workshop, too."

Thoyer started to go. He suddenly remembered the envelopes that he held in his hand. He passed them to Quedden, who noted that they were blank, and lightly sealed. His eyes glaring angrily, Quedden ripped open the envelopes and brought out folded papers.

As before, Quedden's mood changed with the quickness of a summer squall. He indulged in a hearty chuckle when he spread the papers.

"Another joke," he told Thoyer. "Where did you find them? In the mailbox, as usual?"

"Yes, sir." Thoyer craned timidly to look at the papers. "What are they, professor? More of those coded notes?"

Quedden nodded. He was eyeing Thoyer, with that head tilt which The Shadow had noted before. It added to his shrewd expression; but Quedden's attitude seemed unnoticed by Thoyer. Turning to the messages, Quedden scanned them one by one; then placed them in a desk drawer.

"I shall keep them," he decided. "They may prove important, later. Do you agree, Thoyer?"

"I don't know." The assistant was dully doubtful. "It may be that they have simply been left at the wrong house."

"Bah! There have been too many of them, Thoyer."

"Maybe the sender is wondering why he receives no answer."

A pleased smile showed on Quedden's lips, as he arose from his desk. Stepping to one side, he clapped an approving hand on Thoyer's shoulder.

"Good logic," commended Quedden. "You may have struck it, Thoyer. You relieve me of much anxiety."

Thoyer looked blank. The professor explained.

"BEFORE I came here"—Quedden's tone was a confiding whisper—"I received many threats. The Foundation has protected me against such nuisances. Against persons who plotted to steal my inventions. I was afraid that the trouble had begun again."

"I understand, sir." Thoyer was hurried. "You mustn't get started on that again, professor. You know what the physician said—"

"Bah! I trust no physicians!"

"But the Foundation sent that doctor here, sir."

"That's so!" Quedden's wild look faded. His lips took on a childish smile. "Therefore, the doctor's advice was good. The Foundation always advises me properly. I shall worry no longer."

They walked away from the desk. Thoyer was humoring the professor, asking if a lecture he had given in Rochester had been well received. In chuckly fashion, Quedden declared that he had gone over his allotted time; that was why he had missed his train. His late arrival in New York was the result.

Though the professor and his assistant were out of sight, The Shadow could hear them converse at the door. There, Quedden chided Thoyer for not having shut the office. Thoyer excused his oversight by the fact that he had expected Quedden earlier.

"After this," clucked the professor, sourly, "see that the door is shut. Once it is closed, this office is protected. Remember, Thoyer, should an intruder enter this house, the office would be his goal. That is why I have prepared against such emergency."

The door closed. From it, The Shadow heard a loud click that sounded like an automatic lock. The door must have been a tight one, for there were no traces of departing footfalls along the hall. The Shadow was satisfied, however, that Quedden and his assistant were actually gone.

The professor had extinguished the lights. Coming from his hiding place, The Shadow reached the door, made careful inspection with his flashlight. He was correct in his surmise about the door. It fitted so tightly that it could cut off light as well as sound. The Shadow turned on the room lights.

Five minutes later, Quedden's safe stood open. From its interior, The Shadow was bringing stacks of currency and bonds. It did not take him long to identify them. These were spoils from recent robberies in and around New York.

ALL in all, Quedden's hoarded wealth totaled about forty thousand dollars; a meager sum, considering the size of some of the reported hauls.

Crooks had made sharp inroads recently, cracking safes in big business houses as well as those of outlying banks. That, plus unreported robberies of certain gambling places and racketeering headquarters, had put the reputed loot above the half-million mark.

Nevertheless, that was no reason why the Murder Master should have retained a large proportion of the swag. It was plain that many criminals were involved in his enterprises. They could be paid off cheaper by giving them plenty from the earlier robberies.

A mastermind intended greater crimes. That was apparent to The Shadow, without the evidence in Quedden's safe. That night of triple murder, during the broadcast from WQJ, was definite proof to The Shadow that a surge of crime would come. For some reason—as yet, an evasive one—the Murder Master had found it necessary to eliminate three men who stood in the way of his plans.

The Shadow had not forgotten that the Murder Master had planned the finish of a fourth. That last victim was to have been The Shadow. In fact, the Murder Master already believed The Shadow dead.

That was a factor that gave The Shadow a powerful advantage. He had met with such circumstances before. Always, he had been able to play a strong counterthrust against hidden crime, when enemies believed that he was eliminated.

The Shadow intended such measures in this case. Not only was he alive; he was occupying the most unlikely spot where crooks would expect him to be. This office, vital to the crooked game, had become The Shadow's own headquarters. Here, he could analyze crime; plan steps against the Murder Master, with plenty of evidence at hand.

Professor Quedden had spoken of the office's protection. But the shrewd old professor had apparently overlooked the possibility of a person being in the office when he closed it. Like the trap in the cellar, this was a snare that had a loophole.

That was why The Shadow lingered, confident. His laugh was a whispered one, confined to the soundproof office. The Shadow was picturing how easily he had offset Quedden's craftiness.

For once, The Shadow had laughed too soon.

## CHAPTER XI
## FROM THE TRAP

QUEDDEN'S safe contained many items other than the incriminating swag; but little else pertained to crime. In searching, The Shadow found plans for various inventions, along with records of chemical formulas. Few of these were in a complete state.

It seemed that the professor was versatile, as well as creative; but he apparently had the habit of dropping one endeavor to take up another. It was likely, therefore, that many of Quedden's inventions might have flaws that would make them impractical.

They ran a long range, those inventions; and The Shadow immediately saw that they had insidious possibilities, not mentioned in the specifications. Quedden's radio experiments, for instance, involved a system of remote control that had probably been used during the episode at WQJ.

The professor had also experimented with lethal gases. A bulky envelope was packed with data on that subject. Its only relation to crime, however, seemed to concern the handling of criminals. Along with Quedden's own formulas were reports that described the efficiency of existing vapors, from tear gas to the lethal gas used in legal executions.

Like much that pertained to Professor Quedden, these finds were uncertainties. While the funds in the safe were evidence that Quedden had acquired stolen goods, there was no proof that he had put his inventions to criminal use. The radio link was the likely one.

To follow it, The Shadow finished with the safe; as soon as he closed the heavy door, he turned to the desk.

There, The Shadow produced the coded messages and began a study of them. They appeared to be ordinary cryptograms; but the letter frequencies did not check. It was obvious that these must be reports from crooks who served the Murder Master; that made it unlikely that the system could be complicated.

Searching for the answer, The Shadow found it by checking short words in different messages. He discovered that three simple codes were used in every message. In each case, the first word followed one system of letter substitution; the second word, another; the third word, the last system.

The fourth word reverted to the first code; the fifth, to the second; the sixth to the third. The rule of one, two, three was followed throughout. It was a clever idea on the part of the Murder Master, for it made the messages more troublesome than ordinary cryptograms. At the same time, it was easy for the lesser crooks to code their reports; almost as simple as if they had used a single cipher.

The messages were rather cryptic, even when translated. The writers did not refer in detail to deeds that they had accomplished. Instead, they mentioned matters that were evidently understood by the Murder Master, which was proof that he had some method of direct communication with them.

There were references to "garage," to "telegram," to "taxicab"; these, oddly, meant very little to The Shadow, for he had not yet learned the manner wherein victims had met death during the broadcast period from station WQJ.

More illuminating was a message that referred vaguely to The Shadow's own experience. It stated that the "box" had worked; that the body was in the cell.

There was another message, declaring that the machine had been left in the house, but that the record had been replaced where it belonged. To The Shadow, that last phrase signified that the record used in the WQJ broadcast was back in the workshop that adjoined Quedden's lower laboratory.

LEAVING the messages in their drawer, The Shadow folded the odd sheets of paper on which he had decoded the notes. He began an inspection of the desk; there, he found typewritten letters addressed to Professor Quedden. All were from the Foundation for Inventors, but they bore no signatures.

They proved conclusively that the Foundation was a myth. The Shadow had never heard of such an organization; its letterheads bore no address other than New York.

The only other Foundation literature was a printed folder, giving a list of lecture engagements that Quedden was supposed to keep. The Rochester lecture was specified; in his talk in that city, Quedden had discussed the subject of stellar rays.

A clock on Quedden's desk showed that The Shadow's investigation had taken nearly a full hour. The Shadow, however, was in no hurry to leave. Seated at the desk, his long-fingered hand penciled notations of their own. The Shadow was analyzing the situation as the evidence showed it.

Identifying Jerome Quedden as the Murder Master, facts fell steadily in line.

Here was Quedden, posing as an inventor financed by a mythical organization called the Foundation for Inventors. An expert in radio, Quedden could communicate with his followers whenever he chose. They, in turn, could send back coded reports. As for Quedden's shares of stolen wealth, those were left in envelopes that bore the name of the nonexistent Foundation.

Crooks also had access to Quedden's premises, but not by the front door. They obviously used a side entrance that led into the lower laboratory. They could come and go secretly, bringing and taking whatever Quedden's instructions might require. Quedden, himself, could enter that side entrance when he chose.

The one weakness was Quedden's alibi. The fake Foundation for Inventors would not stand the strain, if the law investigated it. Offsetting that was the fact that the law probably would have no occasion to look into the Foundation. If crime continued smoothly, the law would never even hear of the fake organization.

Why, then, should Quedden, as the master criminal, bother with the Foundation hoax at all?

There was a plausible answer to that question. The answer was Thoyer. He was the one man who remained close to Quedden, and never took part in outside crimes. Taking Thoyer for what he looked to be, The Shadow saw how useful the man could prove to Quedden.

The professor needed a competent assistant to work on his inventions with him. Evidently, Thoyer filled such qualifications, while available crooks did not. On that simple assumption, the bluff regarding the Foundation for Inventors was necessary, to keep Thoyer ignorant of true conditions.

It was a curious setup—one of the strangest that The Shadow had ever encountered. To all outward appearances, Professor Quedden was an eccentric inventor; gullible when he trusted people, highly suspicious of all other persons— even imaginary ones.

Thoyer, in contrast, was a slow thinker, methodical and used to taking orders. He was satisfied to stay here constantly, and his one anxiety appeared to be humoring Quedden when the old professor started a tantrum.

Beneath that surface lay a hidden purpose. A schemer was doing his utmost to keep a dupe under complete control. That precaution was constantly successful; it served as vital protection to the Murder Master's game. From The Shadow's viewpoint, it showed a flaw in the supercrook's armor.

This would be the place to have the showdown, with Quedden and Thoyer as participants. If each could be forced to tell only a part of what he knew, while existing evidence lay in light, the criminal career of the Murder Master would come to an abrupt finish.

That climax could wait. There was much to be accomplished before it arrived. Matters would remain static here, during the time that The Shadow required. Meanwhile, The Shadow's task was to delve into other angles of past crime.

Those coded notes told that many dangerous criminals were in the Murder Master's service. Unsigned, printed only in pencil, the messages gave no clues to their senders. The Shadow intended, therefore, to learn who were the members of the crooked band before he made his final stroke.

RISING from the desk, The Shadow did not have to glance at the clock to know that he had stayed a long while. The tight-closed room was becoming stuffy. Its heavy atmosphere produced a physical weariness that brought a tingle to The Shadow's nerves. He realized that his steady concentration had produced a strain, for he could hear a sound that he had not noticed before. It became more distinct as he approached the door.

The sound was the *whirr* of a small fan. The Shadow located it in a box beneath a table near the door. Through holes in the box top, he could see the revolving blades. The fan was controlled electrically.

The device looked like some odd motor that Quedden had put under test. It seemed to have no purpose that concerned The Shadow.

Extinguishing the room lights, The Shadow tried the door. It came open easily; he glided through to the hall. When he tried the outer knob, he gained his first surprise. The knob was loose. The door had not been latched at all.

That was curious, since Professor Quedden had spoken of protection from the closed door. Coupled to the riddle was another factor that The Shadow immediately noticed. The whirring fan was slowing to a stop. Evidently, the door latch controlled it.

There was a way to make certain. The Shadow closed the door from the hallway side. He waited a dozen seconds; then quickly opened it. Leaning into the room, he heard a dying whirr. The fan had started when he closed the door; stopped again, when he reopened it.

This time, The Shadow closed the door and left it shut. He was out of the trap, whatever it might be. He had other matters to concern him; chiefly, an inspection of the downstairs laboratory and the workshop. After that, The Shadow needed a mode of exit. It would not be difficult to find one.

As for the office, The Shadow had left it exactly as he found it. Since the fan was again in motion, Professor Quedden would find no clue to the fact that an intruder had visited the office. The Shadow's campaign against the Murder Master looked like a clear one. It would have been, but for an important fact.

The spinning fan within the office had begun its motion at the time when Quedden had first closed the door. It had not been necessary for an intruder to enter, to put the device in operation.

That fact was springing to The Shadow's mind as he stood outside the door. He dropped the thought almost instantly, as his strained ears caught a sound that made him forget the fan. The noise came from the hallway, near the side door that led to the old storeroom. The Shadow turned, expecting to see Quedden or Thoyer.

Instead, he faced an unexpected challenger. A girl stood in the hallway, covering him with a leveled revolver. Who she was, how she had come here—for the present, both were mysteries. But there was no doubt about the girl's determination. That was told, doubly, by her grim stare and her grip.

To her, The Shadow was an enemy. Her purpose was to hold him helpless.

## CHAPTER XII
### FUTILE BATTLE

THE SHADOW stood motionless at the end of the hallway, his hands half raised. Unarmed, he was forced to that position, until he could parry with this new challenger. Even his breathing was slow; so slight that there was not the slightest sway to his flowing cloak.

That pose puzzled the girl; she showed her uncertainty. It was obvious that she was not a crook; had she been, she would have recognized who The Shadow was. In the half light of the hallway, she wondered whether this strangely silent figure could be human. All that the girl could see of The Shadow's features were his eyes. They had a fiery glow that worried her.

In his turn, The Shadow was taking this respite to decide his next course. He was reading the girl's expressions; from them, he realized the factors that limited her action. Like himself, she was an intruder. Also, she had expected to meet Professor Quedden; not someone else.

She had come from the storeroom; its door was opened wider. Though determined to keep The Shadow at bay, she was anxious to do so without noise, for she had not uttered a word. Only a gesture of her gun had encouraged The Shadow to lift his hands.

That meant that the girl would avoid gunfire, except in an extreme emergency. The Shadow was gambling on that prospect; his best game, therefore, was to lull the girl. Calmly, The Shadow waited. All the while that the girl tried vainly to see his face, he was studying hers.

Her features were well molded; they gave her a definite beauty, marred only by the thrust of her chin. That, however, was only temporary, forced by the girl's effort to be determined. So was the glare of her dark-brown eyes. Naturally, they would have appeared much milder.

The girl's paleness, too, was forced by circumstances. Her skin had a sheer whiteness, against the dark background of her hair. The tight clamp that she gave the revolver was an effort to control her nervousness; not a desire to be quick with the trigger.

Whatever the reason for her expedition to Quedden's, she had carefully prepared for the trip. Her clothes were dark, of rough cloth. They were tight-fitting except for her skirt, which was of an athletic type that allowed plenty of freedom.

As the lull continued, The Shadow saw the girl's free hand clench tightly. She was fighting off her nervousness, more than ever. Her lips opened; she seemed ready to give a command, then changed her mind. Her eyes narrowed, as she stepped slowly forward. Closer to The Shadow, she spoke in cautious contralto.

"Step toward me!" was her command. "Keep close to the other wall!"

The Shadow obeyed. He saw that the girl wanted him to pass her, so that she could force him into the storeroom. She was still too distant for The Shadow to spring to action. Nor did he make any unwise move as he went past the girl. That was the moment when she was most on edge.

It was at the storeroom door that The Shadow halted, his breathing as slow and controlled as before. His hesitation showed no tenseness; on the contrary, it was natural, as though he expected another command. One came—close to The Shadow's ear. With it was the nudge of the gun muzzle against the center of his back.

"Move into that room—"

THE girl's whisper ended with a sharp gasp. Imperceptibly, The Shadow's shoulder blade had edged backward beneath his cloak. The twist that he made was swiftly unexpected. His shoulder blade clipped the gun muzzle, joggled the revolver in the girl's hand.

Before she could recover it, The Shadow's fist was clamping the weapon. His digging fingers forced the girl's clutch from the trigger.

The girl put up a fierce, but silent, struggle. Her left hand clawed for The Shadow's throat, only to be gripped by his free fist. Her efforts to regain the revolver failed; it was slipping farther from her grasp. Frantically, the girl tried to wrench loose toward the storeroom door. The Shadow let her take that direction; in her eagerness, the girl lost the gun entirely.

Once in the storeroom, she tried to gasp a cry. The Shadow prevented it by tilting her head with easy throat pressure. Looking upward, the girl stared straight into The Shadow's eyes. She still had fight, but he held her helpless, with a clutch that was almost velvet.

The girl realized, though, that those easy fingers would turn to steel, if she forced it. She quieted; but her eyes flared with anger, as she panted long deep breaths. It was her turn to play a waiting game. She withheld the useless cry that The Shadow could so easily prevent.

For the first time since he had left Quedden's office, The Shadow took a deep breath of his own. The effect was more startling than his encounter with the girl. Compared with the stuffy office, this air had the sting of tart wine. The strong scent of ozone tinged the entire atmosphere.

Another breath; it came with intoxicating strength. The Shadow found himself gulping the air with an instinctive eagerness that he could not resist. The room swayed; the girl seemed to melt from his grasp. Confused thoughts drilled The Shadow's brain.

He had to hold the girl; to question her. It was vital to learn who she was; why she had come here. With his campaign against the Murder Master dependent upon his own disappearance, The Shadow could not afford to let it be known that he still lived.

Conflicting with those impressions was a flashback to the scene in Quedden's office. The Shadow remembered the dank air; the whirling fan that he had discovered near the door. They fitted with the information that The Shadow had noted in Quedden's safe, but to which he had given too little attention.

The office was a trap; rendered so by an odorless gas that Quedden loosed every night, when he closed the door. That fan had stirred the vapor through the office. A person breathing it would neither suspect it nor feel immediate effects.

It took draughts of clear air to make the gas effective. Anyone who inhaled it would experience the results on the way out from Quedden's office. Had The Shadow gone to the lower laboratory, he would be swaying there, instead of here in this storeroom.

Old Quedden might have lost his faith in that delayed-action gas, had he been here to witness The Shadow's resistance against its effect. The Shadow had been in the office a full hour; hence he had inhaled more than an ordinary quota of the vapor. Nevertheless, he was still possessed of energy.

REELING across the room, shaken by every new breath of air that he inhaled, The Shadow had the strength to guide his actions. If he had been in the lower laboratory, he could have forced his way out to safety before the gas took its full hold. Here, he was restrained by the girl who was still anxious to take him prisoner.

Partly released from The Shadow's clutch, she was battling with new fury. Numbly, The Shadow tried to hold her. He let the gun go from his hand, kicked it mechanically when it hit the floor. If the girl had tried to regain it, The Shadow might have had a chance to rally. Instead, she continued her battle with the cloaked fighter. Her own wrists wrenched free, the girl shoved her hands to The Shadow's throat.

Frail fingers showed remarkable tightness when they gripped. Half sagging, The Shadow was forced to clutch the girl's arms to prevent his fall. The whole room was whirling; his eyes closed, The Shadow sensed nothing but darkness. The hold on his throat was relentless. The girl wasn't handling The Shadow as easily as he had treated her.

Then, while his head roared with rolling throbs like kettledrums, The Shadow felt the floor become steady. The girl, ignorant of what had caused The Shadow's dizziness, was actually aiding him by her pressure on his neck. The Shadow could no longer get the air that he wanted, even though it overpowered him.

Gloved hands tightened. The Shadow's eyes came open, to see the girl against the dim light from the hallway. She was panting, with long gasps of weariness. Her fingers yielded. Again, she was almost helpless. Victory had returned to The Shadow—until he took another breath, which he so badly needed.

That one deep puff of air was charged with all the power that The Shadow had escaped while he choked. It filled his lungs like a tidal wave of ozone. His head split with the crackle of a million insects. The Shadow's hands fell away; his arms spread wide as he rolled to the door. With that fall came blankness.

Steadying, the girl stared at her cloaked adversary, wondering if his sprawl was another ruse. Slowly, she realized that The Shadow was unconscious. Stooping, she listened for his breathing; she could scarcely hear it. The Shadow was no more than a huddled shape, in which life seemed dwindled to low ebb.

THE girl found her revolver. She groped toward the high-placed window at the back of the storeroom. She halted there, to listen for sounds that she heard from the hallway. Tensely, the girl waited, as footsteps came along. When they were almost at the door, she suddenly aimed her revolver.

It was Thoyer, not Quedden, who went past the door. The girl let the gun lower. She could hear the professor's querulous voice from the front of the hall.

"Never mind the door, Thoyer!" Quedden's cackle took on an expectant glee. "The sounds that we heard no longer matter. If anyone has gone in the office, let him remain there! We shall find him"—the chuckle was prophetic—"after he comes out!"

Thoyer returned; he stopped at the storeroom and glanced into its gloom. He did not see The Shadow flattened on the floor. The girl was also obscure; she had pressed close to the wall beneath the rear window. She heard Thoyer go up front, to report to Quedden.

"I guess we imagined things, sir," said the assistant. "I don't think that anyone has been up here."

After the two had gone, the girl peered out into the hallway. She saw the curtains at the front. She knew that Quedden and Thoyer were in rooms beyond them, but she fancied that both might be on guard. Any unusual sound might warn them.

Another look toward the office door; the girl shuddered. Quedden's words had explained The Shadow's plight. Though the office had been her original objective, the girl no longer cared to investigate it. Instead, she returned softly through the storeroom, reached high and flickered a flashlight at the little window.

Soon, her summons was answered. The window was opened from the outside; two men held a whispered consultation with the girl. She moved to the center of the floor, turned her flashlight toward The Shadow. The men came through with a short ladder.

Working with all possible silence, they raised The Shadow and hoisted him toward the window, where they finally rolled his inert form through to the outside roof.

The girl listened at the door to the hallway, ready with her revolver. Hearing nothing from Quedden or Thoyer, she came back and climbed the ladder. As soon as she reached the roof, the ladder was drawn through. The girl lowered the inside shade; the window was closed afterward.

The trio of new intruders had gone, taking The Shadow with them. Quedden's trap had shown its efficiency, for it had caught a victim in the manner that the professor had hoped. The Shadow had been rendered totally helpless by the soporific gas.

That, however, was something that Professor Quedden would not learn when morning came. He would find no evidence whatever to prove that an intruder had entered the gas-laden office.

Whoever the girl and her followers might be, they certainly were not tools of the Murder Master. Chances were that The Shadow's future would prove more pleasant than if he had been left in Quedden's domain.

There, the power of the Murder Master held full sway.

## CHAPTER XIII
## THE SHADOW'S ALLY

WHEN The Shadow awakened, he was conscious of dim daylight, enough to give him an idea of his new surroundings. He was reclining on a couch in a small room that appeared to be part of a large, old-fashioned apartment.

His cloak was still on his shoulders; his hat lay on a chair beside the couch. The dimness of the room was caused by the lowered shades. Rising, somewhat shaky, The Shadow went to the window and raised the blind.

He was gazing from a fifth-story, over low-lying blocks of buildings in the neighborhood of the Greenwich Village section of New York. The spire of the Empire State Building, glistening in sunlight, formed a fairly distant mark that enabled him to gauge his present location.

Air still seemed touched with ozone, but its freshness no longer had that overwhelming effect. The Shadow felt weak; he attributed that to his need of food. In fact, the daylight bothered him more than the air. He decided that it would be best to rest his eyes while the dawn increased.

Again stretched on the couch, The Shadow looked occasionally toward the window. He noticed that the glare was becoming gradually less. That puzzled him, until he made another trip to the window. Noting the glisten on the Empire State Building tower, The Shadow recognized his previous error.

This was not dawn; it was sunset. It had taken him a full day to recover from the effects of Quedden's high-powered gas.

Since dusk was near, it would not be long before someone came to this room. The Shadow thought of that, while he stood beside the window. As he started another trip toward the couch, he heard a soft knock at the door.

There was something hopeful in that knock; when The Shadow replied, he heard a girl's exclamation

**The girl stared at her cloaked adversary, wondering if his sprawl was another ruse.**

beyond the door. She was giving orders to someone outside.

When the door finally opened, The Shadow saw the girl who had battled him the night before. She was bringing a tray holding foods of various sort, that he might choose for himself. There was a small table near the window. The girl placed the tray there, invited The Shadow to a chair.

The Shadow placed himself away from the light. His face was only vaguely visible to the girl as she stood by the window; but her features were plainly outlined. The girl seemed to prefer that situation, for she had much to tell and wanted The Shadow to believe her.

"My name is Elsa Wendley," she stated, as she faced about from the window. "You are known as The Shadow. I am sorry"—her smile was regretful—"that I did not know that when I first met you, last night."

The Shadow did not ask who had given Elsa her information. The girl explained that herself.

"One of my servants had heard of you," she said. "I realized then that you could not be my enemy. I had my servants bring you here. Since then, I have been waiting, hoping, for your recovery."

The Shadow put a calm-toned question: "Why did you realize that I could not be an enemy?"

The question brought a quick flash from Elsa's eyes. It reminded The Shadow of the fury that she had shown the night before. That glare, however, was not intended for The Shadow. It was Elsa's recollection of another personage.

"You are opposed to crime," declared the girl. "You could only have had one purpose in visiting Quedden's house. That would be to expose him as the criminal that he is! Professor Quedden is the Murder Master!"

ELSA picked up a newspaper, spread it before The Shadow's gaze. Shifting from behind the table, The Shadow read the columns by the light from the window. The news interested him immensely. For the first time, he was learning the details that surrounded the deaths of Hyvran, Palbrock and Denniman. He saw how they fitted with the coded messages that he had deciphered at Quedden's.

As The Shadow placed the newspaper aside, Elsa pointed from the window. Her finger indicated a squatty house, set in a nearby block. The Shadow saw a roof that jutted back from a wide window.

"That is where Quedden lives!" exclaimed Elsa. "We have been watching that house for weeks! Last night, we entered by the back roof. I intended to find Quedden's headquarters, to gain whatever evidence lay there.

"After your experience"—the girl turned toward The Shadow—"I knew that it would not be safe to enter the office. Also, I supposed"—her tone was hopeful—"that you had already gathered whatever evidence might be there."

The Shadow was back in his chair. His eyes were steady toward Elsa. The girl met them with a frank gaze. She waited, expecting the command that came. The Shadow's calm tone carried the friendship for which Elsa had hoped:

"Tell me your entire story."

Elsa began the story. It involved her brother, Richard; she winced, at first, when she mentioned his name. Dick had gone from the upstate town where they lived; and he had turned crook, afterward. He had been sentenced for embezzlement; had served a term in the penitentiary.

By the time Elsa completed that portion of the narrative, her reluctance had vanished. Deepening dusk had obscured The Shadow; finished with his meal, he was silent in the chair. All the while, though, Elsa could sense his presence. She knew that he was listening with keen sympathy; that every detail she recounted might prove valuable.

"Dick was given a parole," declared Elsa. "He was enthusiastic, eager for a new life. He didn't come home, because people there would know him for a convict. Instead, he found a job here in New York, thanks to a man who understood him."

This time, The Shadow's voice supplied a quiet interruption, with its question:

"The man's name?"

"Melvin Graham," replied Elsa. "Dick wasn't the only one that Mr. Graham helped. There were others—and they've all gone straight; but Dick couldn't seem to do the same. I learned that"—Elsa choked, to hold back a sob—"the night when Dick came home!"

It was an ordeal for Elsa to describe that night; but she managed it. A car had come up the driveway, stopping with its wheels against the front steps of the house. The grind of brakes had alarmed Elsa; she had reached the door as soon as the servants. Dick had staggered in from the darkness, his hand pressed to a gory shirtfront.

Dick was dying from bullet wounds. There hadn't been time to summon the town doctor. A call to his house brought the reply that he was away on a case. Dick didn't want the doctor. He said there would be no use to bring him; that it would only mean trouble for Elsa afterward. He had time to gasp his story; he wanted Elsa to hear it.

He had gone back to crime, without Graham's knowledge. Old pals had talked him into it; but they weren't to blame. The man responsible was Jerome Quedden, who posed as an inventor and lived in New York. He was the criminal-in-chief to whom chaps like Dick reported.

Quedden's orders came by shortwave radio, over some special apparatus that Dick and the others used. They, in turn, left reports at Quedden's home. They had gone out on ugly jobs; Dick hadn't minded that, until it came to murder. Quedden, it seemed, could cover murder as easily as other crimes.

Dick had broken with the others. He had started home. Outside of town, his car was overtaken. There, his former pals had loaded him with bullets; left him for dead. But Dick had driven the rest of the way, to tell his story to his sister.

ELSA ended her account abruptly. It was almost dark outside; The Shadow could scarcely see the girl, as she took a chair beside his table. The Shadow knew that she expected questions, for her narrative had been a strained one. Moreover, she had not explained why she had come to New York.

"The others," quizzed The Shadow. "Dick's pals. Did he name any of them?"

"No," replied Elsa. "He said that maybe some were as sick of it as he was. If Quedden could be brought to justice, they would have their chance to clear themselves from him. So Dick thought; but I believe that none of them will try to break away as he did."

The Shadow shared Elsa's opinion. He asked the girl how she had explained Dick's death. She hesitated; then admitted that she and the servants had secretly buried the body. That had been Dick's last request. His parole term had ended; hence the parole board did not wonder at his absence.

"I came to New York," added Elsa. "Of course, I feared that I had acted illegally in not reporting Dick's death. That was why I was careful when I went to see Mr. Graham, who had been Dick's friend."

"What did you tell him?"

"I saw his secretary first. I said that I had not heard from Dick for a long while. The secretary produced letters, typed and with Dick's signature. Presumably, Dick had a job in Texas. But I know that those letters must be forgeries. More of Quedden's work."

"And when you saw Graham—"

"I saw him only once. He was too busy to give me a long interview. He promised to write to Dick personally, to ask him why he had not written me. I asked him to find out all he could regarding Dick. My hope was that he would first learn something for himself; after his suspicions were aroused, I could talk freely.

"But I never went back to see Mr. Graham. A few days later, I learned where Professor Quedden lived. From then on"—Elsa's voice had low, cold firmness—"I have been watching Quedden! Always waiting for the time when I could meet him, in his own abode, and there confront him as my brother's murderer!"

Elsa's statement explained why she had not again visited Melvin Graham. Gripped with hope of vengeance against Quedden, she had thought it best that no one should know that she had remained in New York. Perhaps, at first, she wondered if her course could be justified; but it was evident that, at present, Elsa had no doubt.

"When I read of the Murder Master," she told The Shadow, "I was sure that he must be Professor Quedden. I felt that I had made a terrible mistake in not revealing him to the law; then I realized that such a step would have accomplished nothing.

"Quedden's position is too secure. My story is weak—the sort that would not be believed. The Murder Master would be warned of danger, and would easily divert it. My servants advised me against it. I concluded that the way to end the Murder Master was to follow my own planned course."

This time, Elsa waited, hoping for some word from The Shadow. She did not have to tell him that she trusted him. The fullness of her story gave proof of that. Elsa had found The Shadow already at Quedden's headquarters. He had penetrated there ahead of her. She was sure that he could give the advice and aid that she could gain nowhere else.

THE SHADOW arose in the gloom. His hand rested lightly upon Elsa's shoulder. His calm voice was token of his approval.

"Your choice was fortunate," affirmed The Shadow. "It enabled you to bring me away before I was discovered at Quedden's. The Murder Master cannot know that I am still alive.

"But before we can move against him, we must know more. I have learned something of his methods. You have told me other facts. There are ways whereby I can acquire the needed details. When I have them, the Murder Master can be given to the law."

Elsa began a protest. The law had shown its inability to trap the Murder Master. She repeated her belief that proof could not be had. The Shadow's calm tone silenced her. It gave a positive assurance.

"I shall gain evidence," promised The Shadow, "that will link the deaths of Hyvran, Palbrock and Denniman. With it, the law will learn the names of those who serve the Murder Master. He will stand exposed, with his guilty crew. The law will believe the proof that I produce."

Elsa needed no more. She spoke her confidence

in The Shadow's ability, her willingness to accept his decision. All that she asked was how The Shadow wished her to cooperate. She received that, in a single sentence.

"Remain here," came the whispered answer, "and be ready, until you hear from me again."

There was something strange in The Shadow's tone. Its words lingered in Elsa's mind. Particularly, the last word: "again." What did The Shadow mean by it? Puzzled, Elsa spoke a question; she received no answer.

Wonderingly, the girl groped for a lamp cord; she tugged it, to bring a glow to the darkened room. She found herself staring at vacancy. With his last statement, The Shadow had departed.

Elsa Wendley stood alone; but she no longer felt that she was engaged in a solitary cause. She had become The Shadow's ally. When the time came for a meeting with the Murder Master, The Shadow would remember Elsa Wendley.

## CHAPTER XIV
## THE SHADOW'S RETURN

SOON after he had left Elsa's apartment, The Shadow arrived at his sanctum. There, in a room with black-lined walls, he worked at a polished table beneath a bluish light. The Shadow was studying clippings that concerned the three murders of a few nights ago.

The Shadow was considering what the law had learned. Its progress had stopped with the political link that Commissioner Weston had mentioned to Inspector Cardona. That link had weakened the more that it had been tested.

Granted that three murdered men had planned a united campaign involving different factions, none could have made positive statements without talking to some of his own supporters. Nobody close to Hyvran, Palbrock or Denniman had heard of any vote-getting arrangement between the trio. The deeper that the law went in that investigation, the less likely the theory seemed.

That was why The Shadow gave credit to the theory.

It fitted exactly with the methods of the Murder Master—to point the police along the proper trail, then leave them guessing. His talk of murders had sounded like hoaxes; but that talk had teeth, as The Shadow, himself, had learned.

The same with this fading theory. The Shadow believed that the link was there. The Murder Master had faults in his methods. One was a tendency toward too great efficiency. He worked with purposes; then tried to cover them.

Viewing the Murder Master from that angle, The Shadow was digging deep into the schemer's armor. So deep in fact, that it became obvious why the Murder Master had been so anxious to eliminate The Shadow. He had guessed that only The Shadow had the ability to see where a trail went wrong.

Three names appeared in ink, as The Shadow wrote them:

> Richard Hyvran
> Justin Palbrock
> Frank Denniman

The Shadow transcribed those names into a coded message of his own. With the names went brief instructions. All facts concerning the three were to be sifted; particularly the most obvious ones, such as statements that they had made publicly. All, to some degree, had been in the public eye. Newspapers would carry the sort of facts The Shadow wanted.

Those, peculiarly, were the very sorts of facts that the law would overlook. The fact that both Hyvran and Palbrock had been on their way to public meetings, that Denniman had been eager to get with certain politicians, was something that had been taken as a matter of course. To The Shadow, it offered a deeper significance.

Placing his message in an envelope, The Shadow addressed it to Rutledge Mann, an insurance broker who was one of The Shadow's agents. Mann's specialty was the gathering of the type of information that The Shadow needed in this case.

THERE was another detail before The Shadow left the sanctum; one that Elsa Wendley would have appreciated. The girl had given The Shadow a most vital clue, when she had told the story of her brother. It explained exactly why The Shadow had been unable to place his fingers on members of the band that had been so active in recent crime.

Constantly, The Shadow's agents had been scouring the underworld for traces of the hidden crooks. Similarly, the police had been urging stoolies to tap the "grapevine" telegraph. Both efforts had brought nothing. Seemingly, the criminals, now identified with the Murder Master, had been wizards when it came to hiding out.

Elsa's testimony had ended that situation. Her brother had definitely belonged to the group that served the Murder Master. Dick Wendley had been a paroled convict. He had joined up with his old pals; yet the parole board had not discovered it.

There was a lot wrong with the present parole system; but, at best, men on probation could merely get around it, not trample over it. It would have been difficult for Dick Wendley to openly associate with crooks who were under police observation.

Moreover, The Shadow had Dick's record. He

brought it from the files in the sanctum, spread it on the table and studied the names of the dead man's former associates. The majority of them had gone to the State penitentiary, for various offenses.

The list was a long one; with a dozen names were checkmarks indicating that those men had been paroled. That was their most recent link with Dick Wendley. The Shadow remembered Elsa's mention of her visits to Melvin Graham. From all reports, Dick had apparently been keeping out of mischief; yet Elsa knew otherwise.

What applied to Dick Wendley could apply to all others who served the Murder Master.

Paroled criminals were the men he used. The very precariousness of their situation was in keeping with the Murder Master's methods of turning weakness into strength. The Shadow's laugh was a solemn whisper that brought mirthless echoes from the sanctum walls as he pictured the gigantic possibilities of the Murder Master's schemes.

Criminals on parole, with records kept clean, were men that the law had never suspected. The Shadow could not criticize that error. He had also made it. But that stage was past. Beginning with tonight, The Shadow intended to investigate the ex-crooks whose present paths were most pleasing to the parole board.

Behind good records would be clever alibis, hatched by a close-knit crew. Alibis supplied through the ingenuity of the Murder Master, to protect the men he needed. Again, the Murder Master had demonstrated his ability to play a double game.

Not only had he chosen henchmen who could be kept safe through his clever maneuvers; he had been able to pick the types of crooks he wanted. On parole, even the most crafty workers would have to turn down offers from known bigshots. But the Murder Master was unknown. It was safe to work for him.

MORE files were lying on The Shadow's table, when a tiny light beamed from the wall. It signified a call from Burbank, The Shadow's contact man. Word had just come through that Commissioner Weston was on his way to his apartment.

Extinguishing the blue light, The Shadow postponed his present work in order to visit the commissioner. When he left the sanctum, he had little prospect of gaining valuable facts. They did not bob up overfrequently when The Shadow visited the commissioner. Tonight, however, The Shadow was due for a welcome surprise.

At Weston's, he was to learn more than his own files showed. His postponed work would prove unnecessary after the visit.

When he reached the commissioner's apartment, The Shadow was in the character of Kent Allard. He sensed something in the air the moment that Weston's houseman admitted him.

Allard was usually a welcome arrival; tonight, the servant wasn't quite sure how to greet him. He said that the commissioner was in an important conference; that he expected no one else.

In the even tone that suited Allard, The Shadow insisted that Weston be informed of his arrival. The servant delivered the message. There was considerable delay; finally, it was Commissioner Weston himself who returned.

"Sorry to keep you waiting, Allard"—Weston was brisk, almost abrupt—"but matters are rather unusual tonight. Definitely so, in fact. Rather different, you understand, from the evening when I invited you to hear the radio program."

"I was detained that evening," was Allard's reply. His lips showed a reminiscent smile. "Of course, commissioner, I would not care to intrude tonight. I merely thought that you were having another get-together, of the same guests."

There was a peculiar significance to Allard's tone that struck Weston instantly. Bluntly, the commissioner demanded:

"What gave you that impression, Allard?"

"I saw one of the group come in here," answered Allard, calmly. "Let me see—what is his name?—the chap who wears the gold-rimmed spectacles. I have it! Melvin Graham!"

The Shadow was playing a long-shot stroke, on the chance that there was little to lose; much to gain. If Weston said that Graham was not here, Allard could apologize and say he was mistaken. If Graham actually happened to be present, Allard would appear to have an inkling regarding the present conference; enough to worry the commissioner.

The long shot clicked. Weston's jaw stiffened; his fingers plucked the tips of his military mustache.

"I didn't suppose that anyone had seen Graham come here," he declared. Then, anxiously: "Did you see any of the others?"

The commissioner's tone indicated that he did not expect Allard to know who the "others" were. The Shadow parried promptly.

"I saw two other men," he remarked in Allard's tone. "They were strangers; but I would recognize them if I saw them again."

THAT was enough for Weston. He motioned for Allard to accompany him to the office. On the way, Weston confided:

"No one must know of this meeting. I must have your promise, Allard, before I admit you."

Weston's hand was on the doorknob. Calmly,

Allard assured him that the visit would be confidential. Weston opened the door; one minute later, Kent Allard was shaking hands with Melvin Graham, while Weston was waiting to introduce him to three other visitors.

Those three were Ace Curdy, Dobie Kring and Doc Harstell. Although they didn't guess it, the introduction was unnecessary. Kent Allard had recently been viewing their rogues' gallery portraits. Those were in the file that lay on the table in The Shadow's sanctum.

Inspector Joe Cardona was also present. He wasn't worried when Weston explained why the three ex-crooks were there. Of all the commissioner's friends, Allard was the pick, in Cardona's estimation. There were times, Joe remembered, when Allard had supplied some worthwhile ideas to the law. Weston, himself, had thought of that, in admitting Allard.

The three crooks began their reports. Singly, they had visited their old haunts, as they had promised. Ace had tried to get a line on the shooting that had followed the flight of thugs from WQJ; but there had been very few guesses regarding the identity of the triggermen involved.

Dobie Kring had looked up some old specialists among safecrackers; none knew anything about the Murder Master.

Doc Harstell had simply let it be known that his old shingle was out; if needed, he would be ready to look after wounded thugs who came to him.

"It's tough, working like a stoolie," declared Ace. "It never was my line, commissioner. I thought it would be easy; but it ain't. I get an idea every now and then that the guys are wise."

"That's not it, Ace," put in Dobie. "They figure we're regular enough. But they're holding back because they think the parole board is keeping tabs on us. They got an idea they may be reached through us."

"They'll get over that," assured Doc. "I've taken it easier than you fellows. They'll look you up if they need you—just like they will me."

Cardona liked Doc's attitude, and said so. He had a hunch that the Murder Master would plot new crime, more extensive than before. Joe summed his opinion with the statement:

"The guy may be crazy; but what if he is? That's all the more reason he won't stop. His ideas will get bigger and bigger. He'll need more crooks to work for him. He's got feelers everywhere, even though we haven't spotted them. These are the fellows that will hear from him. Our regular stoolies won't."

The three crooks were pleased to hear Cardona term them in a class other than ordinary stool pigeons. Weston gratified them with a handshake

**BURBANK**

all around. Graham told them that his limousine was waiting, that it would take them to their lodgings and return for him.

AFTER the trio had departed, Graham expressed disappointment because the reformed prisoners had gotten no results. Weston and Cardona were still hopeful, however. They felt that the paroled men could produce real information. Kent Allard was a silent listener to that theory. He expressed no opinion.

When The Shadow left, he reviewed the scene that he had witnessed. It was the most brazen sham that he had ever encountered. It stood as new proof of the Murder Master's cunning. The supercrook had unquestionably ordered his choicest workers to offer their services to the law. They, the actual accomplices in murder, were moving about unwatched. Under the circumstances, they could alibi anything that happened.

To the law, perhaps; not to The Shadow. For in the strength that the Murder Master's men had acquired lay a weakness, as apparent as the death trap that The Shadow had escaped. Formerly, such thugs as Ace, Dobie and Doc would have been difficult to watch. Moving in the open, they were easy game.

The Shadow had agents of his own. With tonight, they would begin a new task. No longer would they scour the underworld for facts that never came to light. They would watch the trio of crooks that the law had so obligingly come to trust.

One hour later, Burbank relayed those orders from The Shadow. The campaign against the Murder Master had begun in full.

## CHAPTER XV
## INTO THE MESH

DAYS had passed since The Shadow's return. Tense expectancy gripped Manhattan's underworld, thanks to persistent rumors that were piped along the grapevine. Those referred to the night when crime had gone on the air from WQJ. That night, the Murder Master had announced swift death. Three victims had been found by the law.

The Murder Master had promised a fourth, The Shadow. Since then, The Shadow had been definitely absent. If he had survived the Murder Master's trap, whatever it was, he would be searching for the supercrook and the underworld would know it. The Shadow had a habit of scouring scumland, meeting up with small-fry crooks to make them talk.

So far, there were no such cases. Each day made it more evident that The Shadow must have met with disaster. The Murder Master stood supreme. Seemingly, he had enveloped himself with The Shadow's own cloak, to become as mysterious a figure as the black-clad fighter once had been.

Soon, the Murder Master would move to new crime. How, where, were unanswered questions. These rumors, however, had an authentic touch, because of their repetition. It was plain that they were sponsored by the Murder Master himself.

There was a reason why the underworld had not seen The Shadow. Playing his cool game to deceive the Murder Master, The Shadow was staying close to his sanctum, except when he appeared publicly as Allard. The grapevine rumors were not all that reached him. Day by day, The Shadow was accumulating concise reports from his agents.

Rutledge Mann had provided the newspaper clippings that The Shadow wanted. The Shadow had studied them, and had arranged them as required. From that research, The Shadow had learned the reason why the Murder Master had ordered triple death. It fitted neatly with The Shadow's other facts.

Mann's information could wait. It was ready, when the time came. For the present, The Shadow was concerned with the movements of the paroled crooks who served the Murder Master.

Ace Curdy had been around shooting galleries, winning bets by triggering the spots out of playing cards. Dobie Kring was frequenting gambling joints, playing poker with old acquaintances. It was Doc Harstell who used a different policy.

Doc had chosen an underground stronghold near the border of the badlands. He was ready to take care of crippled mobsters who came his way. Meanwhile, Doc's hideaway served another purpose. It was the one spot where Ace and Dobie could meet with him and be completely in private.

Doc Harstell expected his pals tonight. The Shadow's agents had learned that from casual telephone calls that they had overheard. Moreover, one agent—Cliff Marsland—had provided The Shadow with a complete description of Harstell's hideaway. Cliff had posed as a visiting thug, the sort that Doc was always ready to welcome as a future customer.

THE night was dank and foggy when The Shadow approached the block where Harstell's new headquarters was located. The darkness, tinged with mist, was the sort that best suited The Shadow. This was his first foray since his return; a ticklish one, under present circumstances.

If any shuffling underworld denizen should spy The Shadow and pass that word along, the news would reach the Murder Master. That would ruin The Shadow's entire campaign. Nevertheless, this expedition was essential.

Tonight, paroled prisoners expected word from the Murder Master. Only The Shadow could penetrate to intercept the message. His familiar garb of black was the only attire that could serve him.

There was an alleyway that led to the door of Harstell's stronghold. At present, the windows of a small store cast a light on the front sidewalk. That had been arranged so that watchers across the way could spot any person who entered the alley.

There was another route, however, to the alley's depths; a precarious one, across the roofs. The Shadow chose that path.

Picking an inset fire escape, The Shadow silently drew down the hanging ladder. His weight upon it, he blinked a tiny flashlight as a signal. There was a wait, while a car rolled along the rear street; then two men slid from a coupe and joined The Shadow in the darkness.

One was Cliff Marsland, a brawny chap clad in rough, dark clothes. The other was a hunchy fellow, with wizened face; his name was "Hawkeye." Both were secret agents of The Shadow.

They were the exact pair that The Shadow needed. Cliff, when need be, could match any thug in toughness. Hawkeye was a crafty spotter who could spy danger at almost any range.

The two were provided with bundles of compact rope. The Shadow sent them up the fire tower ahead of him, so that he could raise the lower ladder when he followed them. He accomplished that without noise. When he reached the roof, his agents were awaiting him.

The first need for the rope became apparent

when they reached the gabled roof directly in back of the alleyway. That roof sloped steeply toward the front. The Shadow could gain a grip there, but he doubted that his companions could. That was why he took one end of the rope as he started a lone descent.

The roof was black; the swirling wisps of fog gave added cover, enough for The Shadow's aides to follow later. At the bottom of the slope, The Shadow reached a ledge; there, he stretched over and looped the end of the rope around a rain spout.

A single tug of the rope: Cliff caught the signal and tightened the upper end of the rope to a chimney. The rope had become a taut rail, making the roof a catwalk for The Shadow's agents.

As yet, they were not needed. The Shadow craned from the ledge to learn what lay below. He was above a blank wall—an extension of a house that made the alley a blind one. The wall was about two stories high; approximately sixteen feet.

There were men below—a pair of them, judging from the mutters of their conversation. On watch in the thick blackness at the interior of the blind alley, they could not be seen by those who spied from across the front street. It was obvious that the lurkers in the alleyway were on similar duty to those out front.

No entrance could be effected into Harstell's stronghold without a preliminary encounter with the two guards. That, in turn, was difficult business, for any undue noise would spread the alarm to those out front. The Shadow decided that swiftness would aid silence.

EASING from the front of the ledge, The Shadow lowered himself into the darkness, hanging by his hands. Neither of the watchers guessed that a dangling shape hovered only a few feet above their heads. Listening, The Shadow gauged the position of the watchers. He shifted, hand over hand, along the ledge, until he was directly over one man's head. Stretching, The Shadow tugged the rope twice—a signal for Cliff and Hawkeye to descend the sloping roof.

Two seconds later, The Shadow's hands released.

The first token that told the watchers of The Shadow's presence was the swish of his fall. The first of the pair had no opportunity to look up. The Shadow landed squarely on his shoulders; flattened him to the darkened alley.

The other thug caught a hazy impression of the sprawling figures; he knew that the attacker must be uppermost. He did exactly what The Shadow expected. He piled in, swinging a revolver, hoping to sledge the intruder's head.

The Shadow's arms were crossed above his slouch hat. They warded off the revolver slug. Simultaneously, The Shadow jolted upward, as though recoiling from his plunge. With the rebound, his crossed arms caught the crook's arms.

The Shadow twisted back toward the wall; as he braced himself, he whipped his arms apart. The move spun the thug completely over; he was back upward when The Shadow jolted him against the ground. With arms like steel bars, The Shadow shoved his foeman forward, then did a powerful back buckle. That lashed the crook upward toward the wall. The fellow took the impact head-on.

Letting that foeman slump, The Shadow turned for the man who had taken the first sprawl. He met him, as he came to his feet. The Shadow's fists took the thug's throat, throttled the gargle that came from ugly lips. The crook's hand loosened, to let a half-drawn gun slide back into his pocket.

Deftly, The Shadow changed his grip into a one-hand hold upon his silenced prisoner's neck. His free hand brought out a gun of his own. When that cold muzzle pressed the captive's forehead, the fellow gave up all fight. He knew that his enemy was The Shadow.

There was no mistaking the whispered order with which The Shadow told the mobster to turn about. Keeping his .45 against the prisoner's neck, The Shadow shifted so that his own form was toward the mouth of the alley. Producing his tiny flashlight, he gave blinks from the folds of his cloak.

Those flashes could not be seen from the street, but they were spotted by eyes above. Quick dots and dashes told what The Shadow wanted. A coil of rope dropped down beside him. With whispered threats close to the prisoner's ear, The Shadow withdrew his automatic. The thug didn't budge; he knew how quickly The Shadow could whip the gun forth again.

A few minutes later, the thug lay trussed in the rope, chewing at a gag between his teeth. Muffling his flashlight, The Shadow studied the foeman who had bashed the wall. That fellow would stay silent for the brief time that The Shadow required.

THE door to Harstell's hideout was unlocked. Doc kept it that way as a come-on to crooks. The Shadow entered, moved through darkness, picking the course that Cliff had given him. He saw a light in a little room that served as living quarters; but that was not The Shadow's objective.

He chose a larger room, that Doc Harstell had fitted out with medical apparatus. It was dark; that suited The Shadow all the better. He closed the door; moved about with blinking flashlight. He came to a stack of boxes, carefully unpiled them and worked at one. After replacing the boxes, The Shadow moved elsewhere.

He was busy for about five minutes. After that, he opened the door and glided out again. When The Shadow reached the alley, the stunned crook was showing feeble signs of life. The Shadow blinked his flashlight. The guarded signal brought down another rope; but this time, Cliff held onto the other end.

The loose rope snaked along the ground. The Shadow hitched it under the stunned crook's arms. His next signal was a tug of the rope itself. Cliff and Hawkeye pulled together, while The Shadow shoved upward from below. The only sound was the slight scrape of the rope. It ended when the prisoner went over the roof ledge.

The Shadow released the bound man who lay upon the cement; but the fellow showed no effort to make trouble, not even after The Shadow cut his gag loose. Again, a big gun muzzle was nudging him. The crook couldn't see any advantage in trying to bring the crew from the front street. He knew that if battle started he would get the first bullets, at close range from The Shadow's gun.

Again, The Shadow voiced whispered commands; the surly thug grunted that he understood them. That meant he would follow The Shadow's orders. He had no other choice.

After a dozen minutes, the test arrived. Two men appeared at the alley entrance; from their gait, The Shadow recognized Ace Curdy and Dobie Kring. The Shadow gave his prisoner a gun jab. The fellow growled a challenge:

"Where are you guys going?"

"In to see Doc Harstell," returned Ace. "Say—who's asking us, anyway?"

"Herk Ringey," gruffed the helpless crook.

"Me and another guy was just in to see Doc Harstell. We told him we'd stick around a while."

"Yeah?" Ace started to flash a light. "Where's the other guy?"

"Douse that glim!" put in Herk, inspired by a hard shove from The Shadow's gun. Then, as Ace complied, Herk added: "He's around here somewhere. Go on in and talk to Doc."

Ace and Dobie went through the door. Herk didn't hear the sound that followed the slow thrust of well-oiled bolts, to keep out any other visitors. The Shadow detected it, however, even though he was standing behind Herk. Pressed against the wall, The Shadow had remained unseen during Ace's brief use of the flashlight.

Herk expected The Shadow to follow the pair that had gone indoors. Instead, The Shadow waited, his gun relentless in its pressure. The Shadow simply intended to keep Herk here until the others again appeared.

Whatever the message that the Murder Master might send tonight, The Shadow was satisfied that he would learn its import.

## CHAPTER XVI
## THE MASTER'S MESSAGE

INSIDE his headquarters, Doc Harstell welcomed Ace and Dobie. He took them to the very room where The Shadow had been, a short while before. Turning on the light, Harstell indicated the place with a sweeping arm wave. Ace and Dobie viewed medicine cabinets, operating table, sterilizers and other equipment.

"How do you like my operating room?" he asked.

"More like a hospital," returned Ace. "Say, this is a swell setup, Doc!"

"That's not all." Harstell opened a door to show a room with half a dozen cots. "This is the hospital part of it. Just a ward—no private rooms—but that ought to do."

"A slick come-on," put in Dobie. "I'll bet this layout has started a lot of talk!"

"More apparatus over there"—Harstell pointed to the stacked boxes in the operating room—"but I haven't had time to unpack yet. The main thing right now is to set up the radio."

Harstell went to a corner, where a radio set rested on a large table. A wire ran from the radio to a wall socket. It passed beneath a square box that was beneath the table; but Harstell did not particularly notice that. After he had adjusted the dial, he made a connection with a small box that stood on the floor beside the table.

"I've got the mixer just right," he assured. "I was testing it again, this afternoon."

Ace gave a troubled look.

"What do you leave it out in sight for, Doc?" he asked. "It ain't a good idea to have guys looking at it."

"They don't know what it is. The clucks that come in here never heard of a mixer. I saw one guy looking at it—Cliff Marsland—and he asked if it was a storage battery. So I told him it was."

While Harstell was tightening wires to the mixer, Ace and Dobie indulged in comments on their own recent work. Both had been serving the Murder Master capably. In their pretended search for crooks that were wanted by the law, they had picked men who would be useful to their chief.

Neither Ace nor Dobie had approached any of those candidates. They had simply left reports, telling the Murder Master who the crooks were and how they could be reached. The Murder Master, in turn, had been buying up new talent, as recommended; he had done that through other channels.

"None of them knows we're in it," completed Ace. "That's what makes it jake, Dobie."

"Sure thing!" returned Dobie. Then, doubtfully: "We may run into trouble on account of the guys that Doc has lined up. Like this fellow Herk we saw outside."

Harstell heard that comment.

"Those birds aren't working for the chief," he told Dobie. "They're just part of the gag I'm working here. I've even told the police commissioner about them. This joint's supposed to be a hideaway. So I told that bunch they could case it and make sure the bulls weren't wise.

"The word's gone around that the place is safe. Only the right guys have been here. No wonder—because the cops are laying off! The commissioner fixed that."

There was a whine from the radio. A short-wave broadcast was beginning; it produced a chatter that would have done credit to a flock of blue jays. Ace gave a short laugh.

"Nobody's going to get anything out of that," he remarked.

"Nobody except us," corrected Dobie— "after Doc sets the mixer."

DOC HARSTELL was motioning for his companions to look around the place, to make sure that no prowlers had sneaked inside. Ace looked beneath the cots in the hospital room; Dobie made a trip through the hall, to inspect the living quarters. They returned with the report that the place was vacant.

Though they did not guess it, that proved The Shadow's wisdom. He had foreseen that Doc Harstell would order a search.

The mixer was adjusting to its right rotation period. The chatter from the radio changed, as various sounds were eliminated. At last, a voice predominated—a cackling tone that brought pleased grins from the listening ex-convicts. The Murder Master was on the air; this time for the special benefit of his three lieutenants.

"What a laugh the prof's got," confided Ace to Dobie. "He always cuts loose with it as a starter."

"That gives us time to tune in," observed Dobie. "Listen! Here it comes the dope we want to hear!"

Clucks had lessened. The Murder Master wasn't wasting time with his insidious chortles. His voice was at its lower pitch; precise, emphatic in its delivery. It lacked the insane deviations that had marked the program from WQJ.

Listening crooks were drinking every word. At the end of seven minutes, when the Murder Master finished with a sudden gloating chuckle, they sat in silent admiration of their chief. Every detail of his instructions had registered clearly.

While Harstell was turning off the radio and detaching the mixer, Ace voiced the sentiments that the trio shared.

"What a job!" he expressed. "A cinch, the way the chief has figured it! And what a pile of dough!"

"Ten percent for each of us," put in Dobie. "That ought to come to two hundred grand apiece! The chief is welcome to his seventy percent."

"Only sixty percent," corrected Harstell. "Don't forget, he always has us kitty out ten percent for what he calls the sinking fund. I'd say"—Harstell cut off the radio as he spoke—"that he spends a lot more besides. He's paying the freight on this job tomorrow night."

The three crooks were agreed on that point, until Ace had another idea. He sprang it with enthusiasm that showed increased admiration for the Murder Master's cunning.

"There won't be any payoff!" exclaimed Ace. "None, except to us. Look—there's going to be a bunch of torpedoes there, to fight it out with the cops. But the way the chief has framed it, there's only one triggerman who can make sure of a getaway. I'm that guy.

"The same with the bunch that soup the vault. One man is going to shove the button, and that guy's you, Dobie. You'll be away from everybody else—there's no chance of you getting hooked.

"When the swag comes out, the boobs that bring it will shove it into one car, then make a break in another. That's to fool the cops, only it won't. Those saps will head into trouble. The swag car will get away. The guy driving it will be you, Doc; and Dobie and me will be riding with you."

ACE'S conclusions were accurate. The Murder Master had designed crime to bring in a host of ordinary mobsters and let them take the fireworks, while his lieutenants, their own work unknown, would ride free. Dobie liked the setup; he turned to Harstell and chuckled:

"You'll have a lot of cripples to look after Doc."

"I'll look after them," was the dry promise. "I'll tell the commissioner when they get here. He'll take care of them after that. Which will square me very nicely."

"We'll be squared, too," said Ace, to Dobie. "All we've got to do is tip Cardona off to some of the names we've heard; only we won't know where the guys are. Before he can locate them, the job will be started.

"He'll never guess we were in on it, because we'll tell him that we were up at Graham's. Those birds up there will square us. Graham is going to be out of town tomorrow night, so he won't know they faked it."

Ace and Dobie were ready to leave. Doc Harstell decided to come along with them. It looked like a good time to pay another visit to the police commissioner. There would be nothing to report tonight, but they could at least assure him that they expected results soon. Tomorrow's events would prove the correctness of such a promise.

In the outside alleyway, Herk Ringey greeted the trio with a gruff tone from the darkness. He asked if Doc Harstell wanted him to stick around. Harstell decided it wouldn't be necessary.

"O.K., Doc," returned Herk. "I'll be going soon, then."

Herk was going sooner than he supposed. The trio had scarcely left the alley before The Shadow's flashlight was sending signals upward. The loose end of a rope came down as it had before. This time, The Shadow hooked it to Herk.

The crook didn't give a squawk when he was hoisted upward. He knew that The Shadow was covering him from below. He figured that he might have a chance when he reached the ledge; but Cliff and Hawkeye were ready for him. One had him covered with a gun the moment that he arrived. The other trussed him along with the first prisoner.

Below, The Shadow worked on the door that Harstell had locked. Lacking inner bolts, it was easily picked. When he reached the operating room, The Shadow turned on the lights. He opened the box beneath the radio table. It was a tricky box, that looked tightly nailed, until The Shadow manipulated it.

Inside the box was a phonograph; on it was a cylindrical record. The Shadow changed the needle; he turned on the radio dial and connected the mixer. Immediately, the record began to revolve. The phonograph was connected, through the bottom of the box, with the wire to the radio.

48     THE MURDER MASTER

**The crook didn't give a squawk when he was hoisted upward. He knew that The Shadow was covering him from below.**

The Shadow had shipped this box into Harstell's along with medical apparatus that the fake physician had ordered. On his previous trip into this lair, The Shadow had attached the phonographic device so that the radio connection controlled it. The hidden apparatus had recorded the voice of the Murder Master.

STARTING the phonograph, The Shadow heard a repetition of all that the Murder Master had said. In those seven minutes, he gained vital facts regarding coming crime.

Tacked to the end of the master schemer's message were comments that lieutenants had made concerning their chief. Those ended abruptly with Harstell's mention of a ten-percent sinking fund; for that was the point at which the radio had been cut off. The phonograph had halted with it.

Further statements had not been recorded. That did not matter. Ace Curdy had seen the full purposes of the Murder Master. They were quite as apparent to The Shadow.

Tomorrow night, the reigning king of crime intended a stupendous robbery. One so daring that it made him look like the crazed fanatic that Joe Cardona considered him. Close study of circumstances showed, however, that the Murder Master would not be playing a hit-or-miss game.

He had found a weakness in a hitherto impregnable place that furnished remarkable opportunities for crime. Two million dollars was the stake; but to render his endeavor certain, the Murder Master was forced to marshal hordes from the underworld. Once the expedition was completed, those new henchmen would no longer be needed.

Always crafty, the Murder Master intended to dispose of them afterward. He would sacrifice his new recruits to the law. He would never have to make a payoff for their services. By shoving the burden on them, he would divert suspicion from the paroled convicts who were his permanent lieutenants.

Those three were to take the swag, to stow it in some secure place. Later, it could be left at Quedden's, less their shares. Colossal crime accomplished, the Murder Master could bide his time, thinking out new campaigns. He could always depend on his same lieutenants, for they had gained the law's trust.

The Murder Master had foreseen one obstacle to this superscheme of crime. That was The Shadow, whose far-reaching fingers had so often felt the pulse throbs of the underworld. Unquestionably, the Murder Master was sure that he had eliminated The Shadow; otherwise he would not be launching his coming crime.

A laugh came, sinister, low-whispered, from

The Shadow's lips as he detached the phonograph and packed it. Crime would begin tomorrow, as the Murder Master planned; but before it reached its climax, crooks would learn of The Shadow's return.

That could strike terror into vicious hearts. It would scatter attacking hordes more effectively than any thrust the law could make. It could bring madness to the real lieutenants of the Murder Master. That panic might reach the supercrook himself.

Tomorrow, men of evil would know the power of The Shadow.

## CHAPTER XVII
## THE LAW LEARNS

AT half past eight the next evening, Inspector Joe Cardona was pacing the office in the police commissioner's apartment. At his desk, Commissioner Weston was indulgently trying to calm the ace inspector.

"Compose yourself, Cardona!" urged Weston. "Patience is essential. It is only half an hour since we received these reports"—Weston waved his hand toward the desk—"yet you already expect results."

"Why not?" demanded Cardona, abruptly. "Look at all the names Ace Curdy and Dobie Kring got for us! Enough for us to start a round-up! We ought to have a line on some of them, by this time. I've put twenty men on the job.

"But they haven't spotted any of these fellows at the places where they usually are. That shows just one thing, commissioner. Something's doing tonight, and all of them are in on it."

Weston remarked that the situation proved the efficiency of Ace and Dobie. Cardona agreed; but didn't see how it was going to help, if the law couldn't find the numerous crooks who had been spotted by the paroled men.

Weston suggested that Ace and Dobie might run into something more. Cardona hoped that they would, and expressed the wish that they would accomplish it soon.

There was a knock on Weston's door. It was the houseman, announcing Kent Allard as a visitor. The commissioner went out to greet his friend. They came back into the office together. While Weston was showing Allard the reports, the telephone bell rang. Cardona pounced for the instrument.

The call was not from headquarters; nor were there new reports from Ace or Dobie. Instead, Cardona heard a methodical voice that he recognized from the past. The man on the wire was Burbank, The Shadow's contact agent.

There had been times before when The Shadow had used Burbank to telephone information. Even if Cardona had not previously heard that steady tone, he would have been impressed, for Burbank spoke with a ring of accuracy. The link with the past merely spurred Cardona to hurried action. The moment that Burbank's call ended, Cardona sprang for an evening newspaper that lay on Weston's desk.

"What's happened, inspector?"

Cardona did not bother to answer Weston's question. The ace dick thumbed through the pages; found the paragraph he wanted, to thrust it before the commissioner's eyes.

The item stated that a large steamship company had concluded a transaction that had required the deposit of half a million dollars in the Midtown National Bank.

"What of it?" demanded Weston. "Such occurrences are frequent, Cardona."

"Funny it happened today," returned Cardona. "There's plenty of dough in that bank, to begin with. This makes a lot more."

A faint smile rested on the lips of Kent Allard. That money had actually been intended for deposit today, swelling the cash funds of the Midtown National to considerably more than two million dollars. It happened, though, that the steamship company had postponed the deposit, with the request that the bank say nothing.

Also, a large mining syndicate had privately presented a huge check for payment. Those funds had gone out from the bank. Branch offices, too, had done unusual business. Cash had been shipped to them. Tonight, the vault of the Midtown National Bank was remarkably short of funds. That had been engineered by The Shadow.

"The Midtown National," emphasized Cardona. "That would be a swell nut for those crooks to crack!"

"Too large a nut," returned Weston. "That bank is one of the best protected in the city."

"But where have the crooks dropped to?" demanded Cardona. "I'd be willing to look anywhere for them."

"By anywhere," suggested Weston, crisply, "you should mean anywhere that is logical. The Midtown National is not."

ALLARD was studying the report sheets on the commissioner's desk. In their argument, Cardona and Weston naturally looked to the visitor as one who might decide the matter. Allard had a sensible suggestion.

"Why not summon these informants?" he questioned calmly, as he pointed to the reports. "Ace Curdy and Dobie Kring might piece together something for you."

The trouble was how to reach Ace and Dobie. Again, Allard had a suggestion. Perhaps Melvin Graham would know where they could be found.

Weston put in a hurried call to Graham. He learned that the reformer had left for the Grand Central Station, intending to take a night train for Buffalo. He was stopping at a travel bureau to pick up tickets that he had ordered. There might be a chance to reach him there.

Weston called the travel bureau. In five minutes, there was a return call from Graham. He had no idea where Ace and Dobie could be reached; but he remembered that this was a night when they usually stopped at his home, to make a routine report for the parole board.

"Graham is coming right over," announced Weston, as he hung up. "I did not care to say much over the telephone. He understood that, of course. He says that he can take a midnight train for Buffalo. Meanwhile, he has called his house. If Ace and Dobie come there, they are to call here."

Allard arose, expressing regret that he could not stay to meet Graham. The clock showed quarter of nine when he left; and again, Allard's lips wore their slight smile.

The Shadow had spiked the alibis that crooked lieutenants intended to use. Their story was to be that they were at Graham's before nine, the hour for which crime was timed. Since they were supposed to call Weston's immediately upon arrival, the neglect of such a call would prove later that they had not gone to Graham's.

The telephone bell was tingling as Allard departed. It was another call from Burbank, as The Shadow knew.

This time, Joe Cardona listened to another tip from the methodical informant. Again, he snatched the newspaper to look up a timely paragraph. What Cardona saw there, was a link that nullified Weston's statement regarding the protection of the Midtown National.

"Look at this, commissioner!" exclaimed the inspector. "They're running night shifts on that street-repairing job, working crosstown. That means they'll have the steam shovel operating right alongside of the Midtown National Bank!"

That meant little to Weston, even when Cardona added:

"That's bringing them to the avenue, where the new subway excavation has just been completed. The avenue runs right in front of the bank."

Weston didn't see the connection. Cardona did.

"Don't you get it, commissioner?" demanded the ace. "That's where those crooks have gone for cover! Down in the new subway. What's more, it's the one spot where they could start blasting through into the bank."

"They might attempt it," admitted Weston. He was worried, but doubtful. "It would mean a lot of noise, though, Cardona—"

"With those steam shovels pounding? They'd cover it, commissioner. This is a real tipoff! If we only knew when—"

Again, the telephone bell. This time, Cardona heard a different voice—one that carried a chilling tone. It was the unmistakable voice of The Shadow, providing the last news that the law required.

"Crime will strike tonight," came The Shadow's whisper. "The zero hour is nine o'clock!"

IT was eight minutes before the hour. Cardona snapped a call through to headquarters, letting Weston guess the import of The Shadow's call. There wasn't time to waste in preliminary discussion, even with the police commissioner.

"I'm heading for the bank," informed Cardona, grimly. "We'll have a cordon there inside of fifteen minutes, and it will close in without those fellows knowing it. If there's any orders, commissioner, send them to the radio cars. There'll be plenty of them on the job near the Midtown National."

With that, Cardona was gone, leaving Weston half bewildered at his desk. Though the commissioner commanded the forces of the law, he could see nothing else to be done, until he heard how Cardona fared. Weston decided to curb his impatience until Graham arrived. Then, at least, there would be someone with whom he could talk.

It took Joe Cardona exactly seven minutes to reach the neighborhood of the Midtown National. He dismissed his cab; found a good lookout spot in the corner entrance of a small cigar store. From that point, Cardona studied the entire field of coming action.

The bank occupied an opposite corner; it was a bulky, old-fashioned building, but its grimy granite walls had the look of a fortress. Weston was right; ordinarily, that bank would be too big a nut to crack. But circumstances had altered its normal strength.

The avenue had been excavated; the subway hole was boarded over, on the cut-and-cover system, so that the avenue could be used for traffic. Cardona noted that the tunneled half of the avenue was on the side toward the bank.

There was a deluge of noise coming from that part of the cross street on the other side of the avenue. That thoroughfare, too, was half torn up. A big steam shovel, almost at the corner, was scooping up huge chunks of broken asphalt. Its big arm swung to poise above a truck that stood alongside. The rear of the shovel opened; the huge fragments dropped into the truck with a terrific rattle.

That work would be finished tonight. Already, men farther along the street were laying new paving. There was a steamroller parked in a cutoff space at the corner. It was waiting, with steam up, until the big shovel finished. Then the roller would move through and start its own work on the fresh paving.

Cardona looked at his watch. Three minutes after nine. The zero hour was past. There had been some delay. That would work well for the law.

Within five minutes, the police cordon would be ready, awaiting Cardona's signal to close in. Joe's best stunt would be to move away; give the order for the police to tighten.

With that thought, Cardona shifted from his lookout spot. Just as the steam shovel ripped another clatter of broken paving, Joe heard a muffled sound—one that he would never have noticed, had he not expected it.

There was a tremble, too, of the sidewalk; so slight that it would have escaped Cardona's attention, if he had not heard the muffled blast. Those linked occurrences told their story. Crime was underway.

Mobsters had blown a path into the Midtown National. They had started their thrust for wealth before the law was ready. But they had not outwitted the master fighter who had prepared to break their game.

Across the avenue was a silent figure in black, waiting against a building wall. Burning eyes saw Cardona start off on the run, to hurry up the cordon. A whispered laugh issued from hidden lips.

Events were developing as The Shadow wanted them.

## CHAPTER XVIII
## GUIDED FLIGHT

IF lookouts from the covered subway entrances had spotted police about, crime would have been canceled for tonight. That was why The Shadow had purposely delayed information: so that the law would not arrive too soon. Only Cardona had shown up; he had kept himself inconspicuous. Mobsters had loosed their blast.

Down in the newly excavated subway, gas-masked men were piling through the broken wall where fumes teemed forth. Their flashlights showed the way to the huge vault they wanted. Others followed, bringing new charges of explosives. Working with skilled speed, they prepared to blow the vault.

The word was passed. Criminal workers retired to the subway, following the line of a long wire that they had dragged through. At the end of that wire, tucked in a niche of the subway wall, was Dobie Kring. He pressed the button.

A new blast shattered the vault. Again, a picked crew headed through. When they returned, they were carrying bags and boxes that they had lifted from the vault. They were taking their loot to an opening that led up to the side street. Dobie followed after them.

Like the swag-bearers, the sappers had ripped off their gas masks. The blasting crew had orders to go out by the avenue, where cars would await them. But when they poured from the boarded entrances, a surprise awaited them.

From a lower corner came a siren's wail—the first sound of the police attack. As the sappers tried to enter parked automobiles, police cars whipped toward them. Revolvers barked; tear-gas bombs hit the street.

Trapped crooks had no time to don their discarded gas masks. They were clawing at their eyes, rolling from the car steps to the curb. Officers were piling out to capture them, while more police arrived in cars and on foot.

Perched in a second-story window on the side street, across from the bank, Ace Curdy saw the roundup of the blasting squad. It had come quicker than he expected. Police were here in uncommonly large numbers. That wouldn't matter—not when the triggermen got started.

Down the avenue came the roar of motors. Cars filled with triggermen were driving through in a phalanx, with revolvers spurting from their windows. Those were the prelude to a clatter that never came. The gunners were supposed to use machine guns when they neared the police, but they never found the chance.

From a corner of the avenue, The Shadow tongued the first shots. His big automatics spat bullets that reached the drivers of the leading cars. Two automobiles went skidding in the street. Other cars had to wheel to miss them. They were floundering when they reached the cross street.

From the portion of that thoroughfare where paving construction had not begun came the shriek of police cars. Others answered from a block above, as they roared along the avenue to overtake the crook-manned cars.

The triggermen were trapped between two fires. Police revolvers were dropping them before they could unlimber the machine guns. Their plight was as bad as that of the captured sappers. The Shadow could have added shots from his own direction; but they were unnecessary. Moreover, he had other work ahead.

ACE CURDY hadn't expected such a quick wipeout of the gun crews. There had to be more delay so that the men who had brought the swag could stage a getaway by the avenue. That was supposed to lead the police on a false chase.

Ace had a rifle; he aimed it, intending to snipe all the policemen that he could spot.

Ace never pulled that trigger.

Down at the corner, where wooden horses barred traffic from the side street, Ace saw a figure that he had never expected to view again in life. That was the cloaked form of The Shadow!

Coolly, The Shadow was aiming for Ace's own window. While Ace gawked, the rifle a dead object in his half-raised arms, The Shadow's .45 spoke. With the spurt from its muzzle came a crash above Ace's head. A scatter of glass clattered upon the frozen rifleman.

Ace didn't stop to wonder why The Shadow, usually so accurate in fire, had shattered the window instead of picking off the figure framed within it. Ace chucked his rifle; dived through the darkened room and headed for the stairs. He reached the street in fifteen seconds flat.

Ace's exit brought him to a little alleyway.

There, Doc Harstell was seated at the wheel of a sleek sedan, with Dobie Kring beside him. In back were the piles of swag. Ace leaped into the rear seat, hoarsing the question:

"Why don't you get going, Doc?"

"He's waiting for the other bunch to start," returned Dobie. "They've got to stage their fake getaway, so we can slip the coppers!"

"But they can't pull it!" protested Ace. "The triggermen didn't clear the way for them!"

"They will, all right."

"Not with The Shadow there!"

As Ace spilled that announcement, his companions stared. They thought him crazy; but his face showed too serious. Ace gulped an account of all that he had seen, finishing with The Shadow's lone shot for the window. Doc Harstell stepped on the starter.

"The bulls will be coming through," he declared. "The boys can hold them for a while. That's our only chance!"

MATTERS were proving as Harstell said. On the side street, a touring car was waiting, four impatient men within it. They wanted to make that spurt for the avenue; but it wasn't possible. Worse than that, police had spotted the touring car. A police car was starting to nose past the barricade.

Supposed workmen sprang suddenly to action. They were other thugs, signed up by the Murder Master. They had shoved the foreman and the

**Crooks and cops alike heard the strident laugh above the steam roller's roar. They knew the fighter who was making this lone attempt was The Shadow!**

was slowed by the debris. The steam shovel was scooping more ammunition. Its long arm hoisted another devastating load of paving. The driver of the second car just had time to shove into reverse, when another half ton of paving was dropped.

That load sliced off the radiator, flattened the front wheels. The wrecked automobile bowed forward, as if acknowledging defeat. While another pair of officers were hopping to safety, the steam shovel went after more rock.

Police were firing at the control house of the big scooper; but the mobsters inside were keeping low. Meanwhile, fake workmen along the barricaded street were spattering shots that labor gang into an empty house. These crooks were desperate. They had to stop the law's advance in order to assure their own escape later.

Back at his corner, The Shadow saw sudden action from the steam shovel. It had halted operations during the fight on the avenue, but it was again scooping asphalt. The police didn't particularly notice it as the shovel lifted. They received their surprise when the first patrol car started past the truck that stood beside the steam shovel.

The big crane swung. It didn't stop above the truck. It went beyond; let its load of crushed stone drop for the oncoming patrol car. The cop at the wheel had just time to yank toward the curb.

The chunks of asphalt hit; they shattered the patrol car's hood, ripped away fenders and steps. The car was wrecked, but its occupants managed to dive safely from the far door.

Another car was coming through. Its course prevented an advance on foot.

The derrick was lifting, ready with another supply of stone. The crooks who handled it didn't expect their challenge to be accepted. They didn't figure that any machine could smash their blockade.

They were mistaken. Already they had a challenger who had found a way to meet them. There was a hiss from the avenue corner; a rumble as the parked steamroller lumbered forward.

While crooks and cops stared alike, they recognized the driver who was coming through. He was clad in black; they heard his strident laugh above the steamroller's roar. They knew the fighter who was making this lone attempt. The Shadow!

As the steamroller hit the stone-strewn street, it pressed between the wrecked police cars. Chunks of debris were flattening beneath the roller's pressure. Bullets were flattening too as they hit the steel surface of The Shadow's vehicle.

Low behind the throttle, The Shadow was as secure as the thugs in the control house of the steam shovel.

Those crooks let the loaded shovel open. Big chunks of asphalt showered the steamroller, bounced from its steel sides as uselessly as pebbles. The steamroller was through; up from its helm, The Shadow was firing with an automatic. His shots were for the thugs who had lined themselves along the street. He had passed the shelters that they used as barricades.

The steam shovel was starting again, going after more asphalt in frantic haste. It was too late. The Shadow had smoothed a clear path for the police cars. They were ramming through while the shovel was still scooping stone. Flanking the steamroller, two patrol cars bore down on the touring car that was scheduled for a fake getaway.

The driver jammed that car forward to whizz between them. His pals were exchanging shots with the police as they passed. None of the combatants had time for proper aim, for the touring car was shoving to its limit in second gear.

Ahead was the steamroller, lumbering toward it. The touring car swerved right; but The Shadow outguessed its driver. The Shadow already had guided the roller to the left. The driver of the touring car wrenched his wheel in the opposite direction; his frantic move was badly belated.

The crook-filled car met the steamroller in a head-on crash. The driver was giving it the brakes; but they served him little. The entire hood of the touring car telescoped back into the body. The impact was so swift that a single instant turned the automobile into a mass of wreckage.

The Shadow sprang to the sidewalk. He reached the alleyway, where he knew another car should be. He saw taillights whisking a block away, as the sedan turned into the next street. The Shadow delivered a triumphant laugh, telling that pursuit was still possible. He sped away, on foot, through the darkness of the alley.

Joe Cardona, arriving in a police car, heard The Shadow's laugh. Joe understood. He took a quick glance along the street. Battle was ended. Those in the touring car were crushed or trapped. Those who had fled their barricades at The Shadow's approach were wounded or taken prisoner. The crew that manned the steam shovel had lifted their hands in surrender.

More important to Cardona was the shout that officers were giving as they peered into the wrecked touring car. The swag wasn't there. Cardona knew where it had gone—through the alleyway, in another car.

THE SHADOW had reached the next street. A coupe wheeled up to receive him. Cliff Marsland was the driver. He pointed out the swag car, speeding a block away. The Shadow paused; he stepped into the glow of the coupe's headlights. Cliff saw him raise a beckoning arm.

That signal was to Joe Cardona, whose car was starting into the alley. Three seconds later, The Shadow was entering the coupe; his strange-toned voice ordered Cliff to take up the chase. The coupe lashed forward.

Three blocks ahead, the pursued sedan took to an avenue. As Cliff made the same turn, The Shadow opened long-range fire from his window. Crooks heard the shots; their car wheeled into a side street. Half a minute later, new shots burst behind them. The sedan turned another corner.

Those shots were harrying the crooks into a twisty route; at the same time, they were guiding Cardona and bringing roving police cars into the chase.

Criminals were boxing themselves, although they didn't realize it. Unwittingly, they were playing into The Shadow's hands; he was forcing them to a course that would mean disaster for themselves.

From that forced flight The Shadow foresaw a result far greater than the capture of the paroled convicts.

This chase was the measure that would bring a showdown with the Murder Master.

## CHAPTER XIX
## THE LAST REFUGE

IT was Dobie Kring who voiced the thoughts that gripped the trio in the pursued sedan. As he heard the increasing wails of sirens, Dobie voiced it in a single sentence:

"They're hot after us, Doc!"

That brought a savage growl from Ace Curdy. He wanted Harstell to slow the car, so that he could take pot shots at the coupe that kept so close along their trail.

"The Shadow's in that bus," affirmed Ace. "He's the guy I'm out to get! Give me a chance at him!"

"And then what?" snapped Dobie. "The cops will be on us! What we've got to do is shake The Shadow. Right, Doc?"

A nod from Harstell as he yanked the car around a corner. Half a block, and Harstell heard the shriek of a siren coming toward them. He took the next street to the right. His mutter was a grim agreement with Dobie:

"If I can shake The Shadow—"

"What then, Doc?" Dobie was eager with the question. "Can you make it to the warehouse?"

"Not a chance, Dobie! But we could head for

Quedden's. That's the only direction that's safe."

Dobie started a protest. Ace intervened.

"Why not?" he demanded. "I got there, didn't I—the night I had The Shadow?"

"A fine botch you made that night," retorted Dobie. "You claim you croaked The Shadow—and here he shows up again!"

"That part doesn't matter. I got into Quedden's, didn't I? And away again, afterward. Those crooked streets around his place are made to order for us. Besides, we've got to let the prof know that The Shadow's loose."

That convinced Dobie. He craned from his window for a look backward as they turned a corner. He didn't see The Shadow's coupe. It was off the trail at last. Sirens, though, proved that police were coming in from everywhere.

"You can make it to Quedden's, Doc!" enthused Dobie. "Only don't stop too near the house. We'll have to ditch the bus, so the bulls won't know where we've gone."

The twisty course ended. Harstell took a straightaway to gain the opportunity they needed. Police cars sighted the sedan at crossings; but none was close enough to do more than follow, well behind. When Harstell jammed the brakes, the sedan halted in a narrow street.

The three paroled prisoners piled out. Each bundled a portion of the swag. They rounded a corner, came to another street that went off at an angle. It was only half a block to Quedden's house, but long-drawn shrills from police whistles told that the abandoned sedan had been found.

"I'll get ahead," panted Ace. "I'll hammer at the front door! We can get in quicker that way, if Thoyer shows up! If he don't, we can duck in by the alley!"

ACE was pounding the front door when the others arrived. Impatiently, they pointed to the alley. Ace shook his head. He could hear the slide of an opening bolt. A moment later, Thoyer was blinking at them from the open doorway.

Ace didn't give the fellow a chance to argue. Instead, he flourished a revolver under Thoyer's nose, to shove him back.

The three convicts entered the lower hall, closed the door behind them. Ace grinned when he shoved the bolt. He turned toward Thoyer, who was staring from across the piles of swag.

"Listen, lug!" snapped Ace. "Tell the prof that we want to see him!"

Thoyer tried to protest. It didn't get far. Ace's gun nudged him.

"You heard me! We want to see Prof Quedden!"

Reluctantly, Thoyer started for the stairs. He halted when he heard a sudden stir among the invaders. It was Dobie who caused it. He was leaning his ear against the door.

"There's a car stopping out front! Wait!—it's going away again. Listen! Those whistles—"

The trio was tense. They were beginning to guess what had happened. Somehow, The Shadow had found out where they had headed. His car was the tracer that Cardona wanted. The coupe had suddenly shown up again, to lead the police here.

All three of the crooks were listening at the door. Sounds outside had ended, which made it all the more ominous. Minutes crept along, with Thoyer still standing on the stairs. Ace grunted that maybe the bulls hadn't found the place. Dobie shook his head.

"Cardona's smart," declared Dobie. "If he's spotted this joint, he'll wait until he's got it covered. We may be in for it; tougher than we think. Wait a couple of minutes more. Then we'll know what's what."

More minutes trickled. Dobie stepped away from the door, with a satisfied grin.

"All right," he told the others. "Let's go up and talk to the chief—"

A hammering sound broke Dobie's sentence. It came from the door. Outside, a heavy voice demanded:

"Open in the name of the law!"

Ace sprang toward the door, drawing a revolver. Dobie stopped him.

"Not that way, Ace! We've got to be smarter when we shoot it out!" He swung toward Thoyer; pointed to the door that opened into the lower laboratory: "Unlock it!"

Thoyer came down from the stairs to obey. When the door opened, Dobie nudged.

"Let's get in there and wedge the windows open. Those shutters will make slick loopholes! We'll give those bulls more than they expect! You and me, Ace."

"What about Doc?"

"He can go up and talk to the chief... Tell him the whole lay, Doc. Better take this mug Thoyer with you."

THE evil trio made an odd tableau at that moment. Dobie was standing halfway toward the open door of the laboratory, pointing in that direction. Ace, nearer the front door, was looking in Dobie's direction. Doc was standing by the stairs that led to the second floor; his left hand was half raised to beckon Thoyer.

Each of the invaders held a drawn revolver. Only Thoyer was unarmed. He was standing at the door of the lower lab, but he was facing Doc Harstell. That was why Thoyer, alone, could see new arrivals who had joined the scene.

They were at the top of the stairs. Foremost was a dark-haired girl; her face was pale, but firm; she held a steady grip on a revolver. So did the two men who were on each side of her; stolid fellows, who meant business.

Again, Elsa Wendley and her servants had taken their own route to Quedden's premises. They were here in time to prevent besieged crooks from starting battle with the police. Elsa was covering Ace Curdy. The servants were taking care of Dobie Kring and Doc Harstell.

"Stand where you are!" Elsa was the spokesman. "Let those guns drop!"

She was stepping downward as she spoke. Her right foot went too far; the girl stumbled. Without thinking, one of the servants reached to aid her. Elsa caught herself; but in that brief instant, Curdy saw a chance for fight.

"I'll get the moll!" Ace was coming up with his revolver. "You fellows clip the others!"

Dobie and Doc didn't budge. As for Ace, his gun hand stopped halfway. From the very stair top came a shivering laugh—a tone of mirth that no criminal could forget. The trapped trio saw another figure, revealed by Elsa's advance.

The Shadow had come to support his allies. His automatics were unlimbered, pointing downward toward the lower hall. Those burrowing muzzles seemed double-focused on every crook.

Mechanically, Ace and his pals let their revolvers hit the floor. A moment later, Elsa and her servants were again advancing downward, each covering a prisoner.

THE SHADOW ignored the covered trio. He looked toward Thoyer, whose face showed a mingling of bewilderment and fear. Thoyer was starting to sidle into the lower laboratory. The Shadow stopped him with a sharp command.

Thoyer saw a muzzle tilted toward him. The gunpoint moved; like a magnet it drew Thoyer across the hall, toward the front door.

"Unlock the door!" commanded The Shadow. "Then turn about!"

Thoyer drew the bolt. Police were hammering on the outside; they must have heard something, for their pounding ceased. Meanwhile, The Shadow beckoned Thoyer with a gun. Shakily, the man came up the stairs.

The Shadow stepped aside, toward the direction of the bedrooms, to point Thoyer through the curtained hallway that led to the rear of the house. In sibilant whisper, The Shadow gave the final order:

"Summon Professor Quedden!"

As Thoyer started toward the curtains, someone tried the door below. It swung inward under pressure, revealing a sudden movement of flashlights on the front steps. Police didn't know whether or not the unlocked door was a trap, until they saw the crooks who stood with lifted arms.

Then came a surge of the law's invaders, Joe Cardona with them. The ace inspector saw the heaps of swag; for a moment, he was amazed at sight of the paroled convicts, as prisoners. Joe almost had the whole scene reversed, until he realized that Elsa and her servants couldn't be the persons who had fled here.

Who the girl was didn't matter, for the moment; and the same applied to the men who served her. Cardona had found the real lieutenants of the Murder Master. Men who were supposed to be at Graham's, but who had been at the Midtown National instead.

"Line up!" Cardona told them. Then, to Elsa: "We'll take over."

Relieved, the girl lowered her revolver; and the servants did the same. Trapped crooks backed away sulkily, under cover of police guns, while Joe Cardona called them several kinds of double-crossers. Cardona could be choice in adjectives; but his style was somewhat cramped, with Elsa present.

There was a stir outside as Cardona finished his accusation. In from the street stepped Commissioner Weston, accompanied by Melvin Graham. Both showed astonishment when they viewed the prisoners. It was a shock to both of them to see these captives.

That, however, was nothing compared to the surprise that still was due. The Shadow had stepped from sight, but he still held control. His next move was to be the trapping of the Murder Master.

## CHAPTER XX
### ONE MORE VICTIM

WESTON was brusque as he began a quiz. In a few short minutes, he learned more than he had guessed in days. Sullenly, the paroled convicts admitted that they served the Murder Master. Their first balk came when Weston demanded the name of their chief.

Elsa supplied it while the prisoners glared.

"Professor Jerome Quedden," she stated. "He lives in this house. At present, he is in an office at the back of the second floor. The door was closed; he did not hear us enter."

Since Elsa knew the way, Weston ordered her to conduct Cardona there. As they turned toward the stairs, they saw Thoyer gazing across the banister at the top. The assistant darted a nervous glance along the hall. He was looking for The Shadow; he did not see him.

Thoyer made a sudden dash away from the stairs. Cardona gave a loud shout, then fired.

Those warning shots echoed loudly through the house. Thoyer bobbed back to view again, his arms raised high. Cardona covered him.

"I'll tell everything!" whined Thoyer. "Everything I know! All about Professor Quedden—"

At that moment, a short-built figure appeared behind the rail where Thoyer stood. The man was Quedden himself; his wizened face peered from a level with Thoyer's shoulder. On Quedden's features was registered a wild, fanatic look, yet one that showed harsh glee.

In his hand, Quedden gripped a revolver. He seemed oddly disinterested, though, in Cardona. The man who concerned Quedden was Thoyer; for the baldish professor had overheard his assistant's whine.

"What will you tell, Thoyer?" demanded Quedden. His voice became a hiss, as he added: "The secrets of my inventions? Never! I have trusted you too much, Thoyer! If you speak—"

For the first time, Cardona saw Quedden's gun between the banister rails. Quedden was half behind Thoyer; Cardona couldn't risk a shot at the professor. With a bound, Joe went for the stairs. Thoyer, in turn, became frantic.

Madly, the assistant sprang for Quedden; leaping over the frail professor towards the curtained hallway. Quedden was wiry; amazingly spry. He rallied; made a dart after Thoyer. The assistant had only one route; that was through the upstairs laboratory. He took it, with Quedden after him.

Joe Cardona was too late to overtake them. All that he could do was follow; and behind the inspector came a pair of detectives. Others were busy holding the downstairs prisoners. Elsa decided that she and her servants should join in the chase.

Only Weston and Graham remained, free for action when they heard a sudden clatter from the depths of the lower laboratory. Before Weston could understand the new noise, Graham grasped the answer.

"Quick, commissioner!" Graham snatched up a revolver from the floor. "They are heading down this way! We must block them off!"

WHILE Graham was dashing into the darkened room, Weston tugged at a revolver that he carried on his hip. Unfortunately, the commissioner needed a gun so seldom that he usually forgot to keep his hip pocket unbuttoned. That was the case on this occasion. It took Weston five seconds to yank the gun loose, bringing the button with it.

The clatter had ended when Weston reached the door of the lower lab. It was just when he arrived there that he heard the roar of a revolver. Then came the pound of more footsteps on the spiral stairs; amid it, Graham joined Weston at the hallway door.

"We've got to find the light switch, commissioner." Graham was fumbling along the wall as he spoke. "Ah, here it is!"

The lights came on. At the door of the little workshop they saw Thoyer, gasping on the floor. Beyond him was Quedden, half crouched in the center of the workshop. The professor had his revolver in his fist. He waved it crazily, as he warned:

"Go back! Both of you! Out of this house!"

It wasn't necessary for either Weston or Graham to use a revolver. Men surged from the spiral steps; Cardona pounced first, with the two detectives close behind. They hit Quedden so hard, that he jounced from his feet. His gun scaled from his fist, flew clear across Thoyer, to hit the laboratory floor.

Graham grabbed for the weapon. He was holding it when he saw that Quedden was helpless in the grip of captors. Weston received the revolver that Graham handed him, with the comment that the commissioner would need Quedden's gun as evidence.

Cardona was stooped over Thoyer's body. The dull-faced man was gasping his last few breaths. Cardona reminded him that he had promised a statement. Thoyer managed a nod; then coughed:

"Quedden—Quedden is in—"

That effort finished Thoyer. The flicker of his glazing eyes told that he wanted to reveal all he knew about the Murder Master, but was unable. That shot in the dark had come too close to Thoyer's heart.

SINCE the lower laboratory was the scene of new murder, Weston decided to hold his investigation here. Quedden, clamped with handcuffs, sat in the chair where they put him.

The three lieutenants of the Murder Master, also handcuffed, were brought in to witness Weston's quiz. Meanwhile, Cardona scoured the house in search of evidence.

There was plenty of it in Quedden's office. The old professor wouldn't talk, except to cackle defiance at his accusers. He knew what they were here for, he told them. They were trying to steal his inventions. He had expected this; that was why he had tried to prepare for it.

Quedden's words became incoherent. They let him mutter to himself, since further questioning was useless. The commissioner concentrated on the documentary evidence. He studied the coded notes that had come from Quedden's desk. Cardona had already searched the other prisoners, and had found a code in Ace's pocket. From it, the notes were translated.

Quedden's safe had been open in the office. Cardona also had the meager swag from previous robberies. Summary of this evidence caused Weston to resume his quiz of Quedden. The professor finally became coherent when Weston asked him where the funds had come from.

"The Foundation sent them," clucked Quedden. "My royalties. I suppose you intend to steal them, along with everything else!"

"This Foundation is a palpable fraud!" snapped Weston. "A product of your own imagination! A very weak pretense, to cover up your crimes—"

Quedden interrupted with a maddened shake of his manacled wrists. His rage was directed toward Weston.

"You lie!" Quedden's voice was high. "You say the Foundation does not exist! I knew you would say that! You want an excuse to rob me—"

Again, Quedden's words became a crazy mutter. Weston gave a shrug; turned to Cardona, with the comment:

"Take him away, inspector. We'll charge him with the murder of Thoyer. Remove the body; here is the gun that he used to kill his victim."

"One moment, commissioner." Cardona had something else. "Wait until we try this big record we found with those crazy phonographs."

The record was of the disk type. Cardona fitted it to a suitable machine. Haunting music sounded; its strain carried a creepy spell that listeners remembered. Then came a frenzied cackle, forced to a dramatic pitch.

"Do you hear me, commissioner?" A crazed laugh followed. "Yes—you hear me. You shall remember me! I am the Murder Master!"

Weston couldn't help a shudder as he motioned for Cardona to stop the record. He had heard enough to prove that this was the "canned" program that had cut in on station WQJ. Enough, too, to recognize the similarity of the Murder Master's tone to that of Professor Quedden.

ODDLY, one of the most curious listeners had been Quedden himself. His face had taken on a childish awe. His beady eyes had lost their flash. He was shaking his bald head, as he muttered:

"I don't understand—I don't understand!"

Cardona hoisted the professor by the shoulder. It was Elsa who halted him before he could start Quedden's march from the room. The girl had an important task to perform; one that she had kept until this opportunity. She spoke to one of the servants. The man handed her a small cardboard box.

"I was told to give you this"—Elsa was speaking to Cardona—"told to do so by—by a friend. One who helped us."

The girl was speaking of The Shadow. Cardona suddenly realized that when he opened the box. Inside was a cylindrical phonograph record. Coiled within it was a sealed envelope.

The case against the Murder Master was not yet closed. The law had still to review The Shadow's evidence.

## CHAPTER XXI
## THE MASTER SPEAKS

THERE was an old-style cylindrical phonograph in Quedden's workshop. Cardona put the record on it. Listeners heard a cackly voice issue from the big horn. The tone was much like Quedden's usual speech, until thirty seconds had passed. Then, it took on a lower pitch, free from gloating chuckles.

The voice was giving instructions for the robbery of the Midtown National Bank.

"This dope went out last night!" exclaimed Cardona. He pointed to the paroled convicts and demanded: "You've heard this spiel before, haven't you?"

There were snarls of denial from the trio. They silenced when the proof of their lie came from the horn. Their own voices were registered at the record's finish.

"The Murder Master, talking to his crew," summed Cardona. "Somebody was smart enough to make this record, commissioner."

By "somebody," Cardona meant The Shadow. Weston, however, was thinking of something else. He had clutched an idea of his own. He told Cardona to run the record a second time.

While it was repeating, Cardona opened the envelope that had come with the record. He found a sheet of paper, pasted with fragments of newspaper clippings. They had been cut from various news stories; then pieced together to make a concise report on a single subject.

"Here's the motive for the three murders!" interjected Cardona, when the phonograph had finished. "Parts of talks that Hyvran and Palbrock gave! An interview—or part of it—with Big Frank Denniman!"

Weston didn't respond. He was deep in thought, his chin buried in his hand.

"They'd gotten together on something we didn't know about," went on Cardona. "They all wanted a reform of the State parole system, and they all mentioned it. They'd have managed that reform, too. Hyvran in the State assembly; Palbrock in the senate; Denniman working to get everyone else in back of it.

"The Murder Master had to get rid of them, because he was using paroled prisoners. The new system would have put that bunch under the watch of the parole board, keeping them out of circulation. That would have queered the racket for the Murder Master."

Cardona expected approval when Weston looked up. Instead, the commissioner pointed to the phonograph.

"That record," emphasized Weston, "carried the voice of the Murder Master! But I am positive"—he swung his finger toward Professor Quedden—"that it was not the voice of that man!"

MENTALLY, Cardona compared the record with the broadcast from WQJ. Weston was right; the record had been too precise. The voice had lost its cackle too early. It had been free from absentminded mutters. Those were a habit with Quedden.

Cardona looked at the old professor. Quedden was scowling from his chair. Why should he be, when evidence was favoring him, at present? He wasn't putting on an act; he was muttering, still holding to the idea that his inventions were at stake. Cardona decided that the old man was what he appeared to be: a curious creature who lived with his own thoughts.

"You're right, commissioner," declared Cardona. "That record spills the real story! It wasn't Quedden who fixed that program for WQJ. It was somebody who faked the prof's voice, laugh and all. That's why the disk was planted here along with the other evidence.

"But the Murder Master didn't worry much when he sent out his own orders. Only his own bunch listened. He wanted them to think that he was Quedden; but he didn't bother to go strong with it. He didn't know we were going to get a record of that talk, too."

The Shadow's evidence was coming home. Together, Weston and Cardona had pieced its portions. Their conclusions, however, were nullifying their past accomplishments. Being a police official, Weston was quick to realize the fact.

The commissioner glanced at Quedden. After all, the muttering professor was the law's only suspect. There was plenty of evidence to prove him the Murder Master. It wouldn't do to clear the fellow until someone could be arrested in his place.

That was why Weston quelled Cardona's enthusiasm. Cardona, always fond of hunches, was trying to move too fast, in Weston's opinion. The commissioner wanted conservative advice; particularly, he needed an excuse to withdraw from the theory that he himself had advanced. He turned to Melvin Graham.

"What is your opinion?" Weston inquired. "Do you think that this discrepancy, in the matter of voice, is a sufficient factor in Quedden's favor?"

"Decidedly not," replied Graham. "You speak of a disguised voice. Why wouldn't Quedden have disguised his own, when he talked with the men who served him? He would naturally have wished to preserve his identity from them."

"Of course!" exclaimed Weston. "We had it the wrong way about! Quedden is the man we want, after all! Take him away, Cardona!"

THE logic didn't quite suit Cardona. If crooks had not known Quedden as the Murder Master, why had they headed here with the swag? They certainly regarded him as their chief. It didn't fit—Quedden disguising his voice for the benefit of men who already knew the part he played.

"I'm taking him, commissioner," declared Cardona, as he laid his hand on Quedden's shoulder. "But I'm still not sure that he's the murderer—"

"Graham has settled it, Cardona."

"I have," added Graham, in support of Weston's statement. "Yet my argument was scarcely necessary, inspector. After all, you saw Quedden murder Thoyer. You have the gun with which he did it."

A thought flashed to Cardona's mind. He hadn't seen Quedden shoot Thoyer. Joe had heard the gunshot; that was all. Pulling the death gun from his pocket, Cardona thrust it under Quedden's nose, with the question:

"Is this your revolver?"

The old professor suddenly showed interest. He studied the revolver with beady eyes, then glared, as he shook his head.

"True to form," remarked Graham. "He denies everything. Can't you ever make him say yes, inspector?"

"Maybe I can." Cardona reached in his pocket, produced a box of cartridges that he had found in Quedden's desk. He showed it to the professor with the question: "Are these yours?"

Quedden nodded.

"There's one 'yes' for you, Mr. Graham," declared Cardona, bluntly. "Maybe I can get another from him. If—"

Cardona was hefting the revolver as he spoke. Its weight was the factor that caused his interruption. He looked at the gun; it was a .38 caliber weapon. A glance at the box; its label stated that it contained .32 cartridges. Cardona opened the box; the cartridges suited the label.

"Here's one for you, commissioner!" exclaimed Cardona. "The cartridges don't fit the revolver! Quedden had the gun, though; and the bullets were in his desk."

"May I see the gun?" put in Graham. "I feel sure it is the one that Quedden dropped when you seized him. Of course, there was also the gun that I picked up in the hall."

"Let's see that one," suggested Cardona, "while you look at Quedden's."

Graham produced the hallway gun. He handed it to Cardona.

"This is a .32 caliber!" exclaimed the inspector. "It must be Quedden's!" Joe cracked the gun open. "Say, this gun isn't loaded!"

There was a sneer from Graham. Cardona looked up to find himself staring into the muzzle of the .38 that he had handed Graham. The tall reformer's eyes were brilliant through the gold-rimmed spectacles that fronted them. He had come to his feet; he was stepping back, so that he could cover anyone who tried a move.

"I rather suspected that it wasn't loaded," snapped Graham. "You see, inspector, that gun is actually Quedden's. I fired the shot that killed Thoyer! I handed you the revolver that I used, instead of Quedden's. I am the Murder Master!"

NECESSITY had forced Graham's bold declaration. The Shadow's evidence had brought the trail too close. In a few minutes more, Cardona might have guessed the truth. As it was, Cardona stood cursing his own dumbness. He should have seen it all, before Graham tricked him.

Always, the Murder Master had thrown a trail; then covered it. Paroled crooks had been in his charge; he had made them his aides in crime, without letting them know he was their hidden chief. All the while, he had previewed the prospect that the police might someday close in upon him.

That was why Graham had set up this headquarters for Professor Jerome Quedden, duping the old inventor through a fictitious Foundation for Inventors. That told the part that Thoyer had played.

Thoyer was Graham's man. His dullness was a pretense. Thoyer, alone, had known that Quedden was not the Murder Master. It was part of Thoyer's job to make Quedden fit that part.

It was Thoyer who had decoded the messages from the lieutenants. He had sent them along to Graham, accompanied by the swag that crooks delivered. All except the ten percent, that the Murder Master termed a "sinking fund"; that share was stuffed in Foundation envelopes, for Quedden.

Hoarding that money had kept the old dupe happy. All the while, he had been stowing away the strongest of all the evidence that wrongly branded him as the Murder Master.

Graham had heard Thoyer cry that he would talk. That was why Graham had been forced to boldly slay his accomplice. Even then, true to form as ever, he had seen a quick opportunity to pin his own crime on Professor Quedden.

Right now, Graham was facing big odds; but he did not fear them. He was the Murder Master. His own announcement had given him a menacing prestige. Coolly, he ordered Elsa to get the handcuff keys from Cardona's pocket; to release the crooks who lined the wall. The Murder Master intended to take his three lieutenants with him.

Cardona nodded for Elsa to obey. The girl had long ago discarded her revolver. When she reached into Cardona's pocket, her hand felt the metal of the inspector's gun. Elsa gripped the weapon. She was ready for the Murder Master.

Cardona suddenly felt what was due; he couldn't warn the girl to forget the gun. That would bring prompt shots from Graham.

An instant more, Graham would have guessed it anyway; with that, he would have opened fire. Other eyes than the Murder Master's, though, were watching Elsa. Eyes that Graham did not suspect. He had come here too late to know that The Shadow had been on the premises.

Like others, Graham had failed to hear the silent tread of a personage who had descended the spiral staircase.

A laugh chilled from that gloom. It was perfectly timed. The Shadow had given Elsa the utmost limit to get at Cardona's gun, for he saw likelihood that her shot would be needed. It was. Graham showed all the nerve that suited the Murder Master.

He spun for The Shadow, because he knew that his only chance lay in meeting that challenger. He guessed also that his chance would be slim, unless he added some protection for himself. As he wheeled, Graham grabbed for Weston; he shoved the commissioner between himself and The Shadow.

THE SHADOW fired as Graham spun; but the only target was the criminal's left shoulder. Graham jolted, but showed the endurance that The Shadow expected. Bobbing past Weston, he blasted at The Shadow. His shots were wide, for The Shadow had faded. Graham guessed wrong, when he tried to pick the right direction.

Elsa had the gun she wanted. The girl jabbed a shot while her hand was on the move; but her marksmanship was true. The Shadow had counted upon it. He knew the righteous vengeance that she sought for her brother's death. Elsa had waited long for this meeting with the Murder Master. Graham's scheme to shift the blame on Quedden had added to her intensity.

Elsa's lone shot staggered the Murder Master. He reeled away from Weston. He was an open target for The Shadow; but the cloaked fighter did not fire. He had promised the Murder Master to the law. Graham's gun hand was drooping. This was the chance to take him.

Cardona pounced forward; detectives piled with him. They carried Graham to the floor, where he formed the center of a struggling pack. The crooks along the wall saw a wild chance for escape; they began to sling their manacled wrists at Elsa's servants, who had sprung to guard them.

Graham's lieutenants halted suddenly. Again, they heard The Shadow's taunting laugh. This time, it was meant for them.

Out from the workshop, The Shadow stood in view; his two guns held the three crooks covered, as they had from the stairway when the trio had first arrived at Quedden's. From then on, those crooks were mere spectators; added witnesses to Graham's sudden finish.

One man had watched the battle with strangely gleaming eyes. That man was Quedden; he saw the attempt that the thugs had made to use their handcuffs. He remembered it, when, from the surging group upon the floor, Graham came crawling free.

Despite his wounds, the Murder Master still showed tenacity. He had kept his gun; with bloodshot eyes, he was looking for the nearest victim. He saw Quedden—and the professor saw him.

As Graham strained to lift his revolver, Quedden sprang to meet him. On hands and knees, Graham was down to the midget inventor's size.

Before that lifting gun could aim, Quedden's hands were sledging downward. Quedden did not see The Shadow aim for Graham. The professor could save himself from the Murder Master; and he had his own score to settle with this fiend who had tried to frame him.

No skull could have stood the bludgeoning crash of Quedden's gun. All his nervous strength was in the stroke. Steel drove hard to Graham's head. The blow floored the Murder Master, while excited detectives added gunshots to the sagging body.

THE Murder Master was dead. He had spoken, that master of evil, only to be outvoiced by the master of justice, The Shadow. The paroled convicts who had served Melvin Graham heard the tone of a strange, mirthless laugh. It sounded as a parting knell; for when they stared, they saw The Shadow no longer.

The cloaked avenger had faded to the darkness of the workshop. Silently, he was ascending the spiral stairs, to leave by the route across the roofs. He had left the lieutenants of the Murder Master as trophies for the law.

Their part in crime was known. Soon, they would return to prison walls. This time, their sentence would be one from which they would never find parole.

The electric chair awaited the servers of the Murder Master.

THE END

**Coming in our next volume:**

# THE BLACK FALCON

Lamont Cranston is kidnapped after a master fiend discovers The Shadow's identity, and the Dark Avenger's true face is finally revealed!

Then, through roaring flames and hurtling embers they plied their evil trade:

# THE SALAMANDERS

A group of crooks who found a new way to gain their evil ends; who baffled the police to a finish—but who forgot that The Shadow starts where the police end, and uncovers evil, no matter where it may be. Here is a tale that crackles with interest like a huge furnace fire crackles. And it will thrill you more! Don't miss these two full book-length novels in the next thrilling volume of

Only $12.95. Ask your bookseller to reserve your copy now!

# SPOTLIGHT on THE SHADOW: "ON THE AIR"
## by Anthony Tollin

*There were those, of course, who claimed that they had heard his voice coming through the spaceless ether over the radio. But at the broadcasting studio, The Shadow's identity had been carefully guarded. He was said to have been allotted a special room, hung with curtains of heavy black velvet, along a twisting corridor. There he faced the unseeing microphone, masked and robed.*

*The underworld had gone so far as to make determined efforts to unravel The Shadow's identity—if it were truly The Shadow whose sinister voice the radio public knew: for there were doubters who maintained the voice was but that of an actor representing The Shadow. But all crookdom had reason to be interested: those without the law had to be sure.*

*So watchers were posted at the entrance to the broadcasting chain's building. Many walked in and out: none could be labeled as The Shadow. In desperation, a clever crook whose specialty was wiretapping applied for and secured a position as a radiotrician. Yet questioning his fellow workers brought nothing but guesses to light. Around the studio, The Shadow was almost as much a myth as on the outside. Only his voice was known.*

*Every Thursday night, the spy from crookdom would contrive to be in the twisting corridor—watching the door to the room that was supposed to be The Shadow's. Yet no one ever entered the room.*

*Could it be, then, that The Shadow broadcast by remote control—that his voice was conveyed to the studio by private wire? No one knew. He and his fear-striking laugh had been heard—that was all.*
—The Living Shadow, The Shadow Magazine, April 1931

The Shadow was America's foremost mystery man during the 1930s and 1940s; *The Shadow Magazine* was the top-selling hero pulp and the Dark Avenger also starred in radio's top-rated daytime series. The huge audience of Mutual's Sunday-afternoon broadcasts knew The Shadow as Lamont Cranston who was "never seen, only heard" in his battles with criminals and racketeers.

However, The Shadow's haunting tones, deep and sibilant, had first emerged over the airwaves July 31, 1930 as a phantom narrator: "The Shadow knows, and you too shall know if you listen as Street & Smith's *Detective Story Magazine* relates for you the story of—'The Serpent Stings.'" The host of CBS' *Detective Story Program* was network radio's first mysterious storyteller, paving the way for such sinister successors as the Whistler, the Mysterious Traveler, *The Witch's Tale*'s Old Nancy and *Inner Sanctum*'s Raymond.

Street & Smith's *Detective Story Magazine* had debuted in 1917 as the world's first detective fiction magazine, but a decade later was showing its age. Plagued by imitators like *Black Mask, Clues* and *Detective Fiction Weekly*, the nation's largest pulp publisher decided to promote its flagship magazine through a new advertising medium—radio. The publishing house selected Dave Chrisman of the Ruthrauff & Ryan advertising agency and producer-director William Sweets to adapt their famous mystery magazine to the airwaves. Chrisman and Sweets developed the concept of a mysterious host, who was soon christened The Shadow by scriptwriter Harry Charlot. Broadway actor James LaCurto voiced the mysterious host in the early broadcasts but within months was replaced by Frank Readick, a radio veteran whose venomous tones made The Shadow a national sensation.

Street & Smith discovered that its sinister host had stolen the show when listeners began requesting "that *Shadow* detective magazine." Circulation manager Henry William Ralston decided the time had come for a revival of single-character publications similar to Street & Smith's earlier *Nick Carter*, and a chance visit to the Street & Smith offices led to magician/journalist Walter Gibson being assigned to bring the radio host to literary life. *The Shadow Magazine* debuted in 1931 and introduced a supersleuth who waged war on the underworld. In his first novel, *The Living Shadow*, Gibson established that his master crimefighter was the same mysterious entity who announced the Thursday-night radio series.

"By the time the second issue was out, the first

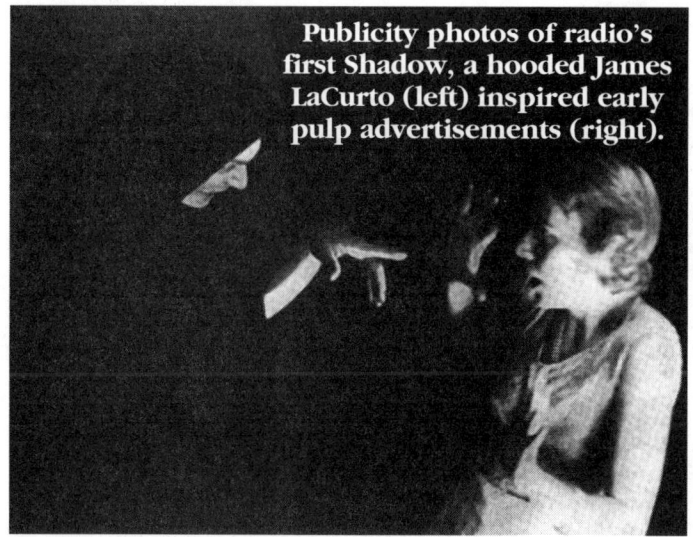

Publicity photos of radio's first Shadow, a hooded James LaCurto (left) inspired early pulp advertisements (right).

**The Shadow DETECTIVE MONTHLY**

Tune in on Street & Smith's sure-fire hit. A great big magazine of detective fiction for a thin dime! Thrills! Action! Mystery! Get your copy to-day!

10c    10c

one had sold out and so did the second one, so they jumped the magazine to monthly with the third and asked me to write one a month, and next thing they wanted them twice-a-month," recalled Gibson. "This was during the Depression, so this was a good thing to be doing. I just dropped everything else and did *The Shadow* for 15 years." Gibson eventually wrote 283 of the 325 *Shadow* novels, creating The Shadow's Lamont Cranston identity as well as Commissioner Weston, Inspector Cardona and cabby Moe Shrevnitz who would later be featured alongside Cranston in the long-running radio series.

After finishing a short run as narrator of *Street & Smith's Love Story Hour*, The Shadow was recruited to host mystery segments on *The Blue Coal Radio Revue*, beginning a long association with sponsor Blue Coal and announcer Ken Roberts. The Shadow returned in subsequent seasons as star of his own mystery anthology, with Readick continuing in the role of sinister storyteller.

Lamont Cranston finally made his radio debut when Blue Coal sponsored a *Shadow* audition over WMCA. The broadcast aired at 10:30 p.m. on June 15th, 1934 over the single New York station, with no advance publicity, but featured the slouch-hatted crimebuster of the pulps (and his agents Harry Vincent and Cliff Marsland) in a script by Gibson:

Frank Readick

Carl Kroenke

I am The Shadow. I seek Kalda, the master of crime. But before I reach him I must thwart his evil schemes. Some fell purpose makes him seek the life of an innocent victim, Carol Croyden. Kalda sent his henchmen to murder her. I, The Shadow, interfered. Carol Croyden is under my protection. Kalda's evil minions lie dead. From this girl I shall learn the truth of Kalda's schemes. I shall thwart them. When his crimes have been defeated Kalda shall meet—The Shadow. (Laugh)

Readick returned as The Shadow to host a final CBS mystery anthology that fall, though the series disappeared from the CBS airwaves on March 27, 1935, due to Street & Smith's insistence that radio's sinister storyteller be replaced by the master sleuth of Gibson's pulp novels. However, radio's most famous laugh would not be silenced.

Just days after Frank Readick's final CBS show, The Shadow's mocking laughter returned to the airwaves in a syndicated serial produced in C. P. MacGregor's San Francisco studios. Twenty-six 15-minute serialized installments were scripted by prolific writer John Eugene Hasty, with radio veteran Carl Kroenke voicing The Shadow. MacGregor's *Shadow* serial remained in syndication through the end of the decade, supplied without charge to stations to promote *The Shadow Magazine* and later sold to American and foreign stations by radio syndicator Charles Michelson.

Street & Smith entered into a new broadcasting agreement with Blue Coal in 1937, and that summer Gibson teamed with scriptwriter Edward Hale Bierstadt to develop the new series. Inspired by the upcoming Shadow radio revival, Gibson submitted *The Radio Crimes* on June 4, 1937, which was published the following year as *The Murder Master* in the February 15th issue. Interestingly, the cackling, self-satisfied tones of the master fiend in Gibson's novel strongly resembled those of the sinister Shadow of Frank Readick's earliest seasons.

*The Shadow* returned to network airwaves on September 26, 1937, over the new Mutual network with Broadway "boy wonder" Orson Welles starring as Lamont Cranston, "wealthy young man about town." However, the 22-year-old Welles was unable to perfect The Shadow's famous laugh, so recordings of Frank Readick's sibilant signatures opened and closed all of Welles' broadcasts.

Orson Welles as The Shadow

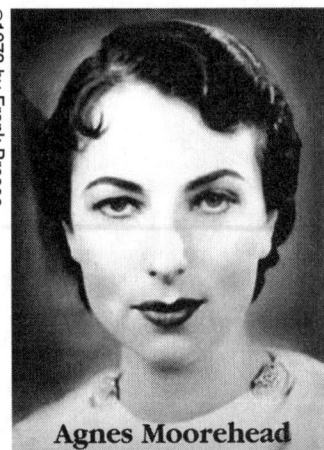

Agnes Moorehead

Margot Stevenson

Bill Johnstone and his shadowy predecessor Frank Readick

Playing The Shadow each week provided Welles a steady income with a minimal commitment of time. "$185 every week, it was marvelous," he later recalled, delighting in the princely sum he had received in 1937 for less than an hour of work. His contract permitted him to skip the show's rehearsals, while he sent his assistants to read his lines and mark up his scripts during the run-throughs. "My God," he explained to Peter Bogdanovich. "I didn't even know what was going to happen to me while I was in 'em. Not rehearsing—which was part of my deal with Blue Coal, the sponsor—made it much more interesting. When I was thrown down the well or into some fiendish snake pit, I never knew how I'd get out."

The Shadow of Gibson's novels blended into patches of darkness, but his radio counterpart had "years ago in the Orient learned a strange and mysterious secret, the hypnotic power to cloud men's minds so they cannot see him."* While the Oriental origins of The Shadow's mystic powers were frequently alluded to, no origin story was ever presented in the MBS radio series, though the story was eventually revealed in an anonymous text feature in Street & Smith's *Shadow Comics* (reprinted here for the first time).

As Gibson explained in 1975: "In the stories, I had The Shadow frequently filter from sight, or blend with darkness and everything of that sort. I put quite a lot of hypnotic stuff in too because he'd been in Tibet, and hypnotism and magical illusions were my specialties, but I didn't overplay them. Well, they liked the idea of The Shadow being invisible. As a matter of fact, [in] that very first script that Bierstadt did we were having a problem: The Shadow was to talk to a man in the death row at Sing Sing. We decided that we would have the guards hypnotized and he moved in in a dim light, and the man heard a voice talking. Bierstadt did a very good job of delineating that. Well, these people just decided to take the short way, which was very good radio, to simply say that he clouded people's minds. They'd say, 'Shadow, where are you?' 'I'm here but you can't see me.' Well, that was wonderful because the people listening over the radio couldn't see him either.... So really the radio was very similar to the stories where I had him use real hypnotism on people except that mine was modified, whereas they made it a standardized thing.

"Now, we didn't try to get some of The Shadow's agents in because there would have been a difficulty with the voice contrast." The Shadow's major agent, Harry Vincent, was edited out of Bierstadt's script before it aired, replaced by the lovely Margo Lane. The new character was inspired by Broadway ingenue Margot Stevenson who succeeded originator Agnes Moorehead to play the role in the 1938 Goodrich-sponsored summer season. Street & Smith eventually asked Gibson to incorporate Margo into his pulp novels, and in *The Hydra* he finally provided a rationale for her introduction.

Bill Johnstone stepped into the shadows in the fall of 1938 after Welles departed to star in *The Mercury Theatre on the Air* on CBS. Johnstone had begun his acting career by accident: "I was standing on West 51st Street in New York, where I lived at the time, watching the workmen complete the new Guild Theatre. Before I knew it, someone yelled at me, 'Stop gazing and get in line with the others.' The teenager obeyed and ended up playing a small role in the Theatre Guild's production of *Caesar and Cleopatra*. A regular in the supporting cast opposite Readick, LaCurto and Welles, Johnstone brought a mature authority to the role that soon eclipsed the performances of his famous predecessor. "Bill Johnstone had an awful time perfecting that Shadow laugh," recalled his friend Kenny Delmar. "I felt so badly for him, because the trick is not to laugh but to have an audible sneer ... it has to be free to flow. Poor Bill suffered every time he had to do the laugh." Johnstone voiced The

---

*By 1944, The Shadow's mystical invisibility had firmly moved into Gibson's pulp novels. In *No Time for Murder*, he wrote: "Either The Shadow had the instinct of a chameleon where darkness was concerned, or he had profited heavily from his sojourns in Tibet, where he had studied deeply into the metaphysical philosophy which declares that invisibility is basically a mental state on the part of the person who desires it. In brief: if you think you are seen, you will be. If you think you aren't, you won't be. The rule worked under certain conditions, of which darkness was the best."

*Marjorie Anderson and John Archer perform before a wartime audience at the Mutual Longacre Theatre.*

Shadow for five seasons before following *The Cavalcade of America* to the West Coast, and in 1948 echoed his earlier shadowy intonations as The Whistler and the Voice of *Suspense*.

Following Bill Johnstone's departure, radio's former Mr. First Nighter Bret Morrison was chosen from more than a hundred actors to voice radio's most famous mystery man. Morrison won the role with a cold reading of *The Shadow*'s opening and closing signatures. "I got a call to come in for an audition," Morrison recalled, "but they were losing the studio at 2 o'clock and I was going to be on the air until 1:45. I finally got there with about two minutes to spare and the director asked me to just read the opening and closing. I took the script, walked into the studio and discovered it was the opening and closing of *The Shadow*. When I had played the 'First Nighter,' we used to follow *The Shadow*, so I always heard the sign-off while we were waiting to go on the air, and I used to imitate it to amuse the rest of the cast. At the audition I read the lines the way I had always remembered hearing it.... A couple weeks later I got the phone call telling me I had the job."

Hollywood star John Archer took over the title role during the 1944-45 season while Morrison focused on his other career as a cabaret singer. Born Ralph Bowman, Archer had won a new name and an RKO contract on Jesse Lasky's *Gateway to Hollywood* radio talent search. Like Welles, Archer had to juggle his busy radio and Broadway careers. "I was rehearsing a Broadway-bound play called *One Man Show*," he recalled in 1985. "We were out of town doing the tryouts in Boston, New Haven and Philadelphia, and I'd have to take a train into New York every Saturday night after the performance so I could do *The Shadow* on Sunday."

Many of Archer's *Shadow* broadcasts featured science fiction themes—not surprising since the majority were scripted by Alfred Bester, an acclaimed pulp science fiction writer who had also penned comic book adventures of Captain Marvel and Green Lantern.

Archer left the shadowy radio role after only a single season due to his growing popularity as a Broadway star. "When a new play came along, I said 'Good-bye' to the radio work, but when the play closed, it was 'Hello, radio.'"

In September of 1945, Steve Courtleigh assumed the famous part.

*Steve Courtleigh*

*Lesley Woods*

The character actor had received glowing notices for his portrayal of Abraham Lincoln in Broadway's *Prelude to Greatness.* Unfortunately, while Courtleigh gave a strong interpretation as The Shadow, he delivered a wooden performance as Cranston, the role which had become the focus of most of the show's airtime. Courtleigh left the series after only a half-dozen shows, replaced by the returning star who would wear The Shadow's cloak for the next decade.

To a generation of listeners, Bret Morrison was The Shadow. He often performed in The Shadow's slouch hat and cape for the entertainment of the audience that gathered to watch the live broadcast each Sunday afternoon at the Longacre Theatre. More than any of the series' previous stars, Morrison lived the role of Lamont Cranston, on-air and off. Since his first successful days in Chicago radio, Bret had been an avid collector of Rolls Royces and other classic cars. He was voted Chicago's "best-dressed man" for five consecutive years and continued his elegant lifestyle in New York. He regularly catered a lavish luncheon for the cast between the rehearsal and the live broadcast, and often arrived at the theater in jodhpurs and equestrian gear after an afternoon of horseback riding in Central Park with his costar, Lesley Woods.

Morrison portrayed The Shadow for the duration of the radio series, appearing in almost as many broadcasts as all the other radio Shadows combined. Grace Matthews *(Big Sister)* joined the cast as Margo in 1946 and costarred with Bret for the remainder of the Blue Coal run, and in 1949 was succeeded by Gertrude Warner, the last and longest-running of the lovely Margo Lanes.

*The Shadow* radio series outlasted *The Shadow Magazine* by five years, leaving the airwaves on December 26, 1954—nearly a quarter century after Street & Smith's *Detective Story Program* first introduced radio's foremost mystery man.

A year later, Frank Readick died alone in his Greenwich Village apartment. The passing of the radio actor who had created The Shadow's haunting laugh went unnoticed by the news media and radio listeners who had earlier been tricked by his superb performance (as field reporter Carl Phillips in Orson Welles' legendary *War of the Worlds* broadcast) into believing that a Martian armada had invaded New Jersey. With the dawn of the TV age, the era of radio drama was coming to an end, and *The Shadow*'s cancellation and the passing of one of radio's finest actors was scarcely noticed.

However, less than a decade later, *The Shadow* returned to the airwaves via syndicated reruns that paved the way for a revival of radio drama that continues to this day.

Bret Morrison and Grace Matthews

Gertrude Warner and Bret Morrison

# THE POWER TO CLOUD MEN'S MINDS

In the unending, daily, deadly war which The Shadow wages on the underworld, he has three weapons. They are his brain, cool, clear and unique in its ability to extract information from the tiniest bit of evidence.

His miraculous ability with guns is the result of a naturally good eye, a strong pair of wrists and constant practice.

The third is his ability to cloud men's minds so that, to all intents and purposes, he becomes invisible.

The whole weird story of how this weapon was won has never been revealed. We are going to give you part of the strange story here.

Deep in the hidden and mysterious fastnesses of ancient Tibet, high in the unconquerable Himalayas lies the incredibly aged, forbidden city of Lhassa.

The reason for The Shadow's pilgrimage to Tibet still cannot be told. It is a tale fraught with a danger that came close to changing the lives of every man, woman and child on the face of the earth. The merest hint of the underlying purpose of the fiends that The Shadow fought at this time might wreak untold havoc.

Let us pass in silence, then, over the reason why The Shadow plodded wearily through the snows of Tibet. Suffice it to say that for the first time in The Shadow's long career of crime fighting he was forced to appeal to someone for help.

That someone was the reason that The Shadow had come halfway around the world. That someone lived high above the eternal hills of Tibet. Lived in silence in the center of the sacred and forbidden city of Lhassa.

One by one the bearers had deserted The Shadow, so that now, as he saw the black old walls of Lhassa rising up ahead, he was alone. Alone in a vast and enduring silence.

He plodded grimly on. Somehow he had to communicate with men who not only could not speak his language—but who had never even heard of it!

In the face of this he had to explain how urgent was the need, how horrible the result if he failed.

He knocked on a wooden door that was the only entrance he could find in the tremendous wall that surrounded Lhassa. The wood of which the door was made was so old and so intricately carved that it made The Shadow's head spin. As his tired eyes followed the strange and curious figures that decorated the portal he nodded and fell to his knees.

When his mind cleared he was still alone. But his clothes were changed. He was in a tiny cell. The only light came from the dying sun, whose feeble rays could barely penetrate the slit which served as a window.

He squatted on the floor and, sitting cross-legged, he brought his mind to bear on the problem. What had happened after he had knocked on that ancient door?

He still sat cross-legged, staring into space, as he grappled with the problem of communication with the men he had come so far to see.

Suddenly a vagrant thought crystallized in his mind. Clearly, in his mind's eye, he saw a child. It was a boy. The boy's eyes were enormous. All else faded into insignificance as The Shadow focused on the tremendous eyes.

Gently, like a breeze on a hot, sultry day, a thought took form in The Shadow's mind. It seemed to emanate from this child.

"I am he whom you sought!"

Bemused as was The Shadow, he still retained enough of his probing mind to object:

"But you are so young—I thought the master was—"

The alien thought was stronger now—

"Youth and age are but different aspects of the same thing. What is it that you seek?"

The Shadow resigned himself to the impossible. Quickly, clearly and concisely, as was his wont, he outlined the hideous plot that threatened the world.

The boy, or rather image of the boy in The Shadow's mind, nodded gravely.

"I see," he said. "And why do you come here?"

"You are my last chance." There—it was done. The Shadow had staked his all. Staked the fate of the world on this child!

The child stared deep into the recesses of The Shadow's mind and asked:

"Why do you think you are the proper person to—"

Now, if ever, was The Shadow glad that his life had been lived as it had. For, like a peering searchlight, the alien mind groped and brought to light the motives, the deeds, the things that made up the Shadow's life.

If there had been one blot, one evil thing reposing in the back of The Shadow's mind, it would have stood revealed.

We who know the facts of The Shadow's blameless life, of his self-sacrificing fight against all that is bad in man, know what the result was. The Shadow, with undue modesty, feared the result of this examination.

Finally it was over. The Shadow lay back exhausted. He had never felt so tired in his life. But—

The child said: "You have found your own path to Nirvana on the grueling wheel of life. We are satisfied!"

For the first time The Shadow realized that the child was just a focal point for a score of brains. The child became shimmering and The Shadow could see that he was just the projection of a picture that ten minds had cast. The ten were old and young, but all wore a look of benign understanding. Their combined thoughts joined in The Shadow's mind:

"Because your life is clear, and devoted to the good of mankind, we endow you with the power to cloud men's minds. Men will think you are invisible. It is a potent weapon, and one that you must use with care. It should, combined with your own powers, enable you to win victory over the menace you fear. Go in peace!"

The fact that you all still walk the earth proves The Shadow won his battle.

That is the story of The Shadow's power.... The right to invisibility was won by The Shadow on his merits.

It is his, and his alone—

**Originally published as "A Plea" in *Shadow Comics*, Volume 2, Number 7, October 1942.**

---

**FROM OUT OF THE SHADOWS**

Walter Gibson helped popularize ancient mysteries and psychic phenomena with his 1924 syndicated newspaper features "Miracles Ancient and Modern" and "Human Enigmas." But in the ensuing years before Lamont Cranston came to radio, public interest in Eastern mysteries had considerably increased. Like Chandu the Magician and the Green Lama, The Shadow's mystical powers were almost certainly inspired by the influential writings of Alexandra David-Néel, whose 1929 book *Magic and Mystery in Tibet* was translated into English in 1932. The landmark study detailed the Frenchwoman's 14-year sojourn in Tibet, during which she had interviewed the Dalai Lama and became the first Westerner awarded the robes of a graduate lama by the Tashi Lama. David-Néel related the Tibetan science of telepathy and of contrivances for creating virtual invisibility similar to the Ninja arts. "But great *naljorpas* and *dubchens* need not possess any magical material implement to make themselves invisible," she wrote. "According to them, it is not a question of juggling oneself away, but of taking care not to arouse any feeling in the sentient beings by whom one is surrounded. By that means one's presence is not detected or, at a lesser degree, one is scarcely noticed by those before whose eyes one passes; one does not excite any reflection in their mind and does not leave any impression in their memory.... At each moment, a large number of objects are within our view, yet we only notice a few of them. The others do not make any impression on us.... Practically, these objects have remained *invisible* to us."

A Complete Book-length Novel from the Private Annals of The Shadow, as told to **MAXWELL GRANT**

**The original Hydra was a beast that grew two new heads for each one that was cut off. The Shadow faced its counterpart—a master villain who called himself the Hydra.**

# the hydra

## CHAPTER I
## MONSTER OF CRIME

GUESTS were arriving at the home of Edmund Glencoe. They came in clusters from taxicabs and limousines that rolled along the curved driveway leading up from the great gates. Dozens of guests were absorbed by the huge mansion, as though it patiently awaited more.

When Edmund Glencoe gave parties, he gave them in a very large way, which was logical enough, considering the enormous size of his Long Island home. As for the expense of such entertainments, Glencoe could well afford it, for he was a millionaire.

Within the house, staid servants were ushering the guests into reception rooms, where the arrivals met other friends who attended Glencoe's parties. Those most familiar with the place became an overflow that trickled into a glass-inclosed conservatory at one side of the mansion, the usual place where the regulars gathered.

Conviviality filled the air. Everybody was happy to be at this party—except Edmund Glencoe.

Not that Glencoe showed it openly. On the contrary, he was all smiles and handshakes as he received the guests and sent them on their way. But when he found his chance for a break, he took it. Timed to a lull among the arriving guests, Glencoe stepped through a curtained doorway to a hall, plucked the arm of a passing servant, and ordered:

"Find Mr. Mance. Tell him I must see him in my study; privately, and at once."

Reaching his lavishly furnished study, Edmund Glencoe sat behind a desk and waited. Alone, he was able to show the worry that he felt, and the effect was very marked. A huddled figure, with drawn face the color of his thin gray hair, Glencoe appeared more than worried. He looked frightened.

The door opened to admit Willard Mance.

At sight of his friend, Glencoe brightened somewhat. Mance was the sort of person who inspired confidence. He was tall, broad of build, a figure of latent strength. His face was tawny, of a chiseled type, the sort that went with a man of iron. His grizzled hair did not detract from his youthful vigor; rather, it marked him as a man who possessed experience, along with force.

Mance's dark eyes flashed a look of understanding at Glencoe.

"I could tell that you were worried, Edmund," spoke Mance in a deep tone. "But don't tell me that it's about those robberies that happened recently. No harm could reach you here."

"That's what the police commissioner says," returned Glencoe nervously. "But those crimes weren't just robberies. Certain wealthy people disappeared."

"Probably as a mere precaution." Mance inserted a cigarette in a holder and reached in his pocket for a lighter. "Very foolish of them to run away from imaginary danger." He paused, about

to flick the lighter, and asked sharply: "Are you intending to do the same?"

Glencoe shook his head emphatically. Leaning across the desk, he tapped it rapidly.

"No, Willard, I'm not," declared Glencoe. "I'll tell you why. There's a rumor around that those persons disappeared not because they feared crime, but because they had a part in it."

Mance furnished an incredulous stare.

"That's what the police commissioner thinks," insisted Glencoe. "He's holding a conference with prominent citizens tonight. Men like Dustin Bardell—"

"An old fogy, if ever there was one!" interrupted Mance. "Come, Edmund, be sensible. There can't be an epidemic of hit-and-run crime staged by reputable people. Granted that a criminal organization exists, it must have a brain."

"There is a brain," declared Glencoe solemnly. "It is called by a very appropriate title: the Hydra."

Mance's eyes took on a puzzled look.

"The Hydra was a fabulous monster," explained Glencoe. "According to legend, it had several heads, with its brains divided among them. If anything happened to any of those heads, the others continued to function. What is more—"

Glencoe was up from the desk, wagging his hand excitedly, when Mance clapped him on the back and laughed in interruption:

"I suppose the Hydra grew new heads?"

"Exactly!" exclaimed Glencoe. "And that is what we fear this modern Hydra is doing. It is a monster of crime that must be stamped out!"

Mance laughed again, said, "Come along, Edmund. Your guests are waiting to have you show them around the house. They want to see what new curios you have collected."

Glencoe gave an obedient nod, but at the door he spoke an earnest request:

"Will you do one thing for me, Willard?"

"Of course."

"Keep an eye on the servants." Glencoe gestured before Mance could interrupt. "I know they're all reliable, but I'm afraid to trust anyone. So please watch all of them."

"Including Selbert?"

"All except Selbert," corrected Glencoe. "After all, he is my confidential secretary. I'd have asked him to perform this duty, but I was afraid it would worry him. He's a nervous chap."

THEY went out to a reception room, where Glencoe summoned the guests to begin a tour of the mansion.

Selbert immediately appeared; he was a dapper little man, who carried a big book under his arm, the volume being a catalogue of Glencoe's curios, antiques, and art treasures.

The first stop was at the music room, which Glencoe unlocked and invited the guests to enter. They thronged after Glencoe and Selbert, because all were anxious to view Glencoe's collection of rare violins and original folios of music created by famous composers.

Looking past the crowd, Glencoe noted that Mance was by the door, near enough to catch any conversation between two livaried servants who were standing there.

Quite pleased, Glencoe left Mance to his task and devoted his own efforts to displaying musical rarities. Nevertheless, when Mance spoke to the two servants, he was careful to do so in an undertone, hiding his mouth under cover of the hand with which he removed his cigarette holder from his lips.

What Willard Mance said was:

"Head No. 4."

"Eye 4C," responded a servant. "The opening beyond the second piano is ready."

"You made it large enough to remove the Borgian harp?"

"Six inches clearance, tested."

At that moment, Glencoe was pointing guests to the Borgian harp that Mance mentioned. The gold decorations of the priceless instrument were alone worth a small fortune, its many jewels another sizeable item. Mance turned to the second servant.

"Ear 4K," the fellow said. "Formerly 2B. The trucks have arrived behind the tennis courts."

"Are any of the guest cars there?" queried Mance.

"None," replied 4K. "All were diverted to parking spaces on the other side of the house."

The guests came from the music room, shepherded by Glencoe, with Selbert following patiently behind his employer, still carrying the bulky catalogue. The next stop was Glencoe's art gallery, which formed a special wing of the house.

While the guests admired a long row of valuable paintings, Mance strolled about looking over other servants.

Near a door, Mance turned his back and identified himself as Head Four to a servant who proved to be Eye 4D. This Hydra spy informed him that the selected paintings were already cut from their frames, but held invisibly in place by tape that would give way at a single tug. Quite intrigued, Mance strolled along the gallery and checked the work himself. It was perfect.

On the way from the art gallery to Glencoe's antique room, Mance paused to contact another of Glencoe's reliable servants. To Head No. 4, the servant identified himself as Tooth 4B. When Mance asked him if he'd done the picture job, the

Tooth nodded, then beamed with pleasure when the Head complimented him on such clean work.

So it went throughout the tour, from Glencoe's antique room to the heavily locked wing on the second floor where the millionaire kept his main curio collection, valued at a hundred thousand dollars.

By then, Mance had finished his survey of the servants, and Glencoe was pleased to see his friend looking over some of the doubtful guests, even sounding them out through casual conversation.

Doubtful, indeed, those guests!

Each one was an Eye, Ear or Tooth, all answering to letters prefaced by the number four, which symbolized the Head they secretly served. Not once did Mance nor any of his helpers overdo the countersign by which they introduced themselves. It consisted merely in spreading a loose-clenched fist into an open hand, the fingers standing for the Heads of the Hydra.

At the finish of the insidious parade, Glencoe bowed his guests into reception rooms, remarking that servants were busy setting supper tables in the conservatory. Plucking Mance's arm, Glencoe drew his friend aside for a few words.

"You did nobly, Willard," complimented Glencoe. "All my qualms are ended. Wait—here comes Selbert. We can discuss the Hydra matter later."

GLENCOE turned one way, Mance the other, but after a few paces, the latter paused. Mance's loose fist opened as Selbert approached; the dapper secretary gave a similar gesture with a hand that clutched Glencoe's private catalogue.

Mance's undertone was a quick statement of identity.

"Head No. 4."

"Tooth 4A," whispered Selbert. He opened the catalogue showing where he had torn pages from it. "I marked the wanted items, and left the sheets in their proper rooms for the Eyes, Ears, and Teeth to find."

"All are Teeth from now on," declared Mance. "And you, Selbert—are you ready?"

"I have the combination to Glencoe's safe," replied Selbert. "Ear 4B reports that the light switch in the study is properly connected to the oil tank."

Mance frowned, whereupon Selbert quickly informed him that the light switch was seldom used, Glencoe preferring his desk lamp. When Selbert added that he could rifle Glencoe's safe within the next ten minutes, Head No. 4 nodded his complete approval. Selbert continued to the study, while Mance strolled off to find Glencoe.

The trouble was, Mance didn't find Glencoe. The host wasn't with his guests. Mance's emotionless face began to show worry of its own, as he detached himself from friends and made a side trip to the study. The door was ajar, so Mance pushed it open. By the glow of the big desk lamp, Head No. 4 saw all that he expected.

Glencoe's safe was open. In front of it stood Selbert, his hands raised. The desk was strewn with the contents of the safe—cash, stocks, and bonds already stacked in separate piles. In front of all was Glencoe, nervous no longer.

The gray-haired man was covering his treacherous secretary with a revolver. Hearing Mance enter, Glencoe sped a quick look across his shoulder.

"I'm glad you're here, Willard!" exclaimed Glencoe. "Look what I found! Selbert, the man I trusted most, robbing my safe! I'll hold him while you summon the servants—or, better still, call the police."

"A little more light would help," spoke Mance coolly. "Where is the light switch?"

"Right by the door," began Glencoe. Impatiently, he added: "No, never mind the switch. It isn't important."

"I think it is," argued Mance, "and so is this!"

With a darted glance, Glencoe saw what Mance meant by "this." It was a revolver that Mance himself had drawn and was aiming straight at Glencoe. With a fierce gasp, old Glencoe swung about to meet his false friend's aim.

There wasn't a chance for Edmund Glencoe.

Mance's trigger finger tugged, while the thumb of his other hand pressed the light switch that he had found.

The gun burst that dispatched a bullet straight to Glencoe's heart was drowned by an exploding roar that shook the very foundations of the massive mansion. The floor of the study was shuddering when it received Glencoe's sprawling body.

Crime had struck in a titanic way, as planned by Willard Mance, Head No. 4 of evil's manifold monster: the Hydra!

## CHAPTER II
### ENTER THE SHADOW

SELBERT was right. The light switch on the study wall was connected to the tremendous fuel tank supplying the furnace of the great mansion. A big furnace like Glencoe's took a lot of oil, a liquid that could explode with wrecking power when pepped up with high-test stuff, as Glencoe's fuel happened to be.

Teeth of the Hydra had seen to that, along with other important details. In fact, the full preparations for this tremendous crime hadn't more than begun to show themselves. The explosion from the cellar merely primed the holocaust to come.

Glencoe's mansion was built of stone, its walls as thick as bastions. If it hadn't been of such strong construction, Mance and his Hydra helpers wouldn't have risked a heavy explosion while they were still in the place. Thus, though the building shuddered, it did not cave in. However, floors heaved when timbers buckled; partitions split asunder, while cracking ceilings delivered deluges of plaster.

Every light in the house was extinguished, but darkness did not take over. Up through rifts in the floor, writhing in from broken partitions, came great licks of livid flame like the tongues of Gargantuan gas jets. Guests shrieked at sight of the searing fire which should have subsided, but didn't.

It wasn't just oil that fed the flames. Those hungry tongues found much to gobble. In one reception room, a whole stretch of paneling spurted into blaze. Recently varnished by one of Glencoe's servants, the woodwork had been treated with pure collodion, which ignited like a mammoth sheet of celluloid.

As guests fled to another reception room, the conflagration pursued them. They fled from its hellish midst through the only remaining route, a wide doorway to Glencoe's great front hall.

There the fugitives found that a mass of flame had cut off all exit except through the front door and a few adjacent windows. They saw a grand staircase transformed to a huge torch, the reason being that combustibles had been stored in a closet beneath it. Most of the fugitives didn't worry over that. With door and windows available, they took those routes to safety.

Some, however, remained to battle the holocaust. What happened to those few was tragic. Two guests grabbed buckets of sand that they happened to see in a vestibule. Sand buckets had been ordered months ago by Glencoe as a precaution against air raids, and sand could prove a big help in ease of fire.

This sand *was* a big help—to the fire.

As each man chucked a load of sand into the flames by the staircase, there was a brilliant puff, like a bursting skyrocket. That sand was stuff of which fireworks were composed. It obliterated itself and the hapless men with it, at the same time spreading the flame to new portions of the hall.

Similar was the experience of loyal servants who tried to use fire extinguishers on the flames. The extinguishers were loaded with explosive mixtures that blasted the moment that they sprayed. Other victims vanished with the fiery torrent that was now engulfing the great mansion with volcanic fury.

Yet amid that sea of blaze were paths that the roaring flames had not reached. Byways through a literal hell, free for travel by a host of lesser demons who knew their pattern. Demons who in their human form had announced themselves as servers of The Hydra.

FROM the door of Glencoe's study, Willard Mance, Head No. 4, was shouting orders to those workers between the crackles of the flames, while behind him stood Selbert, top man of the Teeth. Their stretch of hallway was free from the seething fire, and they knew the routes to safety.

For along those routes Mance's workers were carrying the most valued of Glencoe's treasures. Folios, violins, the great Borgian harp, were coming through the rear gap of the music room. Two men with packs of rolled paintings were leaving by one door of Glencoe's art gallery, while the fire swept in from the other direction to gorge itself on carved wainscoting and empty frames.

The best of Glencoe's antiques were being removed bodily, the rest remaining as added fuel for the mighty fire; while from the second floor, servants laden with the finest curios were coming down a rear stairway which the flames hadn't quite surrounded.

All these routes were converging to one goal—a side door that opened behind the conservatory and afforded a direct route to the trucks beyond the tennis courts.

This explained why Mance, the Hydra Head, had ordered the holocaust so arranged that fugitives would be cut off from all exits except the front. He didn't want them to go through the conservatory, from which they could view the looting of Glencoe's treasures. Fire, a mighty mass of it, lifted to staggering proportions, was to be the cover-up for murder and robbery.

As yet, the conservatory was unscathed, but the time had come to add it to the pyre. Like a satanic majesty in the midst of his favorite element, Mance ordered Selbert to that task, while the Hydra Head personally stepped into Glencoe's study, where flames were beginning to appear, and gathered up the accumulated wealth that strewed the desk.

Viewed from the front driveway, Glencoe's burning mansion was a most horrendous sight. It formed a great pyramid of tapering flame, the fire streaming up from the sides into long tongues that were lashing through the roof, giving the effect that the whole interior was ablaze, though such was not the case.

At the right of the building was the only untouched portion—the glass-inclosed conservatory, two stories high, filled with grass rugs and wall hangings, wicker furniture and potted plants, the exterior adorned with pillars of dry, clinging vines.

The lurid glare revealed a garage to the right of the house; near it were parked a few of the guest cars. But the glow did not show the parking space beyond the tennis courts, for that area, the courts included, was directly behind the great conservatory.

All over the front lawn were scattered guests. Some of them were burned or injured, and these were being helped off to the left of the house by chauffeurs who had come running from the dozen limousines parked there. One more car was coming in the driveway, bringing a belated guest to Glencoe's ill-fated party.

The arriving car was a limousine, its passenger a gentleman named Lamont Cranston.

A world traveler of repute, Cranston was a man who had seen many things and always took them calmly. He instantly sized Glencoe's mansion as a total loss, but at the same time recognized that it might still have occupants in need of aid. There was just one way to reach such persons—through the conservatory, which, so far, was undamaged. Since the driveway skirted in by the conservatory, Cranston spoke to his chauffeur:

"Stop here, Stanley."

The voice was calm, and so was Cranston's face. Reflected firelight showed a visage that was serious and masklike, carrying a hawkish profile that fitted a man who could combine action with reserve.

The door of the limousine opened and Cranston stepped out. His calculating survey of the situation offset the fact that he wasn't attired in firefighting garb. Lamont Cranston was immaculately clad in evening clothes.

The car had stopped just past a line of very bushy shrubs that skirted the driveway. It was only a few dozen yards to the conservatory, but the windows there were fairly high above the ground.

WHILE Cranston was taking a quick look for something that resembled a door, only to see none, an odd thing happened at the corner windows of the inclosure.

A man arrived within those windows and began to hammer frantically against the panes. The fellow was Selbert, and Cranston recognized the secretary from a previous trip to Glencoe's.

Apparently, Selbert was trapped; but if so, he wasn't using his head about it. All he had to do was yank a window open and jump out. If he happened to be worrying about someone else inside the house, Selbert should by rights be opening the window anyway, so that his shouts could be heard.

At least, someone did see Selbert's actions. A stocky chauffeur was hurrying over from a car parked near the garage. Why that chauffeur should be staying there, while all others were on the front lawn helping the guests, was only a short-lived mystery. As he reached the corner wall, the chauffeur stooped and grabbed up the nozzle of a big hose. In heroic style, he smashed the corner window with the nozzle.

Then came a shout from Selbert, words which Cranston could hear beside his car, though he was the only person close enough to catch the call that Selbert addressed to the stocky chauffeur.

"Turn it on, Kirthle!" ordered Selbert. "Make it quick! I'm going back through!"

With that, Selbert turned about and picked a path through a flame-bordered doorway that led from the conservatory into the mansion. At the same time, Kirthle beckoned and a pair of servants sprang into sight from the outer corner of the conservatory. Kirthle handed them the nozzle, while he dived to a water spigot where the hose was already attached!

In through the conservatory window went a long stream that reached the outward-lashing flames. Instead of subduing the blaze, the stream fed it. The spurt from that hose wasn't water; it was gasoline, piped from an underground tank near the garage!

It seemed that half the fire in the mansion came out to engulf the conservatory. New fuel for the holocaust, delivered by design! The servants knew that it was coming, for they fled around the house, leaving the hose thrust through the broken window to continue its devastating work.

About to follow, Kirthle saw Cranston. Realizing that this lone witness could testify to the incendiary origin of the giant conflagration, Kirthle yanked out a revolver. He was aiming the gun at Cranston when the latter turned, saw the menacing weapon, and made a quick dart toward the open door of the limousine as though to seek the shelter of the car.

Before Kirthle could follow with his aim, a strange thing happened; something all the more amazing because the sweep of flame through the conservatory was adding a tremendous burst of light. Amid all that glow, Cranston was swallowed by blackness before he reached the car door.

Blackness that seemed to swoop at Cranston's beck, envelop him and take him off to nowhere! As blackness whirled, the door of the limousine slammed, but the inky mass remained outside the car. Living blackness of human size, that issued a weird, challenging laugh which Kirthle knew was meant not alone for him, but for the Hydra.

For that blotting shape had turned itself into a

cloaked figure, whose eyes, beneath the brim of a slouch hat, caught the glow from the fire-swept mansion and transformed it into a burning gaze that promised ill to crime.

In a manner so swift that the transformation seemed under way before it happened, Lamont Cranston had completely vanished, to be replaced by that superfoe feared by all men of evil:

The Shadow!

## CHAPTER III
## MASTER OF FLAME

THE SHADOW was surging forward, intent upon taking Kirthle alive, to make the fellow talk about the Hydra. Kirthle fired one frantic shot, missing The Shadow by three feet. The bullet didn't even wing the limousine, for it was gone from behind the path that The Shadow had retaken.

Kirthle wasn't the only smart chauffeur on hand. Stanley, Cranston's man, was trained to pull away when he heard shooting start. Though Stanley regarded it odd that a complacent gentleman like Cranston should be in the vicinity of gunfire so often, the chauffeur never questioned his master's orders, nor did he link Cranston with The Shadow. Among other elements in Stanley's training, he'd learned to mind his own business thoroughly.

As for Kirthle, he was thinking only of The Shadow. Under the muzzle of an automatic that the cloaked fighter aimed, Kirthle tried another gun stab, that didn't deliver. The first shot from The Shadow's gun preceded Kirthle's tug of the trigger.

The leaden slug found Kirthle's forearm, just above his gun hand. Jounced by the impact, Kirthle staggered around, his arm flinging wide, while his loosened hand let his revolver scale against the wall below the conservatory windows. Wounded and unarmed, Kirthle turned to run; then, seeing The Shadow looming hard upon him, the stocky man turned back.

Diving for the wall, Kirthle grabbed up his gun with his left hand and swung triumphantly, hoping to cripple The Shadow in turn. Within reach, The Shadow made a swoop to grab Kirthle's arm, but the fellow made a successful dodge along the wall, escaping the cloaked fighter's clutch.

It was death for Kirthle.

Down came a great chunk of the conservatory wall, a mass of molten metal and white-hot glass. Kirthle hadn't realized how quickly the conservatory had become a furnace under the feeding spray of gasoline which he himself had started. Probably Kirthle never realized it, for he was buried out of sight in an avalanche as deadly as a flow of volcanic lava.

Only by a long, swift dive did The Shadow escape the fiery debris. Wheeling from the scorching flames that now were climbing the vine pillars, The Shadow made a wider circuit toward the rear of the mansion, hoping to overtake the two treacherous servants who had helped Kirthle with the hose.

They were beyond the tennis courts, those crooks and others. The Shadow couldn't see the trucks because of an intervening wall, but he did spy the last of the men who were bringing burdens from Glencoe's side door.

The Shadow gave them a weird laugh that made them falter; then, in response to the mirth, came a deluge of gunfire from beyond the tennis courts.

That barrage was meant for The Shadow. Though it didn't reach him, it allowed the burden carriers to escape. Attacked by the whole Hydra tribe, The Shadow needed shelter of his own in order to fight back. He took the only spot he saw, which happened to be the best, the very door from which the Hydra's men had brought the last of Glencoe's curios!

Once within that shelter, The Shadow jabbed a few shots toward the distant marksmen. Dropping deeper to let them spot themselves with unwary shots, The Shadow suddenly lost interest in such random battle. Here within the fire-gorged mansion, The Shadow was viewing the pathways through which The Hydra's workers had maneuvered their departure with a vast supply of loot.

It wasn't a question now of rescuing helpless persons who weren't even likely to be around. Here was The Shadow's chance to trap some of the Hydra's clan in the very pitfall which they had designed as coverage for crime!

ONE candidate was already in sight. Turning a corner toward The Shadow was the very man who had signaled the destruction of the conservatory—Glencoe's false secretary, Selbert!

Mere chance warned Selbert of danger ahead. Dropping back as a stretch of floor gave underfoot, Selbert looked up and saw The Shadow bearing straight toward him. With a wild look, the dapper man turned and dashed back around the corner.

With a leap, The Shadow was across the cavity. Around the corner he sidestepped as Selbert peppered frantic shots in return. Scrambling for Glencoe's study, Selbert stumbled on the threshold. He was up again, clutching his gun and a precious bundle, when The Shadow overtook him. With a wild wrench, Selbert went through the doorway, right into the arms of Willard Mance.

The Hydra Head was perfect in his pretext. He didn't waste half a second asking any questions. One look told him that Selbert had met with something supernormal, and Mance acted just as though he expected someone like The Shadow. He pinned Selbert against the only stretch of wall that the flames hadn't reached, grabbed the man's gun, and tried to get the bundle.

"I've got him!" bellowed Mance. "The traitor who murdered Glencoe and robbed him! Help me ... somebody!"

It wasn't just anybody who appeared. Staring across Selbert's shoulder, Mance looked amazed when he saw The Shadow enter.

It looked like Selbert's crime, even though he hadn't done it. To all appearances, Mance had reached the study too late to aid Glencoe and was now demanding vengeance for his murdered friend.

That fact, plus The Shadow's own wish to check on Glencoe's death, worked in favor of the Hydra's cause. The Shadow turned toward Glencoe's body and saw the desk beyond it, strewn with papers that the flames had just begun to devour. Mance had stayed to see that Selbert had missed nothing of value and that sudden doubt flashed to The Shadow. He wheeled, automatic ready in his fist.

Mance and Selbert were already gone, the Hydra Head shoving the Tooth through the doorway to the hall, their departure drowned by a sudden crackle of flames that poured through the study walls. If Selbert had paused long enough to fire, he might have clipped The Shadow; but the secretary was too fearful, too amazed by Mance's sudden shift.

As for Mance, his gun was out, but he didn't have it aimed when he fired. His shot was wide, and he was smart enough to duck through the door ahead of The Shadow's reply. Then Selbert was dashing for the corner with Mance behind him, but all the while, the rugged Hydra Head was shooting back, hoping to nail The Shadow in the doorway.

From that shelter, The Shadow fired as Mance turned the corner. Again, flames rallied to a criminal's aid. These were the flames that roared through the study walls, flaring up from the supporting beams. Literally that fiery mass swallowed the floor of the entire room, and The Shadow plunged as the whole room caved into a flaming pit.

CLUTCHING the doorway as he went, The Shadow clung there watching the collapse. Glencoe's body, the desk beyond it, finally the big safe, went splashing into a sea of red fire that spouted like a mighty geyser, seeking another victim in the person of The Shadow.

One heave and The Shadow was clear of the lashing flame, safe in the hallway that formed a last oasis amid disaster.

The Shadow reached the corner of the passage, only to find it transformed to another pit of flame that Mance and Selbert had just managed to bridge. The route to the conservatory was cut off; it was from that direction that new waves of fire had reached the doomed study. One path alone remained: the back staircase to the second floor.

It led up and down; nevertheless, The Shadow took the stairs ahead of a rising wall of fire. On the floor above, he saw the outline of a window through a raging torrent of smoke-clouded red. Floorboards cracked and fell as The Shadow dove across them, but his lunging arms reached the window and drove through the space from which glass had already cracked and fallen.

Again, The Shadow's hauling hands made up for lack of footing. Over the sill, he struck headlong on a small, sloping roof of slate that held the temperature of a griddle. That ordeal was short, for the roof gave as The Shadow struck it and he scaled off to the ground, landing clear of burning porch posts and a shower of loosened slates that seemed to hiss their heat as they knifed into the turf and stopped there, upright, like Druid monuments in miniature.

Cars were spurting away through a back driveway, off to the left of the house. Seeing an abandoned sedan, The Shadow reached it, found the keys that the frightened owner had left, and started the blistered car away from the tremendous mountain of flame and smoke that now entirely obscured the whole of Glencoe's home.

The chase, however, was short-lived. It ended at the emergency entrance of a hospital two miles from Glencoe's. The vehicles ahead weren't trucks, nor even the sort of getaway cars that crooks might use. They were limousines piloted by faithful chauffeurs, who had brought the burned and injured guests from Glencoe's fiery party.

Mance and his Hydra followers had gone the other direction. With many roads to choose, their four-mile start would be sufficient. Dealing with them would be a matter of the future. Such was The Shadow's verdict as he turned the borrowed car about and started back toward the mighty beacon that had once been Glencoe's home.

Great flames lashing to the sky, billows of smoke that rose to heights of clouds, were symbols of the wrath that the Hydra, vast organization of evil Heads, could wreak upon whatever men of wealth it chose to devour as its victims. Never in

the history of modern crime had there existed so terrible a menace as the Hydra.

But there was something that all Hydra Heads, Mance included, could remember, along with those workers who termed themselves Eyes, Ears, and Teeth. With all their individual effort, plus the fury of the holocaust they had created, these men who formed the Hydra had failed to obliterate a lone foe who tonight had challenged them with single-handed might.

He could still rise to challenge them, should the Hydra foment new crime.

He was crime's nemesis: The Shadow!

## CHAPTER IV
### CRANSTON AND CRANSTON

LAMONT CRANSTON woke up and wondered why his head still whirled. It took him about half a minute to learn that the motion came from the fact he was riding in his limousine. Which didn't make sense at first, because the last thing Cranston remembered, he'd been out of his car watching Glencoe's mansion go up in one great blanket of flame.

Slowly, reflectively, Cranston nodded. Someone must have put him back in the limousine and Stanley was driving him home. He didn't have to guess who had helped him on his way, for at that moment Cranston heard a low-toned laugh beside

**It was death for Kirthle—Only by a long, swift dive did The Shadow escape the fiery debris.**

him. He turned to see the black-cloaked figure of The Shadow.

"What did you hit me with?" asked Cranston. "All four of your automatics?"

"I'm only carrying a pair tonight," replied The Shadow, "and they were inside my cloak when I tossed you in the car. Your head must have struck the opposite door."

"A bit overzealous, weren't you?"

"Hardly. A chap was aiming at you with a revolver. I had to send you away fast, which I did. So rapidly, that he thought you turned into me."

Cranston chuckled at The Shadow's statement.

"That's quite all right," declared Cranston. "A lot of people think they've seen me become The Shadow."

"And others," added The Shadow, "are quite sure that I have become Lamont Cranston."

"But no one knows that there are two of us."

"No one except the two of us."

The big car was rolling along a country road. Cranston was surprised to note that it was the highway leading to his New Jersey estate. Calculating the distance from Glencoe's, Cranston realized he'd been out of circulation quite a while.

"That fellow who was taking a shot at me," inquired Cranston, reminiscently. "Who was he?"

"His name was Kirthle," replied The Shadow. "He worked for the Hydra. I was trailing him from the last case, the only lead I had. I didn't know that crime was due at Glencoe's; otherwise, I'd have gone there in place of you. The Hydra is assuming larger proportions than I expected."

"You mean this Hydra business is on the level?" demanded Cranston. "Why, I thought it was just another of Commissioner Weston's pipe dreams!"

It was The Shadow's turn to laugh, which he did, though his low-throbbed tone lacked mirth.

"Frankly, Cranston," stated The Shadow, "I classed those recent crimes as individual cases. One night when I was you, I told Weston that they seemed the work of a group with multiple heads, like a Hydra. I simply wanted to stir our friend, the commissioner, to furnish more cooperation from the law.

"But I struck the thing right on the head—or Heads. There is a Hydra, and tonight its work was managed by a head named Willard Mance. That fire was of incendiary origin, intended to cover a big robbery. It finished by masking murder as well. Edmund Glencoe is dead, slain by the man he called his best friend, Willard Mance."

For the rest of the ride, Cranston sat in stupefied silence. Knowing both Mance and Glencoe, he wouldn't have deemed the thing possible but for the fact of his own narrow escape from death at the hands of Kirthle. Cranston was still pondering deeply when the car pulled up in front of his own sizeable residence.

"After you, Cranston," undertoned The Shadow. "Only one of us can go in the house openly. I shall meet you in the trophy room."

Going up the front steps of his house, Cranston looked over his shoulder, hoping to catch some token of The Shadow's exit from the limousine. All that Cranston saw was blackness, thick within the car, and likewise on the ground where the car had been after Stanley swung the limousine around the corner of the garage.

Meeting servants inside the house, Cranston was detained a few minutes before he went upstairs, as he had to inquire about phone calls during his absence, particularly because some might be of importance to his friend, The Shadow. At last, Cranston reached the second floor and opened the door of the trophy room.

There Lamont Cranston found himself.

Seated in a comfortable armchair, languidly smoking one of Cranston's favorite cigars, was his double. Feature for feature, pose for pose, the man in the chair was Lamont Cranston. Actually, he was The Shadow, who through perfect make-up and long practice had become as much Cranston as himself.

This had been going on for years, so it should have been perfect. But when Cranston thought back to the time when he had first met The Shadow as himself, he remembered that the impersonation had been flawless, even then.

"I SUPPOSE I owe you an apology, Cranston," declared The Shadow in his friend's own calm tone. "When I first decided to supplant you, it was purely because you were away from home for such long periods. It was very convenient to be someone who wouldn't show up for a year or more."

"No fault of mine that I came back to stay," returned Cranston. "Globe-trotting is an obsolete sport nowadays, with world conditions as they are. However, I still enjoy our little game. I've made a lot of real friends through you."

"And enemies, perhaps?"

"Plenty of enemies," laughed Cranston, "but they haven't been permanent! You seem to have the habit of writing them off."

The Shadow joined in Cranston's laugh. It was singular, how their tones blended into a single voice. When the mutual mirth ended, it was The Shadow who remarked:

"Speaking of friends, Cranston, you have made a few for me. One in particular—"

"Margo Lane," interrupted Cranston. "I knew

we'd get around to her. But how did I know that I was going to meet her on that Caribbean cruise I took? How could I guess that she would run into you at a nightclub two days after we landed? Naturally, she mistook you for me. I even would myself if I could forget who I am. Anyway, you've found Margo useful."

"Very useful," agreed The Shadow. "Whenever trouble is coming up, I know it from the way Margo gets into it. It's a wonder she didn't get tangled in this Hydra business."

The Shadow had risen from his chair. He was strolling the room in slow, easy fashion. Watching his double, Cranston caught the mood and began a stroll of his own. He came face to face with The Shadow in a doorway and waited for his impersonator to speak. When The Shadow did, his voice came from behind Cranston's shoulder.

"When did you install that door mirror?" asked The Shadow. "You should have told me that you were having the trophy room remodeled."

Cranston spun away from his own reflection. His face showed blank surprise as it met The Shadow's, who copied the expression to show Cranston what he'd missed by not continuing to watch the mirror. Finding his wits again, Cranston gestured about the room.

"I had the place repapered," he explained. "I'd forgotten about the mirror. It was fitted only a few days ago."

"Where have you put your rifles?" asked The Shadow, studying the blank wall. "In the gun room?"

Cranston nodded.

"I think I'll leave them there," he said. "There won't be room for them when the trophies are hung. Of course, I'll keep the cup cabinet here."

He pointed to a corner where a huge cabinet showed shelves that were laden with dozens of cups, all tributes to Cranston's skill as a sportsman. The Shadow smiled when he noted that one shelf was devoted to the trophies that he, The Shadow, had personally won during times when Cranston was away. Nice of Cranston to arrange a special Shadow shelf.

"Keep me posted on all changes," suggested The Shadow. "I might come home while you are out and find myself a trifle confused. By the way, you hired a new houseman lately. What is his name?"

"Kendrick," replied Cranston. "He always answers the door, so you'll probably meet him if you forget your passkey. A rather stolid chap, but capable—"

The Shadow raised his hand in interruption. He could hear slow footsteps coming up the front stairs. Plucking his hat and cloak from a chair, The Shadow passed them to Cranston and gestured toward the door with the mirror.

"Step in the closet a minute," suggested The Shadow. "That must be Kendrick coming upstairs, because the footsteps are new to me. I might as well get acquainted with him while I'm here."

A big surprise was due.

What caused it was the fact that The Shadow was totally off guard. He had to be so because he was posing as Cranston. There wasn't any reason for Cranston to be alert, or even abrupt, when opening the door of the trophy room to admit an arriving servant. Since The Shadow was playing the part of Cranston, he opened the door in most deliberate style.

Then The Shadow's hands were rising, shoulder high. The back steps that he took were forced upon him by the pressure of a revolver muzzle planted squarely in his chest. And the stare that The Shadow gave was Cranston's blank one, that he had imitated only a few minutes earlier.

The man behind the gun was the murderer who had tricked The Shadow at Glencoe's. Not satisfied with that exploit, Willard Mance had sprung another clever stroke. Linking The Shadow with Lamont Cranston, the belated guest who had come to Glencoe's home, the Hydra Head was here for a final showdown!

## CHAPTER V
## DOUBLE DEATH

HIS eyes fixed on The Shadow's, Mance gave an ugly laugh. Not for an instant did the killer relax his gun hand, even when he reached behind him to close the door. There was murder in Mance's glare. It stood for the future as well as the past.

"I'm going to kill you, Cranston," informed Mance in a deep undertone. "You crossed my path at Glencoe's, and that was once too often!"

"Too bad what happened at Glencoe's," parried The Shadow calmly. "I suppose you escaped with the other guests. But your attitude puzzles me, Mance. Did the heat of the fire affect you?"

"Now, I *know* you're bluffing, Shadow," sneered Mance. "But you don't do it well without your cloak and hat."

In a bland fashion that suited his impersonation of Cranston, The Shadow stepped back so that Mance could have a better look at him.

Like Cranston, The Shadow was attired in evening clothes. Protected by the cloak, the full-dress suit hadn't suffered during the episode at Glencoe's. If Mance sought evidence to prove his claim that Cranston and The Shadow were identical, he wasn't getting it.

"Naturally, you've hung your hat and cloak somewhere," Mance told The Shadow. "What is more important, you had them with you when you came to Glencoe's. Selbert told me that he saw your limousine arrive out front. You're the only person who could have spotted Kirthle's work.

"First Cranston, then The Shadow. Quite a coincidence. Kirthle must have seen you switch from one into the other. It meant nothing to the rest, except possibly Selbert, but it meant enough to me. So much, that I decided to settle the problem quite on my own."

"You need a drink, Mance," suggested The Shadow indulgently. "Unless you've already had too many—"

By interruption, Mance pushed his gun forward, thrusting The Shadow hard against a chair. Whipping his free hand beneath The Shadow's evening coat, Mance hauled out an automatic from its holster and sent it thudding to the floor. In the same quick sweep, he reached across The Shadow's body and pulled out the other .45. The second weapon hit the floor just as The Shadow regained his balance.

As he drew back, Mance gave a triumphant sniff. He'd caught the trifling odor of smoke from The Shadow's evening coat. It was helpful, though, that discovery, for it caused Mance to pause and gloat.

"That covers your case, Shadow," was Mance's verdict. "I'm going to kill you, like I did Glencoe! Not that you matter, because you never could defeat the Hydra. You've heard of the original Hydra, with its many heads—and more."

The Shadow acted as though he hadn't, so Mance explained what he meant by "more."

"Everytime you lop off a Hydra head," gloated Mance, "two others grow in its place. That was the legend of the original creature called the Hydra, and our system is the same. If you'd killed me tonight, Shadow, the other Heads would have elected two more of their kind.

"It happens that I'm going to kill you. When the police commissioner finds his friend Cranston murdered, he will never blame me for it. I happen to be a man who has a perfect alibi. That is, I'm sure to have one when you're no longer alive to dispute it.

"But you can die with the satisfaction that, sooner or later, the Hydra would have finished you. It was just a question of time, Shadow, and that time is now!"

THE word "now" was The Shadow's cue. Expecting it, he knew the gesture that would follow it—a forward thrust of Mance's gun, even though the muzzle was less than a foot from The Shadow's chest. Likewise, The Shadow foresaw that Mance would withhold his trigger tug just long enough to see if his victim yielded to the emotion of horror.

Had the Shadow lowered his hands or made any move other than a slight waver, Mance would have fired instantly. So all The Shadow did was waver, and it proved quite enough. He faltered sideward, then forward with a trifling twist. Mance's gun was closer to his tight-drawn arm than to his chest, when The Shadow suddenly clamped biceps against forearm.

Right in the groove about his elbow, The Shadow caught the barrel of Mance's revolver. Not once did his hand signal what was coming, nor did that hand stir after The Shadow gave the arm clutch. It couldn't, for The Shadow's arm stayed rigid like a gripping vise.

What The Shadow did was spin full about, packing all the weight of his body into the leverage that whipped the revolver from Mance's clutch and scaled it into the corner by the trophy case!

Finishing his twirl, The Shadow lunged for Mance. Though tricked, the killer was already on the move. Stooped to the floor, Mance was snatching up one of The Shadow's automatics. As Mance swung the gun toward its rightful owner, The Shadow sped a hand for the killer's wrist. Life or death were hinging on a split-second, the question being whether The Shadow could stop Mance's gun hand before it completed its aim.

A split-second with inches at stake! Inches that might spell the end of The Shadow's duel with the Hydra! The Shadow's fate depending on the first spurt of his own gun, now in the grip of an enemy's hand!

The automatic tongued flame, but its burst was unheard. Just as with Mance's earlier shot at Glencoe, so was this report drowned out by a much greater roar. The whole room shuddered, its very walls seemed to split. The Shadow reeled from the concussion almost at his elbow. He didn't feel the bullet that seared his shoulder when it passed—proof that Mance's shot had missed.

Staggered by something really tremendous, The Shadow grabbed for Mance, only to find that his foeman wasn't there. The murderer was gone with the blast, and the discordant clatter of metal that followed was something that The Shadow couldn't connect with the killer's disappearance.

Then, across the room, The Shadow saw Cranston rising from the floor beside the open door of the closet. Cranston looked dazed, too, for he'd taken a kick as hard as the toss that The Shadow had given him earlier. From the floor, Cranston picked up a mammoth weapon, more sizeable than a one-man burden. The thing was an old-fashioned elephant gun.

"I found it in the closet," explained Cranston. "It was the only gun left here. The cartridges were on the shelf. So I let Mance have one. He went over there while I was coming here."

"Over there" was beside the trophy cabinet. The charge from the elephant gun had given Mance a permanent wallop, along with the temporary kick it handed Cranston. Folded right in half, Mance had hit the cabinet and overturned it. His crumpled body was covered with a blanket of cups, which accounted for the clatter that followed the gun blast.

Mance hadn't heard that belated crash. He was dead when his body started it.

RELIEVING Cranston of the elephant gun, The Shadow steered his friend into the closet. Hauling the big weapon with him, The Shadow opened the door to meet arriving servants who had dashed upstairs when they felt the house quake.

In Cranston's calm style, The Shadow inquired who had left the elephant gun loaded. The servants looked at one another as they shook their heads, so The Shadow coolly dismissed them, saying that he would take up the matter later.

"Whenever I see this gun," began Cranston, coming from the closet, "I'll remember what I did with it—"

"Quite right," interposed The Shadow approvingly. "What you did to Mance will make amends for any elephants you may have killed. Too bad Mance didn't bring along a few more Hydra Heads. At that close range, you could have bagged a batch with one shot."

Slowly, understanding dawned on Cranston. He'd never compared his big-game hunts with The Shadow's quests for men of crime. He felt that The Shadow's cause was justified, but it had seemed outside the field of sport. It still was, but Cranston, now that he had dealt with a murderer who deserved to die, was realizing that his game hunts were more deserving of rebuke.

Bringing his cloak and hat from the closet, The Shadow put them on. Gazing at Mance's body, he spoke in the whispered tone that suited his black garb:

"Mance mentioned an alibi. He said he could kill me and never be called to account—"

There was a radio in another corner. The Shadow tuned in for a news report and waited silently until it came. The first flash was a summary of the fire at Glencoe's, listing the victims who had perished there. Heading the list, next to the name of Edmund Glencoe, was that of Willard Mance. More names followed, among them Selbert's.

No wonder Mance had come to Cranston's bent on murder! Already marked as dead, Mance would never have become a murder suspect. Clear of blame in Glencoe's death, he could have killed at leisure, beginning with The Shadow.

Though Mance hadn't known it, he would have needed to do a double murder to dispose of both The Shadow and Lamont Cranston, the two that he believed were one. Justly enough, the matter of double death had boomeranged on Mance. Already counted dead, the Hydra Head had met with actual doom.

"This solves our present problem," The Shadow told Cranston. "Since Mance is already dead, there is no need to report what happened here. It is better to let the other Hydra Heads believe that Mance is still at large, rather than have them elect two more to replace him. Be ready later to admit my agents. They will remove the body after your servants have retired."

While The Shadow was descending by the window route, Cranston went downstairs inside the house and informed his servants that he would need them no more this evening. Outside, Cranston walked along the driveway toward the gates, listening for other crunches on the gravel. None came; instead, Cranston heard a whispered voice beside him. The Shadow had arrived silently, an invisible companion in the darkness.

"I've been thinking over what you told me," Cranston confided. "It's given me a new definition of sport, though I always did argue that it wasn't the kill that counted. Hunting big game seems small compared to tracking down criminals."

The Shadow's responding laugh told that he had found it that way for a very long while.

"I seem to have moved in on this hunt," added Cranston, "so I feel entitled to see it through. Whenever you sight the other Hydra Heads, give me a tallyho. Meanwhile—"

"Meanwhile, you can still be yourself," inserted The Shadow. "As such you may be the first to meet another Hydra Head. I often find a trail when I am you, Cranston."

They were at the gate. Turning, Cranston started to ask another question, only to learn that The Shadow was no longer beside him. The proof was a whispered laugh that floated back from the night.

Encouraging, that laugh. More than a token of departure, it carried The Shadow's full approval of Cranston's offer to continue in the quest against the multiple monster of crime that called itself the Hydra!

## CHAPTER VI
### THE LONE TRAIL

TWO evenings later, Lamont Cranston learned what it could mean to be himself. In response to a phone call from The Shadow, Cranston went to the Cobalt Club to meet his friend, Police Commissioner Ralph Weston. It was a long while since Cranston had seen the commissioner, because The Shadow had monopolized those meetings.

From the moment he reached the club, Cranston realized that Weston hadn't asked him to a social session. Crime was on the board, and the commissioner was actually asking Cranston's advice. Moreover, there were two others present who seemed to value it.

One, of course, was Inspector Joe Cardona, a swarthy man of poker-faced expression. Though Joe said little, he was always interested when Cranston spoke. Cranston knew that The Shadow had often sided with Cardona when the commissioner disputed his ace inspector's judgment.

The other man was Dustin Bardell, chairman of a citizens' committee that had convened with Commissioner Weston on the evening of the Glencoe tragedy. He was a serious man, Bardell, past middle age but very active, and at times dynamic. He seemed as determined to ferret out the Hydra business as was Weston.

Square of face, sharp of eye, Bardell did more than come bluntly to the issue. In slam-bang style, he thwacked his hand upon the table and fairly rumbled at Cranston:

"Come! You were at Glencoe's. You can tell us if incendiaries started that fire!"

"I wasn't there when it began," pleaded Cranston. "They say there was an explosion that caused it."

"If so, the explosion was arranged," argued Bardell. "Glencoe isn't the first wealthy man who has been subjected to attack. There was something wrong about that whole business. You must find more evidence, commissioner." Bardell paused, about to bang the table again, then held his hand poised. "Ah! Here is the man who can help us!"

The man in question was a tall, sharp-faced individual who entered the scene with a long, brisk stride, opening a brief case as he arrived. He spread a batch of papers on the table between Weston and Bardell, then turned from one to the other, giving each a decisive gaze.

Cranston recognized the newcomer as Charles Medor, head of the United Insurance Bureau, which made a business of investigating claims against large insurance companies. Impartial in its decisions, the United Bureau was never questioned in its verdicts. Noted for his thorough work, paid highly for his services, Medor was the final authority on insurance claims.

Medor's report was a bombshell that turned out to be a dud when he delivered it.

"The explosion was an accident at Glencoe's," asserted Medor, referring to the report sheets that he brought. "A faulty valve in the oil pipe to the furnace, slow seepage from the storage tank were the contributory causes.

"The quick spread of the fire was not surprising, considering that hundreds of gallons of oil were in the tank. All testimony proves that the flames spread too rapidly for any of Glencoe's furnishings to be saved.

"Since the insurance companies have a full inventory of Glencoe's treasures and their value, I have recommended that all claims be paid, particularly as the guests at Glencoe's home have stated that every item named was in the house when the fire started."

Bardell came to his feet angrily.

"You can't do this!" he stormed. "Why, suppose that fire was meant to ruin Glencoe! Enemies might even have wanted him to perish, along with poor Mance! Suppose, for example, that Glencoe had been blackmailed, but had refused to pay—"

"I do not deal in suppositions," inserted Medor icily. His eyes were very cold under his bristly brows. "I go by facts, and in this case they are plain. Any delay in settlement of Glencoe's just claims would injure the reputation of the insurance companies that I represent."

"But who could object, now that Glencoe is dead?"

"Certain new corporations in which Glencoe had an interest," returned Medor. "Glencoe had agreed to finance several budding industries. He had even given his notes, pending the issue of stock in those companies."

Bardell nodded slowly.

"I know about those companies," he admitted. "I'd hoped to buy into some of them myself. Still, Medor, if this could only wait!"

"It can't," emphasized Medor. "The law has provided no evidence of crime directed at either Glencoe or Mance."

Commissioner Weston sat as though handcuffed. Medor was right; too right. Even the bodies of Glencoe and Mance had not been recovered from the heaped ashes and cinders that represented all that was left of Glencoe's mansion and its treasures. Even to suggest that the pair had been murdered, would be preposterous, if voiced publicly.

As for Lamont Cranston, he sat back wishing that he really were The Shadow. He was sure that his uncloaked double could have found some way to change Medor's set opinion in a case where The Shadow knew that crime had been committed on three counts: arson, robbery, and murder!

PERHAPS if Cranston had reasoned a bit

further, he'd have realized why The Shadow hadn't chosen to come here in his place. Actually, The Shadow was taking the best of steps to unveil the true facts of crime at Glencoe's. He was using the same system as before—that of trailing a worker of the Hydra, as in the case of Kirthle.

This time, however, The Shadow was doing more than haunt the footsteps of a mere tool.

He was trailing Selbert, Glencoe's "dead" secretary!

Only a few nights ago, Willard Mance, a supposed dead man, had tried to trick The Shadow. The result had proven disastrous for Mance, establishing him as really dead; still, Mance had won a point. He'd shown, for instance, that a man supposed to be dead would not have to worry over alibis for murder.

The same applied to Selbert. Like Mance, he could feel secure, except for one proviso.

If publicly recognized by anyone, Selbert would be in a serious plight. The fact made him an outcast with the rest of the Hydra's tribe. He couldn't go around with them in the mobile fashion that they preferred, because if marked, he'd make trouble for the rest.

There was another interesting slant in Selbert's case.

Unquestionably the Hydra, through its various Heads, owned hideaways of the deepest sort. Pooled wealth could give the lesser workers benefit of many advantages that ordinary criminals did not possess.

But it would be folly for the Hydra to waste any such assets on Selbert. The dead man wasn't hunted, not to the Hydra's knowledge. All Selbert had to do was stay someplace where he wouldn't be recognized. In brief, Selbert was on his own for the present.

For two days, The Shadow had been working on that theory. From his sanctum, a black-walled room deep in the heart of Manhattan, the cloaked investigator was keeping contact with many secret agents skilled in locating men that their chief wanted found.

It wasn't like looking for a needle in a haystack, not the way The Shadow handled it. On the table beneath the bluish light that formed the only illumination in his sanctum, The Shadow had spread a large map of Manhattan, divided into many squares, most of which were shaded. The rest were the ones that counted.

This was a map that covered cases like Selbert's. A man in his situation would stay in Manhattan rather than go to one of the other boroughs. He would avoid Chinatown and the other numerous foreign quarters where he would be too conspicuous, so those were shaded off.

Naturally, business areas were out. So were hotel sections, amusement centers, even big apartment sectors, where people often had chance meetings with acquaintances.

Conversely, Selbert wouldn't be around old-fashioned neighborhoods or in the realm of cheap rooming houses where strangers attracted attention. He'd probably picked an apartment larger than a converted house, yet one that didn't have an attendant on duty. Preferably a furnished place on a month-to-month basis, which narrowed the field even more.

Such were shown in the comparatively few squares that remained unshaded on The Shadow's map. There, his agents were scouting for someone who looked like Selbert. And now, even while The Shadow was tapping new squares with his finger, a tiny light glowed on the wall.

Reaching for earphones, The Shadow heard from his contact man, Burbank.

Selbert was found. Clyde Burke, an agent who worked as a newspaper reporter, had spotted the former secretary leaving a delicatessen with a three days supply of food. He'd watched the small apartment house where Selbert went, and had seen lights come on. Selbert was living in Apartment 3D of a side-street apartment house known as the Monolith Arms.

The bluish light clicked off. There was a crinkle as the map was folded in the darkness. A whispered laugh stirred the sanctum, its tone so shivery that echoes answered in repeated sibilance, only to fade into a silence as solid as the blackness, a double proof that The Shadow, master of night, had left his hidden domain.

AT the same time, Lamont Cranston was dropping Charles Medor at the office of the United Insurance Bureau. Alighting from the limousine, Medor smiled as he thanked Cranston for the lift.

It happened that Cranston had left the Cobalt Club at the same time as Medor. The reason was that Cranston had received a telephone call from a very insistent young lady named Margo Lane.

Commissioner Weston had griped about the way Cranston's girlfriend so often talked him out of conferences, but it had done no good. For a week, Cranston had been promising to take Margo to a nightclub, and always something had postponed it. He'd said that if he didn't keep the date tonight, Margo would be through with him.

That had brought a grunt of "Good riddance" from Weston, but Cranston hadn't seen it that way. Medor's office being on the way to the place where Cranston was to meet the Lane girl, the insurance man had gotten a ride.

Though Cranston had said little during the trip,

Medor watched the car until it was out of sight. Then, striding into his office, the rangy man nodded to his night clerk and went on through.

Reaching his private office, Medor locked the door behind him and sat down in front of a square-shaped instrument that looked like the microphone of an interoffice communication system.

First, Medor pressed a button. A curious *whir* came from the device. Medor spoke aloud, and waited. A garbled voice responded, its words chopped to nonsense by the *whir*. Medor turned a dial until the voice was clear.

This instrument was a shortwave radio set, fitted with a mixer; only the two persons who held a conversation could shift the whirring sound so that they would hear their statements ungarbled.

Interrupting the other voice, Medor spoke again, his sharp face pressing close to the microphone, until its flat top was on direct level with his bushy eyebrows. The words that Medor uttered were:

"This is Head No. 7."

## CHAPTER VII
## CRIME'S STRANGE LAIR

FROM the vestibule of the Monolith Arms, Selbert poked his pale face and gave a wary look both ways along the street. Two nights ago, Selbert's manner had been dapper; this evening, he looked scared. Maybe his fright at his first meeting with The Shadow was the reason, for Selbert's glances were the utmost in suspicion each time he studied a darkened patch of street.

Any of those blotted-out segments might be The Shadow. So thought Selbert, until he counted so many splotches that he suddenly changed his mind. Quite sure that The Shadow couldn't be around, Selbert stole from the doorway and off along the street. His anxious eyes were set straight ahead, as if his fear had become a matter of the future.

It would have made no difference if Selbert had looked back. The particular clump of darkness that moved did so in a style that no one would have noticed. The solid gloom of a basement doorway seemed simply to surge forward, then spread; not for an instant did it reveal itself as a figure cloaked in black. Rather, it drifted into the surrounding gloom, to be absorbed like a cloud of dispelling smoke.

Selbert's hurry, his anxiety, both made it easier for The Shadow to stalk him. Turning a corner, Selbert threw a furtive glance at a subway entrance in the next block, then decided that he couldn't afford the benefit of a nickel fare. His picture had appeared in the newspapers as one of

**MARGO LANE**

the victims at Glencoe's house. Though small and a poor photograph, the resemblance might strike some subway rider.

A cab was the only vehicle that Selbert could safely use, so he took one. Which suited The Shadow, because he had stationed that cab for Selbert to find.

The cab belonged to The Shadow and its driver was Moe Shrevnitz, one of The Shadow's capable secret agents. Accepting Selbert as a passenger, Shrevvy stalled a bit while starting his motor, which gave The Shadow time to enter a cab across the street.

The driver of the other cab was quite astonished by the whispered voice that told him to follow the cab ahead, because he'd seen no one enter from the darkness.

But the tone wasn't the sort to brook an argument, so The Shadow won his point, while Moe, up ahead, saw that the trailing cab didn't lose him.

Maybe Selbert suspected something, for after a dozen blocks he paid Moe off and transferred to another cab. That old trick didn't help him. The Shadow paid off his cabby and shifted to Moe's waiting cab. From then on, Selbert couldn't know that he was trailed, for The Shadow had trained Moe to such business.

Moe ducked around through other streets and picked up the trail on another avenue. Sometimes he would get ahead of Selbert and let The Shadow check on the other cab. On avenues, Moe would lose his cab from sight behind trucks and busses, like a porpoise playing amid a school of whales.

Thus when Selbert reached his goal, The Shadow still was right behind him. On foot, the cloaked trailer merged with a building wall until Selbert entered the side door of a large building. After a brief pause, The Shadow took the same route.

SINGULAR was Selbert's choice of destination. He had picked the promenade of a huge office building that was much like an arcade, with rows of shops on each side. Few of the shops were open in the evening, but there was an arrow ahead that pointed to a door with the sign:

MUSEUM OF MECHANICAL SCIENCE

The museum was due to close within an hour; hence it was almost deserted. Selbert paid fifty-five cents, for admittance and tax, to a uniformed gatekeeper, who watched him go through a railed entrance fitted with a photoelectric beam. A recording device gave a sharp click, then another, which caused the gateman to turn in sudden surprise.

For the first time in its history the beam had worked twice when only one person went through, and the keeper couldn't understand it. He looked toward the beam, then shot a long glance after Selbert. Finally, he gazed in other directions, but by then it was too late.

As he had boldly stepped from darkness, so had The Shadow returned to it. Openly visible only when the gateman's attention was diverted, The Shadow had promptly veered to a space behind a huge exhibit case that showed an enlarged mechanism of an automatic lock. Selbert having gone the other way, the puzzled man at the gate took his first look in the wrong direction, and that was enough for The Shadow to complete a glide to cover.

Shifting to a deeper corner next to a big case that inclosed a large model of an ocean liner, The Shadow watched Selbert move around the wall and stop at exhibits whenever other customers came by.

At one case, Selbert dropped a nickel in a slot to watch a model locomotive run on treadmill tracks. While that was going on, The Shadow saw an attendant pause and take a steady look at the drab secretary.

Similarly, another attendant checked Selbert when he was going into an adjacent room, where The Shadow followed as soon as the way was clear. Whisking into a farther room, The Shadow looked back from the doorway to see Selbert finishing a quick round of exhibits under the scrutinizing eye of a third attendant.

The far room was empty of people, but it lacked suitable cover for The Shadow. At one side were a few steps leading down to a door that bore the sign:

CHAMBER OF MARVELS

Reaching the door, The Shadow was opening it and shifting though when Selbert came in sight. Fortunately, the fellow stopped to play with a hand-crank movie machine, otherwise he might have caught his first glimpse of The Shadow entering the marvel room.

In fact, The Shadow was just working the door shut to the slightest crack, when Selbert left the movie machine and came directly to the Chamber of Marvels itself.

Completely closing the door, The Shadow turned about. The first thing he saw was a robot standing on a platform against the far wall. It was a large, cumbersome thing, its limbs, body and head nothing but cylinders of considerably more than human proportions. Hung from its neckless head was a placard, reading:

OUT OF ORDER

Gripping the robot, The Shadow found that it came apart. Evidently its machinery had been sent away for repair, for the interior was quite empty. So the Shadow stepped into the robot's legs and eased the lightweight body and head down over him.

From within the thin-shelled contraption, he peered out through tiny holes that were drilled to make an ornamental pattern.

When Selbert entered, The Shadow was able to take stock of the room as well as the man, for Selbert began a tour of the chamber. It didn't take him long, for the square room was quite small, but its exhibits were highly interesting, all being of a freakish sort.

ONE corner formed a railed square, wherein a huge metal rim was slowly spinning in a mysterious fashion, covering a circle about equal to its own five-foot diameter. It was obviously controlled by an electromagnet that revolved beneath the floor, but the effect was surprising, nevertheless. Selbert stared, quite fascinated, at this marvel, then moved along.

Next was an exhibit case containing a model stratosphere balloon. Selbert pressed a button and the balloon inflated with gas, to rise to the top of the high case. There a valve was released and the balloon came down again.

Another corner contained a combination dredger and sifter. It was much like a full-sized scoop seen on a steam shovel, but its edges were like teeth. The thing was used for dredging coal from riverbeds, since the fine particles of coal would sift out through the teeth.

He spoke again, his sharp face pressing close to the microphone: "This is Head No. 7."

This device was in operation. Each minute it would open its great steel jaws like Jonah's whale, and clamp them shut again.

Leaving that corner, Selbert passed the robot, giving it a mere glance as he went by. He came to another case, containing poison gases and their various reagents. Here were half a dozen slots, each calling for a nickel for the privilege of seeing gases travel through spiral tubes and produce bubbles or color changes in glass jars containing liquids of proper chemical content.

Selbert didn't waste any nickels. He was turning to the final corner to look at an automatic metal crusher, when the door of the marvel chamber opened and three attendants filed into the room. They were the same trio who had eyed Selbert during his earlier tour. Each man had a fist slightly clenched, and all let their hands come open.

In response, Selbert spread his fingers to give the Hydra signal.

"Tooth 4A," spoke Selbert, as soon as the door was closed. "Awaiting new assignment."

"Ear 7C," replied one of the attendants. "We have heard from Head No. 7, telling us to expect you, but not so soon as this. We understood you were on vacation."

Selbert nodded. Then:

"I guess you know all about me," he said. "I'm supposed to be dead, so I have to stay out of sight. But my former Head, No, 4, told me if I didn't hear from him, I'd be transferred to Seven. I was to make contact here."

The Ear knew that such were Selbert's orders. He said that he had heard from Head No. 7 only a short while ago and that Tooth 7A had been mentioned. Proper arrangements had been made on Selbert's account.

"We're pulling out of here tonight," explained the Ear. "Our Head has rigged a job for us. We're going to clean out the Paragon Trust Co. sometime tomorrow."

"You'll come back here then?" inquired Selbert.

"No," replied the Ear. "The museum won't be staying open evenings, so we're no longer needed. The Head was just waiting until we could quit. Working here was soft for us, and saved expenses. Besides, we were ready to help anybody in a pinch, like you."

With that, the Ear gestured to the robot that formed The Shadow's hiding place.

"We took the guts out of old Roger," continued the Ear, "so we could use him to hold a stowaway. That 'out-of-order' sign is so people won't bother him. If you'd come racing in here, we'd have piled you in Roger, clamped the catches tight and chucked away the sign. A guy inside can do the robot act as good as any machinery. You tell Roger to raise his right hand, he does it. Simple stuff like that."

The Shadow resisted the impulse to prove that Roger was an obedient robot. Selbert gave the metal man a stare, as though glad he hadn't been called upon for robot duty. Then the Ear was plucking Selbert's arm, gesturing to a device that stood on a table between the gas case and the crusher.

The thing looked like an ordinary radio set, but it was labeled:

RADIO MIXER
Hands Off

"You'd better talk with Head Seven direct," the Ear told Selbert. "Make it short, though. We're closing the dump soon."

Selbert began to thumb the dials of the mixer. One of the attendants showed him a hidden switch that started the *whir.* Another turned to the Ear and asked him if he wanted to turn off the perpetual lamp, which was an object like a gas jet, burning in a glass cylinder on a shelf above the radio mixer.

The Ear shook his head. He said the perpetual lamp could burn out for all he cared, since this was their last night on duty. With that, the Ear gestured his companions out through the door behind them, leaving Selbert to hold a private interview with his new Head.

An interview that would be overheard by Roger the Robot, in the person of The Shadow!

## CHAPTER VIII
## MACHINES GONE MAD

IT took Selbert several minutes to get the hang of the radio mixer. He kept talking to it while he played with the dials, but everything sounded garbled. At last, a voice spoke in response to Selbert's efforts. It said:

"This is Head No. 7."

As occupant of the robot, The Shadow could hear as well as see, but he wasn't able to identify the voice of Head Seven. The *whir* from the mixer disguised the tone, making it quite crackly. That didn't matter to Selbert. Knowing that he'd opened conversation with a new chief, Selbert began to talk.

First, he expressed loyalty to the Hydra and all its heads. That seemed to impress Head Seven, who announced that he could use the services of a capable Tooth. Then the voice that really belonged to Charles Medor put an important question.

"Why have you not heard from Head No. 4?" was the query. "We who form the Hydra expected more from him."

"So did I," returned Selbert. "Something must have happened—"

"Because Head Four met The Shadow?"

"That might be it," replied Selbert. Then, a bit puzzled, he added: "How did you know about The Shadow?"

Head No. 7 gave a cryptic chuckle. It didn't perplex The Shadow, because he knew that others of Mance's followers had seen him around Glencoe's, something that Selbert probably had not learned before Mance sent him away alone.

"The Hydra is everywhere," spoke Head No. 7. "His Heads are many, his Eyes numberless, like his Ears and Teeth. The Hydra cares for all who obey his mandates."

"I know," said Selbert gratefully. "I could have hidden here, had I been in danger. No one would have found me."

"No one *could* have found you," stressed the whirring voice of Medor. "Turn to the robot that was to be your hiding place."

Selbert turned to face Roger.

"Beside the robot is a lever," continued Head Seven. "Take hold of it and draw it toward you, hard."

As Selbert gripped the lever that projected from the robot's platform, The Shadow not only voiced a warning hiss, but he raised the shell arms in hope of stopping Selbert.

The Shadow's intuitive brain had grasped a thing that hadn't struck Selbert. A menace was at hand, and though The Shadow held no regrets for Selbert, he didn't want to share the consequences.

The crackly laugh of Head Seven's voice was a giveaway to The Shadow, though not to Selbert.

Unfortunately, The Shadow's hiss and the sudden movement of the robot's arms failed utterly to halt Selbert. The dupe simply thought that the robot's machinery was in action, for Selbert's own problems had caused him to pay little attention to the things that the Ear mentioned. This lapse on Selbert's part was fatal.

Selbert pulled the lever. It came loose in his hand the moment it released a mechanism beneath the floor.

With that, the room went mad.

All the machinery cut loose at once. The huge revolving hoop began to spin at stepped-up speed. The stratosphere balloon puffed, shot upward, deflated, and filled again, within its tall glass case. The toothed scoop clapped open, clanged shut, and began to jab forward on a long rod, like a crane in action.

Poison gases were seething in their case. A heavy crusher in the last corner banged down, popped up, banged down again in tremendous fashion. Fully five feet square, that crusher was horrendous when it began to act that way.

The perpetual lamp did nothing; it simply continued to flicker in the glass case on the shelf above the radio mixer. The fact that the robot hurled itself apart and clattered in sections on the platform, was simply part of the chaos, so far as Selbert was concerned.

The dazed man didn't see The Shadow come from the robot's interior, for Selbert had swung back to the mixer, shrieking that the lever had broken loose and hell along with it.

To which came Medor's response, the triumphant crackle of Head No. 7, delivering words that were wrong in every fact until the final statement.

"You tricked us, Selbert!" accused Head Seven. "We know you for who you were, The Shadow in disguise! Clever of you to play the part of a simple secretary. Things went further than you thought they would, but you did manage to finish Mance afterward; otherwise we would have heard from Head No. 4.

"Now you are back again, trying to trick the Hydra. We were waiting for you, to make this effort the last. It is death for you, Selbert! Things have gone too far again. This time, they are designed for doom—to The Shadow!"

DOOM to The Shadow!

The whole mistaken motion of the Hydra was bearing fruit, for The Shadow himself was in the very trap designed for Selbert, the man the Hydra Heads had marked as the black-cloaked warrior in disguise!

**MOE SHREVNITZ**

Terrible, indeed, was that trap! Famous waxwork museums of the past had held their so-called Chamber of Horrors. This modern museum of mechanical science had a Chamber of Marvels that inventive genius had transformed to one of real horrors. It didn't take the statement of a Hydra Head to prove it.

Mere delivery of high speed did the trick.

Spearhead of the mechanical attack was the great rim that normally kept spinning in its corner. The huge hoop weighed at least a quarter of a ton, and the hidden electromagnet that controlled it was on a greater eccentric than the corner confines. It was geared to cover the whole room when the power was on in full.

Smashing through the wooden rail that hemmed it in, the mighty hoop cut a swath across the room. Its spin was still moderate, but its force was terrific. It simply chopped down anything it struck. The Shadow dodged it, as did Selbert, and the hoop struck the table that held the radio mixer. Medor's whirry voice chopped off as table and cabinet went to tinder.

Grabbing Selbert, The Shadow flung him sidewards. The massive hoop, slashing past the platform, crunched the shell of the robot into a flattened mess of metal. But in flinging Selbert, The Shadow saved him from a menace equal to the whirling hoop.

The toothed scoop was shoving forward with its hungry jaws, hoping to gobble a human victim. All that it gained was The Shadow's cloak, as he dived along with Selbert. The massive teeth chewed the cloak into shreds.

Up again, The Shadow hauled Selbert away from the hoop's path. The smashing rim took the stratosphere cabinet instead and broke it all apart. A fierce hiss told that hydrogen was coming in quantity from the crushed tank. Still, there wasn't a chance for The Shadow and Selbert to reach the door. The hoop was after them, forcing them to another dodge.

As the two figures rolled in the center of the room, the hoop went past and smashed the cabinet of poison gases, releasing them as another surety of doom. The Shadow tried to haul Selbert toward the door, only to be blocked by the rim in its next circuit.

This time, The Shadow barely saved Selbert from the crusher in the other corner. All that the crusher caught was the brim of The Shadow's hat. Flipping beneath the crusher, the slouch headpiece became the replica of a pancake.

Grabbing the lever that Selbert had wrenched and dropped, The Shadow took a slash at the revolving rim. Playing hoop with that thing didn't work. The lever flew away like a feather and landed on the platform belonging to the ruined robot.

Away again went The Shadow, dragging Selbert with him. It was lucky they didn't head toward the platform, for the rim cut through it like a buzz saw hitting a pine board.

All the while, the toothed scoop was clamping, the crusher bashing, ready for their deadly work if the mighty rim failed.

How long those menaces could be dodged was something that hardly mattered, for the gases would bring death within a few more minutes. The Shadow reached the door and tried to open it, only to find it bolted on the other side. He dodged back to avoid the metal rim's gyration and came into Selbert's clutch in the middle of the floor.

Having realized that his companion was The Shadow, Selbert had gone as mad as the machines. The crazed man still had faith in the Hydra, and seemed to think that by fighting the uncloaked Shadow he could win favor with the multiple master who had disowned him.

Not to be bothered with Selbert, The Shadow hurled him over by the demolished platform. Grabbing the discarded lever, Selbert drove for his human foe.

With mere minutes to live, it was a question of one life or the other. Selbert, accomplice in murder, deserved to die. Still, The Shadow was ready to go the limit to keep the dupe alive. He grabbed at the lever when Selbert swung it, locked with the madman and reeled him away from the approaching hoop.

Selbert wouldn't have it that way. He fought back, and thereby finished himself. The hoop glanced him, sent him against the scoop, which chopped him hard. Mangled, Selbert went shrieking forward, to meet the hoop again. This time it threw him to the crusher, which sprawled him, and more.

What was left of Selbert rolled, or rather slid, away dead. The hoop came slashing around again to make worse pulp of the victim's body. The Shadow had scarcely any time to glance at Selbert during those devastating stages. Still carrying the lever, The Shadow was dodging the hoop and its allies: the long-necked scoop and the hammering crusher.

PRECIOUS minutes were gone. The Shadow couldn't survive another in the gas-filled room. His own brain was whirling madly, but one thing stuck. That lamp on the shelf, the only thing undamaged! The Hydra's men had mentioned it, but hadn't thought it important.

It could be important to The Shadow. Among the deadly gases that were filling the room was an oversupply of inflammable hydrogen!

Finding himself near the remnants of the platform, The Shadow turned and flung the lever at the glass cylinder on the shelf. Even before the iron rod reached its mark, The Shadow saw the great hoop on a new eccentric, coming straight at him across the room, to block the one place that he must reach, the door.

The rim was endwise. Instinctively, The Shadow took a dive straight at it. He was arrowing one way, while the hoop revolved, coming from the opposite direction. Straight through the great rim went The Shadow. His feet were grazed by the edge as it finished the turn, but they came clear. In the midst of that long slide toward the door, The Shadow heard the iron lever crash the glass cylinder that housed the perpetual lamp.

When the glass shattered, the flame was bare. The flame spoke with a mighty puff as it ignited the gas that filled the room. The gas produced a terrific blast that packed more wallop than all the mechanical contrivances put together.

The room didn't blow apart. Instead, its weak spot gave, and that weak spot was the door. It burst like a safety valve, and with the flame that hurtled through went The Shadow!

So swift was the explosion, so complete its result, that The Shadow wasn't scorched by the vanishing flame. He landed clear across the outer exhibit room, and came groggily to his feet while men were dashing in from the other door. They didn't even see the rising shape that looked like Cranston. They were on their way to stop the mechanical madness in the Chamber of Marvels.

When the current was turned off, the arrivals found Selbert's body, or what was left of it. Certain men, workers for the Hydra, also discovered tiny shreds of black cloth and a flattened piece of felt. That settled them in their opinion regarding Selbert.

The Hydra had eliminated The Shadow.

A certain cab driver named Moe Shrevnitz would have disagreed. At that very moment, he was carrying a very groggy passenger to the hospital. Having had both Selbert and The Shadow as passengers earlier in the evening, Moe knew which was which.

This person who had stumbled out of the building and collapsed in the waiting cab was certainly The Shadow. Moe's chief had taken a terrific beating, but he would come through. Moe knew it from experience. Whenever The Shadow muttered, he was all right. He had a way of pushing every ounce of strength into words that were important.

Moe caught those words. It was his business to catch them at a crucial time like this.

"Paragon Trust," came The Shadow's mutter.

"Robbery tomorrow. The Hydra—"

That was all, and it was enough. Loyal agents would pick up where The Shadow had left off. Wheeling the cab in through the hospital gates, Moe was grimly sure that crime would be stopped cold when the time came.

Tonight's events should have told Moe that he was being overhopeful. One thing had been proven very definitely by The Shadow's masterful escape from the lair of murderous machines.

The logic was this: the Hydra hadn't managed to stop The Shadow.

Therefore, only The Shadow could stop the Hydra!

## CHAPTER IX
### CRIME WITHOUT CRIME

IT was noon when Dr. Rupert Sayre told the nurse to remove the oxygen tent. That done, Sayre had a look at his patient, Lamont Cranston. The oxygen had proved efficacious, the best of treatments, considering that Cranston had been treated to about every other kind of gas, the night before.

Of course, the hospital reports did not indicate it. Only Dr. Sayre knew what The Shadow had gone through. Sayre had heard the true facts from Burbank, as relayed by Moe, who had learned something of what was happening inside the scientific museum, while waiting for The Shadow to rejoin him.

Burbank had stressed one point. If possible, Sayre was to suppress the fact that Cranston was hospitalized. Sayre managed to do this because he was Cranston's private physician. Moreover, Sayre knew that his present patient was The Shadow, to whom he owed a great debt. Not only had The Shadow once rescued Sayre from death, he had set up the young physician in a Park Avenue practice.

Thus Sayre would go to any limits for The Shadow, and in this instance the doctor was keeping to himself a thing that he had long suspected: namely, that there were two Cranstons—a real one, and another who used Cranston's personality when occasion required. Sayre also was convinced that none of The Shadow's other agents, with the possible exception of Burbank, knew that there were two Cranstons.

To preserve The Shadow's all-essential secret, Dr. Sayre announced that the patient could be discharged from the hospital. He said he'd call for Cranston personally, but that until he returned, the oxygen treatment could be continued.

Sayre gave the impression that he would be back very shortly, but when he left, it was with the actual intention not to return until late in the afternoon. Knowing the whole story of this case,

**There wasn't a chance for The Shadow and Selbert to reach the door. The hoop was after them, forcing them in another dodge.**

Sayre felt that the more oxygen his patient received, the better.

Thanks to Sayre's system, it was quite all right for the real Lamont Cranston to keep a one-o'clock luncheon appointment with Commissioner Weston. Should the matter ever be uncovered in the future, Weston might be surprised to learn that Cranston had come straight from a hospital cot to lunch with him. But there would be no question of an overlap. The hospital records would show that Cranston had been discharged in time to keep his appointment.

During lunch, Weston spoke briefly of a strange accident that had occurred the night before. He told how the mechanical marvels at the scientific museum had gone berserk and killed an unidentified visitor who had been in the place.

Mangled beyond recognition, the victim had paid a ghastly penalty for toying with a power lever that shouldn't have been touched. The attendants had done their best to save the fellow, but without avail.

Next, Weston shifted to a far more important subject, a tip-off that the police had received.

"It may have been a crank call," declared the commissioner, "but we didn't ignore it. Our informant claims that criminals intend to stage a robbery at the Paragon Trust Co. sometime today."

Cranston looked interested as he inquired: "More of the Hydra's work?"

"Very probably," returned Weston, "unless the whole thing is a hoax. But I can assure you that robbery will be impossible. Inspector Cardona is watching the bank building with a dozen plainclothes men. He has two armored cars bristling with machine guns. They look like bank cars, nothing more. Crooks will be due for a real surprise if they start anything."

Weston was adding that they'd start down to the Paragon Trust after they finished lunch, when Cranston was informed that he had a phone call. Answering it in a booth, he was a bit startled to hear his own voice over the wire. Then, realizing that it must be The Shadow, he relaxed.

"Hello, Cranston," said The Shadow. "Where do you suppose I just woke up? In an oxygen tent, of all places!"

"I envy you," replied Cranston. "You must be far more comfortable than I am in this phone booth."

"I won't keep you long," The Shadow promised. "All I want you to do is give our friend, the commissioner, the slip after you finish lunch."

"So that you can take my place?"

"Exactly! I'll show up outside the club after he begins to get tired waiting for you."

"Very good," agreed Cranston. "Anything else?"

"One more thing," stated The Shadow. "Insist upon an extra cup of coffee, and make sure it disagrees with you."

"But coffee never disagrees with me—"

"A bit of spoof, old man," The Shadow interrupted. "I'm likely to have a dizzy spell in the commissioner's car. I'd rather he attributed it to an overdose of caffeine, instead of too much oxygen. I'll see you later, Cranston—*much* later."

DOWN at the Paragon Trust Co., the tellers were returning from lunch, one by one. They worked in relays early in the day, but all were in their respective cages during the final hour from two o'clock to three. They had to be, for the Paragon Trust was always flooded with customers near closing time.

Stolid fellows, these tellers. They didn't even nod to one another as they took their places. Each simply opened his window, hung his nameplate on the bars, and went to work taking in deposits and paying out checks.

The tellers hadn't been informed of the robbery rumor. It wasn't necessary to bother them. Each had a revolver within reach of his hand, an alarm treadle where his foot could press it. Two watchmen were on duty, ready with guns and tear gas at instant call. The bank was set to stave off any average robbery.

As for the sort of crime that the Hydra might order, the police could take care of that. As Weston had told Cranston, they were all about the place. Certain plainclothes men took their places in the long lines of customers leading to the tellers' windows, then stepped out again and reported to Inspector Cardona across the street.

It was business as usual at the Paragon Trust Co. Others besides Cardona's men could so testify. The others were The Shadow's agents. Three were on the job. One was Rutledge Mann, an investment broker; another, a friend of his named Harry Vincent. They had business in the bank, arranging a loan through the cashier.

The third was Clyde Burke, present as a reporter at Cardona's invitation, since Clyde had somehow learned about the threatened robbery.

Going in and out, Clyde not only caught nods from the other agents; he checked on Cardona's men and carried messages from them to the inspector.

There were some odd-looking characters in the lines outside the windows, but that was to be expected, since this was a wholesale district representing a cross section of Manhattan life. None of those customers ventured a false move. They were here only to deposit cash or withdraw it.

Some of the deposits were very large; so were the withdrawals. Many of the customers had bags into which they dumped big bundles of banknotes and rolled-up stacks of change. Clyde didn't bother to count those sums. The mere fact that a customer's check was accepted by a teller marked the man as honest.

Such was Clyde's estimate of the customers. As for the tellers, he didn't give them a second look, nor did the headquarters men bother to watch them. The tellers were just so many human machines, going through the same old routine. They all looked alike, except for the nameplates on their windows. Skilled men who could count out money, so trained in the work that they lost all individuality.

Even when they went out to lunch and came back, they followed an identical routine. True, one wore tortoise-shell glasses, another was rather baldish, while a third had hunched shoulders with a broad chin squatting between. You could tell them apart when you studied their features closely, but no one ever did.

Through the barred windows, their faces weren't easy to discern, while the sides of their cages were so heavily grilled that each teller had but little chance of recognizing the man next door to him, except by voice. Occasionally, one needed more money and asked his neighbor for it, whereupon a wicket opened and bundles of cash were pushed through from one cage to the next.

From the customers, the tellers received only glances, along with an occasional nod. During this rush hour there wasn't time to chat with the men in gray tellers' jackets. They were too busy, and other customers became annoyed if persons ahead of them held up the line. Yes, the men in gray were very busy.

And their business was the Hydra's!

THE three tellers in the middle were the Teeth. All servers of the Head who styled himself No. 7. They weren't the men whose names were on the windows, though they were made up to resemble them. Nor were certain customers who thronged those windows regular depositors in the Paragon Trust.

Checks were coming through those center windows made out for sums like fifty thousand dollars, bearing such signatures as John Doe and Mary Lamb. Some checks were even inscribed in jestful fashion, saying "Diller Dollars and Nonsense," or anything else that pleased the Eyes or Ears who presented them.

To every one of these fake customers, the false tellers shoved big bundles of currency wherein large bills were hidden by small ones that were on the top and bottom of the packets. Rolls of coin went along, just to make it look as though the customers were bona fide wholesale merchants.

An apt term, for the Paragon Trust Co. was being robbed wholesale under the eyes of its guards, the surrounding police, and the watchful agents of The Shadow!

Robbed in a fashion as simple as it was unique, through the process of pushing all the available cash right through the tellers' windows into the hands of ready takers who had come here by design. The Paragon Trust was paying through the nose and under it!

Occasionally, the middle teller left his window and went to the vault, to come back with more bundles of money for the bags, briefcases, and wallets of the pretended customers. Usually that central man supplied the tellers on each side of him, though they were also drawing heavily on the bona fide tellers who flanked them.

So heavily, that the men on the flanks had to go to the vaults themselves; but by then it was closing time and the lines of customers were thinning. First, the central teller slapped the front of his window, gesturing customers to the others. Before the lines could shift, two more windows were shut.

That sent the customers to the extreme flanks, to stand in front of the vacant windows, for both genuine tellers had gone to the vault. They hadn't returned because they couldn't find any funds, which was why the middle three, the Hydra's men, had decided to close shop so suddenly.

They didn't even stop at lockers to change from their gray linen cloaks. Coming out through a door near the cashier's office, the three fake tellers filed right past the watchmen and Cardona's detectives, and went out to the street.

Simultaneously, several customers with empty bags decided that they didn't need any money after all and headed for that same side door. They had a right to leave if they wanted, so no one tried to stop them until Clyde Burke, who had a reporter's eagle eye, realized that what looked usual was producing the unusual.

Clyde gave a signal. Up from beside the cashier's desk swung Harry Vincent, leaving Rutledge Mann to talk of loans. The Shadow's two agents could have stopped the sudden exit of tellers and customers, if they'd only been able to draw guns. But that mere action would have brought the guards their way, instead of sending them after the departing crooks.

Reaching the door together, Harry and Clyde sprang to the sidewalk, their hands going for their pockets. There they were caught flat-footed, too late to drop back.

Flanked by the bag-carrying customers, three crooks in gray were displaying revolvers borrowed from the bank itself. Sensing trailers from the bank, the fake tellers had their guns close to their hips. Their faces were no longer placid in expression. The need for disguise was over; these men could show the savage looks that went along with murder.

Murder it would have been, but for a rapid intervention—a startling episode in full daylight. A door flipped open from a big, official car that was stopping near the corner. From it lunged a man who looked like Lamont Cranston, but wasn't.

The arrival was The Shadow. He wasn't clad in black, nor did he grip an automatic. The gun in his fist was a stubby Police Positive that he had snatched from the handy pocket of the police commissioner in the car beside him. Nor did the quick-flinging attacker deliver The Shadow's famous laugh.

All that this rescuer did was open fire, and it was enough. As the gun barked in their direction, murderous crooks forgot the helpless men beside the bank door and swung to do battle with The Shadow!

## CHAPTER X
## DOOM'S INVITATION

THE moment that strife began, Commissioner Weston was quite sure that his friend Cranston had gone mad. Even the fact that The Shadow's fire was returned was not enough to convince Weston that crime was on the loose.

How could there be crime where there was no crime? Such was the commissioner's logic, based on the fact that all was serene around the Paragon Trust Co. until his mad friend flung himself into a self-made fray.

Weston made two very bad guesses.

First, he thought that the shots directed toward The Shadow were being fired by some of Cardona's men, it being natural enough that they should mistake the berserk fighter for a troublemaker. Second, Weston thought that his friend Cranston had been clipped by the gunfire that he drew, for The Shadow took a long sprawl when he reached the curb. Frantically, the commissioner hopped from the official car and bellowed for the shooting to stop.

Weston's shouts were drowned by new volleys. Not only were The Shadow's agents shooting at the fake tellers and their companions; Cardona and his squad were really in it, piling from across the street, loosing long-range fire at the men in gray. Amid the mixed barrage, the excited commissioner thought that he heard a peal of challenging laughter, incongruous in daylight. That weird sound belonged to darkness, for it was the mirth of The Shadow!

Whence it came, Weston couldn't guess. He wrote it off as something inspired by imagination, for his nerves had been on edge over the Hydra business. Weston felt that something superhuman was needed to counteract the Hydra, so maybe he had The Shadow on his mind.

Shaking off such thoughts, Weston looked for Cranston, never suspecting that the man he saw was The Shadow. The commissioner's friend was still in the thick of things, using Weston's gun from a propped-up hand and elbow. It struck Weston then that the sprawl had been caused by a stumble across the curb, which was true, though it was only part of the answer.

The Shadow was really dizzy in the open air. He'd jumped from a moving car and he had felt his legs going from under him. So he'd purposely hooked the curb when he reached it, knowing that a fall would make crooks change their aim.

It had, with double results. Not only did The Shadow's enemies miss their mark; his quick subterfuge gave others time to join combat.

With it, The Shadow turned police guns in the right direction. He knew the rule that cops invariably applied. In a gun duel between unidentified parties, police always went after those who felled their rivals. By playing the part of victim, The Shadow put Cardona's men straight.

Crooks took the hint immediately. Turning, they ducked through an alley just below the bank. They were away before anyone could clip them.

Even The Shadow's shots were belated. After all, he'd stumbled, and in recovering he had to remember that he was Cranston. Using a strange gun, particularly a type that wasn't suited to long range, he couldn't be expected to do miracles of gunnery.

There were plenty of other persons handy to round up the fugitives, and besides, The Shadow had visions of reserve crooks who might pop out and need attention.

Among the men with the fake tellers, The Shadow recognized one of the ex-attendants from the scientific museum, who had been posing as a bank customer. Knowing the brutal way of those fellows, The Shadow wanted to be ready for any others who might be around.

None was around. The rest who served Hydra Head Seven were gone with the loot that they had rifled from the trust company—a thing that The Shadow had not yet learned. But when he saw the size of Cardona's squad, with the armored trucks serving as mechanized units, The Shadow no longer worried over a counterattack. The thing to do was scour for the fugitives, three men in gray who looked like bank tellers being the ones most easily marked.

ON his feet, The Shadow found himself gripped by Commissioner Weston, who wanted his gun back.

Rutledge Mann came dashing from the bank, accompanied by the cashier, and together they began to pour out their story, which made Weston forget the gun.

The cashier, though quite bewildered, was stating that everything had been all right when the tellers returned from lunch, though they might have hatched up something at the little cafe around the corner of the next street.

When Weston turned to ask Cranston's opinion, his friend was gone, gun and all. Such was The Shadow's way, even when he posed as Cranston, though in such guise he didn't fade from sight, but merely moved away when he found an opportune moment.

Having heard what the cashier said, Cranston had started for the corner. Around it, he saw the cafe in question, a neat though unpretentious eating place. The personnel, consisting of proprietor and waiter, were outside, wondering about the shooting. They didn't notice the calm-faced customer who went past them, through the door, much faster than his strolling gait indicated.

Noting that the cafe had an upstairs room, The Shadow ascended the steps that led to it. Arrived there, he saw a door, opened it and entered a storeroom. A low laugh issued from the lips that resembled Cranston's when eyes that carried The Shadow's gleam saw the sight that they expected.

Three men wearing gray linen coats were lying bound and gagged upon the floor. They were the real tellers, waylaid in their favorite eating place, that crooked substitutes might take their place after lunch. But The Shadow didn't release them. He preferred not to spoil their alibi.

Footsteps were coming up from below. The Shadow slipped behind a door as two men entered. The Shadow recognized them as a pair who had been finishing lunch down in the cafe. One was for unbinding the prisoners, on the chance that it would hurt their story. The other was more concerned about a stranger who had just come upstairs.

"He was a tall guy," the fellow said. "Kind of important-looking; at least, as if he thought he was. Suppose he came in here—"

"Why should he?" demanded the other. "How could he know about these dopes?"

"Where is he, then? Answer me that!"

The Shadow wasn't waiting for one man to answer the other. Out from behind the door, he was poising Weston's gun to land it on one crook's skull as a starter. It would take a deft swing to score a sure knockout with Weston's stubby revolver.

The poise lasted too long.

A window shot open from the rear of the storeroom, revealing two men, a gray-clad crook and an ordinary companion, both fugitives from the police chase. They had guns, and they were entering this room from a low roof. They saw The Shadow about to make his swing. They yelled.

Immediately, The Shadow was mingling in new battle. He swung for one man, gave him a glancing blow as he turned, then dodged as the other made a grab. Quickly, The Shadow blasted the last few of Weston's cartridges, aiming at the window, but his shots were spoiled when his adversary jogged his arm.

Odd, that jog! The Shadow didn't realize that his own waver had allowed it. Sayre was right; his patient had needed a further dose of oxygen. Then men were piling through the window and The Shadow was a lone fighter in the midst of four. It was only fair to count the fellow that The Shadow had partly slugged, for groggy though he was, the crook didn't stagger much more than the uncloaked fighter.

LUCKY these thugs didn't know they were tackling The Shadow—or was it?

If cloaked, The Shadow could have given them a laugh. With a brace of automatics, his glancing strokes might have counted when they landed, thanks to the weight. Crooks would have mistaken his reeling strides for clever tactics. But in Cranston's guise, The Shadow was just a meddler who needed attention of a permanent sort.

One to another, The Shadow's adversaries were snarling to "give it." They weren't limiting the idea to their lone foe. They meant to give it to the tellers, too. Men of the Hydra were in a mood for murder, now that their work was uncovered.

With a wild lurch, The Shadow carried grapplers with him. He took them in the one direction that counted, toward the bound men on the floor. Those chaps could help, though they didn't know it. In fact, they were better bound than loose.

Headlong, The Shadow and his foemen went tripping across the prisoners. It was enough of a surprise for the crooks. Though his knees buckled in keeping with his swimming head, The Shadow still had strength enough and wits to roll from the pileup that he caused. Then, with his head half buried in his arm, The Shadow did deliver his famous laugh.

Low, sibilant, it rose with sinister quiver, its effect increased by the surrounding gloom. The muffling arm gave it a peculiar effect, that of a voice rising from a tomb. There being no tomb in this vicinity, the mirth could only have come from beyond the half-opened door, which was where crooks faced as they scrambled to their feet.

Just as Weston had rejected Cranston as a giver of that laugh, so did the Hydra's men. To them, The Shadow was an approaching menace, not one in their very midst.

They shifted to take aim through the doorway. As they did, The Shadow's hand pushed beyond the feet of a bound teller. Fingers stretching to their limit reached the door and pressed hard against its lower corner. The door creaked shut, exactly as if someone on the other side had chosen to draw it as a shield.

Again the laugh, muffled more deeply in a coat sleeve. It was enough for men of crime. They dived for the window, shooting back at the closing door, jabbing bullets through the woodwork to prevent The Shadow's entry. Headlong across the roof, down to a courtyard in back, went those enemies who had actually trapped The Shadow, only to believe him still at large!

Footsteps were pounding on the stairs. The door flung wide to admit Inspector Cardona, followed by members of his squad. They sprang to the window and took a few shots at the disappearing fugitives. Cardona growled when he realized that his men had overrun the chase, giving mobsters a chance to cut back into safety.

Then Joe took a look at the men on the floor. He was surprised to find Cranston among the bound tellers. But the very plight of the commissioner's friend, the fact that he'd blundered into trouble, was quite enough to divert any thoughts that he could be The Shadow. To add to that much-desired impression, The Shadow thanked Cardona in a manner befitting Cranston.

When Cardona's men helped The Shadow downstairs, along with the released tellers, Weston met them and began to chide his friend. In Weston's opinion, Cranston's whole behavior had been an invitation to doom. The commissioner suggested that his friend return to the car and wait there until he felt better—and more sensible.

Actually, The Shadow did need a rest, and it was policy to follow Weston's orders. Cranston would have done it under circumstances like this. So The Shadow was piloted to the car, and once there, he settled gratefully in the rear seat, letting his eyes go half shut. He watched until the door closed, and he saw that he was alone.

Then came an undertoned laugh, a mere echo of The Shadow's former mirth. He was thinking of Weston's term, an invitation to doom. Sometimes the commissioner could produce very apt expressions. This was one of them.

An invitation to doom was exactly what The Shadow wanted, and he intended to get one—from the Hydra!

## CHAPTER XI
## THE SHOW GOES ON

AFTER ten minutes' rest, The Shadow felt rested enough to emerge from Weston's car, under the watchful eye of detectives posted to see that Cranston didn't get himself into more trouble. All he wanted to do was make a telephone call, so the detectives steered him to a booth in a corner drugstore.

Returning, The Shadow stated that he'd called for his own car. It would be here soon, so the detectives wouldn't have to wait. Cranston was going to sit down in the drugstore to drink a bromide that the druggist was mixing for him. So the detectives went over by the bank, but they kept a watchful eye on the drugstore.

When Cranston's car arrived, it stopped just around the corner. Soon The Shadow came from the drugstore and entered it, first noting that Stanley, the chauffeur, was looking over toward the bank.

The Shadow didn't want to give Stanley too much of a shock, which the chauffeur, a very sober man, might have received if he'd found himself seeing double.

Lamont Cranston was seated in the limousine.

Briefly, The Shadow told his replica what had happened at the bank. Next, he asked Cranston what had come of last night's conference. Thereupon Cranston unburdened completely, telling how his hopes had risen only to dwindle.

"Dustin Bardell was really getting somewhere," declared Cranston. "He was urging Commissioner Weston to open Glencoe's case. He classed the fire as the work of the Hydra, even though he couldn't offer any proof. Bardell was guessing at what we know was fact.

"Then Charles Medor arrived with his report. You know how exacting Medor is when working for insurance companies. His bureau never misses a chance to dispute a claim. Of course, it would happen that Medor was on the job in one case where crime was really covered.

"Medor said the fire was an accident, and that settled it. After all, he can't be blamed, for the facts were quite positive—unless you want to call them negative. Either way, it's just the same. Poor Medor! He couldn't have covered crime any better if he'd been working for the Hydra!"

For once, Cranston saw himself in a most singular mood. As he turned toward The Shadow, Cranston was met by a burning gaze that he never could have duplicated. He saw his own face as a mask rather than an image. Something was striking home to The Shadow's keen mind.

"So you dropped Medor at his office," remarked The Shadow. "I hope he appreciated the ride."

"He did," assured Cranston. "He invited me to a theater party this evening. Margo Lane was delighted when I told her that I had two tickets to Medor's private box."

"Medor's private box?"

"Yes. He's interested in the Stage Group. You know, those amateur players who have come up so rapidly."

The Shadow remembered the Stage Group. He asked what play they were producing this evening.

"I don't know," replied Cranston, "but it's probably a costume piece. They go in for that sort of stuff. It's apt to prove rather boring."

"Quite," agreed The Shadow. "Why don't you pass it up?"

"I can't very well," said Cranston ruefully, "because Margo wants to go. Personally, I'd rather go over to New Jersey and finish arrangements in the trophy room. By the way, I want to thank you for the prompt disposal of the debris."

"I take it you mean Mance," remarked The Shadow, with one of Cranston's smiles. "The thanks still are mine, on that score. Suppose I sub for you at the theater party. That will help even things."

"But I'm to take Margo to dinner—"

"I'll relieve you of that burden, too. Still, Cranston"—The Shadow's tone was whimsical—"that would put you under obligation to me.

Suppose you make it really even by spending the rest of the afternoon with Commissioner Weston, while he checks over the list of depositors at the Paragon Trust, in case they start to raise a fuss. I'll have to spend a few more hours sulking in my oxygen tent, or I won't be able to survive this evening's ordeal."

DUSK was clouding the hospital windows when The Shadow finished a delightful whiff of oxygen and reached for the ringing telephone. Cranston was on the wire, ready to call off the list of depositors. The Shadow told him to go ahead, but to limit himself to those he thought the most important.

After about twenty names, Cranston stressed one.

"Here's a coincidence," he said. "The Stage Group was a depositor at the Paragon Trust Co."

"Too bad," returned The Shadow dryly. "I hate to see a struggling young organization suffer a financial loss."

"They won't lose anything," informed Cranston. "All depositors were insured up to five thousand dollars. They didn't have that much in the bank. Each day, somebody deposited the receipts of the previous night, and they used the account to pay current expenses."

The Shadow seemed pleased that the Group was not in financial jeopardy. But it struck him that such a worthy organization ought to be farther ahead than it was.

"Do me a favor, Cranston," he suggested. "Send Stanley to some of the ticket agencies and have him buy about fifty seats for tonight's Group show."

"Fifty tickets!" echoed Cranston. "Why—"

"They will cost a lot," interposed The Shadow, "but I'll send you a check from the special account that I carry in your name. Now about those tickets, Cranston, and what I want you to do with them. On your way home—"

The rest of The Shadow's statement was audible only to Cranston. Someone was stopping at the door of the hospital room, so The Shadow lowered his tone to a whisper and confined it to the mouthpiece.

Cutting off Cranston's good-bye, The Shadow settled the telephone on its stand and rolled back beneath the oxygen tent just as Dr. Sayre entered.

Finding his patient much recuperated, Sayre took him to the Cobalt Club on the promise that he'd return home shortly. After that, Sayre made a few late calls. He was swinging into Park Avenue in his coupe, when he saw Cranston's limousine stopped by a corner curb.

The big car was New Jersey bound, but Stanley must have violated some traffic rule, for Sayre saw Cranston leaning from the window trying to square things with a cop. It made Sayre smile to think of The Shadow disputing such a trifling matter as a traffic ticket.

Apparently he was making out all right, for the traffic cop was beginning to nod. So Sayre continued on his way, glad that his patient had taken his advice about going home.

This simply proved that Sayre was forgetting his own theory regarding two Cranstons. Otherwise, he might have realized that his ex-patient wasn't the man in the limousine. The real Cranston was homeward bound, but the double who had done a stint in the oxygen tent was elsewhere.

The Shadow was dining with Margo Lane under the lights of a sidewalk cafe, where he could sniff the pleasing aroma of exhaust fumes from passing cars and reiterate how much he enjoyed fresh air.

Margo didn't share his opinion regarding the atmosphere, but she naturally wouldn't appreciate it, not having occupied an oxygen tent that afternoon.

Besides, Margo had other things to think about. Most important was Lamont Cranston himself.

Margo Lane allowed for people's moods, since her own were inclined to vary. Indeed, it was Margo's ability as a listener that made her popular in cafe society. Physically, Margo was a very attractive brunette, with a photogenic face that required only a minimum of makeup to show it at its best.

Usually, conviviality formed a portion of her charm, but she could go soulful quite as readily, and her serious manner generally brought a response when she turned it on. Sometimes it worked with Cranston, but that was the odd part. Just when Margo was most sure that she really understood Lamont, she'd find out that she didn't.

LAST night, Margo had learned that her complacent friend didn't care for old-style theatrical performances. He'd termed them "too artificial." This evening, his opinion was changed. Lamont was actually showing enthusiasm over the current production of the Stage Group, which was a drama of the French Revolution.

Thus Margo's eyes were tending toward perplexity when The Shadow, sensing the reason, supplied a simple answer.

"I've been reading up on Carlyle," he remarked. "Spent half the morning—the half I was awake—digging through his 'French Revolution.' The title of tonight's show, 'Robespierre,' began to intrigue me. I wouldn't want to miss it."

Margo's perplexity changed to understanding. "So that's it!" the brunette laughed. "I'd been wondering how to account for your sudden Parisian tastes, Lamont."

The Shadow's eyebrows gave a Cranston query.

"Your picking this sidewalk cafe for dinner," explained Margo, with a gesture. "Last night you insisted that such places were abominable, with the noise from automobile horns and the stares of passersby."

"So I did," remarked The Shadow in a recollective tone. "Do you know, Margo, sometimes I feel that I'm a split personality. I really should discuss matters more fully with my other self."

Margo smiled. She thought her friend meant The Shadow, not the actual Lamont Cranston. For Margo Lane had long identified the black-cloaked fighter and the leisurely clubman as one and the same. A situation which was so intriguing in itself that Margo never dreamed that there could be a further riddle within the enigma.

Why should she even imagine that there could be two Cranstons, when one was so amazing?

The answer was, Margo didn't imagine it— which suited The Shadow perfectly. Nevertheless, it wasn't good policy to get out of character while playing the part of Cranston. So The Shadow emphasized his new interest in historical dramas by glancing at his watch and remarking that it was time to start to the theater.

There was a good crowd at the Victoria Garden, the playhouse used by the Stage Group. The theater was so named from a courtyard entrance that lay between two streets. Something of a garden, the courtyard not only gave access to the main entrance, but to a short inner alley that led to the stage door.

Charles Medor was waiting for the members of his box party. Hardly had The Shadow arrived with Margo, before Commissioner Weston appeared, bringing Dustin Bardell with him. Weston was in one of his most impatient moods, stating bluntly that he wished the show was over, an opinion in which Bardell solemnly concurred.

"We'll have to hold another conference," ordained Weston. "I want you there, Cranston, and you too, Bardell. This robbery today—a hundred thousand dollars rifled from the Paragon Trust—it was outrageous!"

"Particularly since we were there to see it happen," put in The Shadow. "That made it worse, commissioner."

"We didn't arrive soon enough," argued Weston. "I'd have identified those tellers as criminals. I can tell a crook at a glance!"

Only Margo saw the slight smile that appeared on the lips of the man she thought was Cranston.

Then they were entering the theater and being ushered to their box, while Weston was remembering that he'd brought along Cranston's briefcase from the Cobalt Club. Handing the bag to The Shadow, the commissioner said:

"It's lucky your broker phoned me. Careless of you, Cranston, to leave a briefcase lying about, filled with valuable stocks and bonds. But they're all there. I checked them over the phone with Mann."

Houselights were darkening as they reached the curtained box. Casually, The Shadow glanced over the audience and saw that the seats were well filled. Buzzing conversation ceased as the curtain rose upon a scene that was a mass of blackness.

There was something prophetic about the blacked-out set. It seemed to welcome more than mere actors. Blackness was The Shadow's favored habitat. This was the sort of stage that he might choose for action. For the present, however, The Shadow retained his Cranston pose.

The Shadow was letting the show go on. He wanted to be sure of certain things before he projected himself into a play that had been advertised as a drama of death. An apt term, that: one that promised The Shadow another meeting with the master mob that operated as the Hydra!

## CHAPTER XII
### INTO THE BASKET

A SPOT of light picked out a figure on the left side of the stage, an actor attired in royal regalia of the seventeenth century. He represented King Louis of France, complete to ruffles and ornamental wig. In stentorian tone, King Louis announced his identity and proceeded to recount what he had done for France.

At the finish, the actor solemnly declared:

"These were my crimes—"

A great crash sounded from the rear of the stage. Its clangor was unmistakable. It was the dropping of a guillotine axe, its echoes chilling as they rang through the startled audience.

Then the spotlight was picking up another man, to the right of the stage. He, too, was made up in seventeenth century style, though his garb was simpler than court dress. He was the famous Danton, great sponsor of revolution. He declaimed upon his deeds, and finished:

"These were my crimes—"

Again the smash of the unseen axe, bringing new shudders to the audience. Each fall of the hidden chopper seemed to be wrenching a human life. Whoever designed this prologue knew his stagecraft.

The lighted circle reached the center of the

stage. There stood Robespierre, a hunched man with his chin buried in the ruffle of a more fastidious garb than Danton's. A good touch, this, for Robespierre was usually portrayed as chinless, and the neckpiece was a token of his vanity.

A man of oratory, this Robespierre. He told his tale as had the others, and finished with the guillotine cue:

"These were my crimes—"

The third whack of the axe brought more than clatter. It produced light that flooded the entire stage. A grim scene, this, with an actual guillotine its backdrop. A huge frame more than twenty feet in height, with a broad, sharp blade climbing slowly up the vertical tracks, to preen itself for a swoop upon another victim!

Onto the stage stepped other actors, one by one. Characters male and female, all from the pages of horrible history. Silent, these, which made their appearance all the more impressive, now that the guillotine had been unveiled. For each newcomer was hardly posted before the axe descended with its furious slash, to cut off any words that might have been said.

The allegory was excellent. These characters were to appear in the ensuing acts of "Robespierre," and their fate was predetermined. The audience was to remember throughout the play that over each person in the drama loomed the hideous specter of the guillotine. They would disappear from the cast one by one, always to the tune of an offstage crash of the mammoth chopper.

In front of the guillotine, and below its pedestal, lay a shallow basket, the common receptacle for the heads of the doomed. Somehow, that wicker container was more terrible than the mighty cleaver—at least to Margo Lane, who was staring, transfixed, like the rest of the audience. Even Weston and Bardell were impressed, forgetful of the things that they had intended to discuss during the prologue.

One person in the box was speaking, now that the heavier dramatics were through. In an undertone, Charles Medor was excusing himself, stating that he'd be needed in the office for a short while. Then he was stepping out through the box curtains, not bothering to count the heads of his companions.

They were one head short, as surprisingly as if the guillotine had reached out to the box and claimed a victim.

The Shadow had opened his brief case, not at the top but underneath, to reveal a section shaped like an inverted V between the normal compartments that were filled with stocks and other papers.

From that hidden section, he had produced a thin black cloak and a slouch hat. Those garments were already obscuring the figure of Cranston when Medor turned away.

Laying the briefcase aside, The Shadow followed Medor. He already had his guns; they were in well-fitted holsters beneath the evening jacket that The Shadow wore when doubling as Cranston. They'd be needed, those automatics, because Medor wasn't going to the office as he claimed. The man that The Shadow suspected as a Hydra Head was taking a passage that led backstage.

The curtain was falling on the prologue when Medor reached the wing. The play called for a five-minute intermission after the prologue, to allow the audience to catch its breath and the stage crew to rig another set.

The last part was simple, for all the stagehands had to do was lower a backdrop that showed the fountains of Versailles, where the first act was laid.

But no one was bothering about the curtain that was to hide the guillotine. Like the actors, the stagehands were crowding about Medor, who, with a cunning smile upon his overhandsome face, was producing a suitcase from a locked closet near the wing.

Opening the bag, Medor began to count out sheaves of banknotes, the loot from the Paragon Trust Co.!

THREE actors edged forward to assist. King Louis, Danton and Robespierre forgot their historical animosities, while their deft hands thumbed through money the way they had that afternoon. Three of a kind, these thieves. In order from left to right, they were the fake bank tellers who had swindled the Paragon Trust. And of them, the middle man was Robespierre, hunched exactly as he had been in the central teller's cage!

A repressed laugh trickled from The Shadow's hidden lips as he moved forward from darkness. He was timing his personal appearance until the payoff. He wanted all hands to be present, which they were. Even the stagehands!

They were three, those stagehands, the former attendants at the scientific museum. Along with a dozen actors, they were getting their cut of two thousand dollars each, the rest to be retained by Medor, the Hydra Head, for benefit of himself and the other leaders of the sinister organization.

Forward moved The Shadow. His laugh grew as he came. Plotters heard it when he was almost among them. Like Medor, the rest wheeled to find themselves under the muzzles of two moving automatics that threatened all with the doom that they thought they had already delivered to The Shadow!

By then, The Shadow's laugh was striking a strong pitch. Strident, it hurled its sinister mirth for the audience to hear. Beyond the curtain were people who should be told what the real crimes of the actors were. Not fanciful exaggerations of French Revolutionary lore, but modern, streamlined villainy done by criminals who used a theater as their hideout and fancy costumes as their disguises!

Fiercer, more chill-inspiring than the crash of the guillotine was that accusation of The Shadow, a mocking laugh for the world to hear. Persons out front didn't have to see what was happening backstage to know that crime was uncovered. With one mighty taunt, The Shadow was shattering the Hydra's latest game, throwing Head Seven and his followers into complete panic.

They did just what a disorganized group would do: some lunged forward independently, others dodged for shelter, while a few actually fled. Some let their money flutter in their excitement; the rest clung to their share of the stolen funds, tightly and grimly. All, however, were yanking weapons of their own. Nobody who served the Hydra ever went unarmed.

The Shadow's guns blasted first. Tongues of fire stabbed the nearest foemen before they could jab their own revolvers in return. Tongues of flame with bullets of metal that cut a swath through the ranks of murderers. Asking for such treatment, they were allowing The Shadow no choice but to give it.

The principal members of the cast were the ones who took the brunt. Across the sprawling forms of King Louis, Danton, and Robespierre sprang The Shadow, wheeling to a better vantage point where he could deal with the rest. In particular, he wanted Medor, but it wasn't judgment to forget the others.

Guns were popping from all about the stage; even those who had started to flee were rallying for the fray. And Medor wasn't where he could be touched.

Clutching the great bulk of the bank swag, the Hydra Head was keeping behind his followers as he shouted for them to flank The Shadow and thus dispose of their mutual menace. Time was short, and Medor wanted to keep it that way for The Shadow.

Wheeling toward the center of the stage, The Shadow was revolving like a human gun turret, but there was still a chance to trap him. Keeping behind a screen of charging followers, Medor continued his urging shouts.

Bullets were chopping hard into the stage. They were coming from many angles, including balconies that led to the dressing rooms. Scattered, The Shadow's enemies were dangerous, a thing he had foreseen. But he was keeping them here on this battleground until aid arrived. Still, with metal slugs whistling through the folds of his cloak and slicing his hat brim, mere dodging wouldn't be enough.

THE SHADOW saw a vantage point: the rear of the stage beyond the hovering guillotine. He feinted toward the footlights, then reversed while gunners were peppering along the lowered curtain. He'd fooled the Hydra's crew that time—with one exception.

Namely, Medor.

Head No. 7 made a perfect guess. His hunch was that The Shadow wouldn't go stage front; otherwise, stray bullets would cleave the curtain after missing him and produce casualties in the audience. Hence Medor, playing still farther ahead, swung about and barked an order to a henchman near the rear corner of the stage.

"Pull it!" called Medor, with an appropriate gesture. "The guillotine release!"

The fellow paused only for a quick glance at The Shadow, now in his rearward whirl. At another gesture from Medor, the fake stagehand tugged the cord. There was a tremble from the guillotine frame as the great axe wavered for its downward journey.

At that moment, The Shadow was right beside the wicker basket. Guns were swinging in his direction, more of them than he could put out of combat with a single volley. To The Shadow, the drop of the chopper could prove fatal, because the broad axe, once down, would block off passage to shelter beyond it.

Again The Shadow did the unexpected, this time with a risk so great that aiming foemen stopped with staring eyes, their guns idle in their fists. Finishing his whirl with a dive, The Shadow cleared the basket and shot headlong between the uprights of the guillotine while the mighty axe was sizzing down those very rods!

A thing amazing, that mass of human blackness arrowing beneath a dropping juggernaut of sharp-edged steel. Head, shoulders, body, feet—all were vulnerable to the murderous blade. It was a matter of split seconds, sliced to the fraction of an inch. A frequent hazard with The Shadow, but never on such a gruesome scale as this.

Blackness disappeared as though banished, as it was cut off by the scintillating chopper. But it was cut off intact, that blackness. Smash!

Foemen were staring at a three-foot expanse of glittering steel, with no fragment of The Shadow

**The mighty chopper was again on its way
... and the great bladc found its mark.**

in sight. Unless they chose to count the mere patch of black cloth, a bit of sweeping cloak fold that the knife edge clipped and let flutter as testimony that The Shadow had split his escape to the thinness of a hair.

Then guns talked, too late. Bullets were flattening against steel from beyond which came The Shadow's laugh. He'd turned the menace into a bulwark, and from near one post, his gloved hand poked a gun to jab responding shots across the top of his steel barricade.

Medor was hopping over to haul up the guillotine blade. He took that duty for himself, because the man in the corner had ventured too far out and was staggering from a bullet that The Shadow gave him.

Medor was too late with his haul. His horde had begun to scatter under The Shadow's fire. The cloaked fighter could afford to let them flee, for aid was arriving in plenty.

In from both wings of the stage, from the alley door that afforded the only exit, came brawny men by dozens, most of them with guns. Thanks to Cranston, The Shadow had stocked the house with them. They were the recipients of the fifty theater tickets, friendly traffic cops that Cranston had contacted all along the avenue, inviting them to a show after they finished duty!

The chopper was up again, with Medor clinging to its rope. Shoving the cord into the hands of the wounded man beside him, Medor ordered him to hang on. Savagely, Medor dashed across the stage, to meet The Shadow coming through the guillotine posts.

They met gun for gun, but The Shadow's trigger finger had already begun its squeeze. Medor staggered sideward, clutching his mass of currency beneath a wounded shoulder, while his other hand kept stabbing with its gun.

Fading from Medor's fire, The Shadow supplied a return jab just as Medor sprang between the posts to gain a deeper shelter. Money fluttered from Medor's clutch as he clamped his hand painfully to his side. He was spinning like a faltering top, weakening beyond the guillotine. His turn finished with a forward sprawl, as his gun dropped from his slipping fingers.

Another hand was failing, that of the man who held the release rope. Fingers gave and the mighty chopper was again on its way.

Medor heard the horrendous rattle from above him and voiced a terrified scream, but he couldn't pull himself forward when he tried. Small wonder, for Medor's head was coming over the baseboard of the guillotine's base and his shoulders wouldn't follow. Medor started to raise his neck too late.

The great blade found its mark. It didn't even quiver as it made the slice. Something plopped and landed in the basket. It was a Hydra Head, chopped off literally. The slice not only ended Medor's shriek; it left stout cops and their prisoners staring at a thing that gave them a deadly leer from a blood-bathed wicker basket.

From the stage door came a strange grim laugh, The Shadow's. It wasn't just a knell to mark the passing of Charles Medor, man of murder. That tone marked The Shadow's recollection of the Hydra's ways. For every head chopped off, two others would arise!

The Hydra would avenge its seventh Head with a new and wider campaign of relentless crime, with every stroke an effort to dispose of the perpetual monster's one invulnerable foe: The Shadow!

## CHAPTER XIII
## HEAD NO. 10

CRIME was striking everywhere at once.

For a week, such crime had seethed, hissing like the tongues of a dozen snakish heads about to rear themselves. There had been run-ins between The Shadow's agents and workers of the Hydra, but with no avail. Eyes and Ears had always been backed by Teeth who maneuvered their escape before The Shadow arrived upon the scene.

Then the strokes.

Sudden attempts at robbery, efforts at murder, always directed against wealthy men. All the more insidious, those crime strokes, because the hidden brains behind them were of the same class—men of substance and standing.

So greatly did the Hydra admire and seek wealth, that it enlisted money-minded men as Heads. That went without saying; the thing to prove was who these men might be. They were the sort who had always upheld the law because it protected their property.

Finding something bigger than the law—the Hydra—they embraced it and became its Heads because it also promised to protect their wealth and gain for them that of others.

Separating the good from the bad was the peculiar province of Commissioner Weston, and he was at a total loss. At a secret conference in the Cobalt Club, he expressed his opinions to The Shadow, who had come there as Lamont Cranston.

Present also was Dustin Bardell, the one man of affluence that Weston could trust, because Bardell had been suspicious of Medor. Even though Glencoe's case was written off and its claims paid, Bardell was to be praised. If Medor hadn't been wrong on the Glencoe matter, he had been plotting against the Paragon Trust Co.

Thus Bardell was the nucleus of a group that Weston wanted to organize into a civic committee to help against the Hydra. So far, except for Cranston, who belonged without question, there had been only one safe candidate. He was present tonight, a man named Lloyd Casler, who couldn't be under the Hydra's influence, because he was bringing data that might ruin the insidious organization.

A broad-built man with an austere countenance, Casler looked both blunt and honest. Further, he preferred to sit back and listen to what others said, before pressing his own opinions.

"So far, we've blocked everything since the Paragon Trust robbery," affirmed Weston. "We stopped a penthouse robbery, a Wall Street holdup, and stalled three attempted murders. But we answered a thousand crank calls managing it. The trouble is, the crimes we did stop looked like feelers. The Hydra is too smart to let a whole crew be annihilated again. Lately, they've pulled out when things didn't seem too pleasant."

The Shadow could have corroborated that statement. The crimes mentioned, and several others, had been forestalled largely through his vigilance. But they weren't just feelers, as Weston chose to term them.

"Big crime needs opportunity," remarked The Shadow. "As soon as the right time arrives, you'll be in for it, commissioner."

"I know we will," groused Weston. "Gad! If we could only think ahead of these chaps. Remember, Cranston, how they tricked us at the Paragon Trust?"

"But The Shadow settled that one, commissioner. The crooks are dead or captured and the funds were regained."

"Yes, The Shadow did well," conceded Weston. "He used the facts that we overlooked. He realized that only clever actors could have impersonated those bank tellers; more than that, they would have had to visit the bank often, to study the men whose places they were to take.

"Somehow The Shadow learned that the Stage Group made steady deposits at the Paragon Trust. That was the vital link he needed. He did a fine job at the theater, while I was sitting in the box looking right at the criminals we wanted!"

The Shadow smiled.

"Remember what you said beforehand, commissioner?" he asked. "How you could tell a crook when you saw one? You saw three, but you didn't tell them anything."

"You wouldn't have known if I had," snapped Weston. "Why, the first shots from backstage must have blown you right out of the box! You were gone when I started to find what the trouble was. The next place I saw you was in the front courtyard!"

The Shadow acknowledged Weston's skill at repartee, whereupon the commissioner returned to business.

"SOMETHING may happen tonight," predicted Weston. "It's the opening of the jewelry show at the International Antique Gallery. The display of European crown gems alone would satisfy the Hydra."

"What precautions are you taking?" inquired Bardell.

"Every precaution," returned Weston. "Detectives inside and outside; armored cars like we had at the bank; patrol cars and motorcycles. Every visitor has to show a special pass, and they've all been warned that if the alarms go off, they'll have to take their dose of tear gas. It may cut down the attendance, but it certainly will prevent crime."

Bardell agreed that it would. Whereupon, Weston added that Inspector Cardona was in personal charge of the jewel show. If no one had any better suggestion to offer, the commissioner thought it would be a good plan to go over and view the arrangements he had mentioned, though everything was under complete control.

Commissioner Weston had just about forgotten that Lloyd Casler was present. The blunt man reminded him of it.

"I have something better," insisted Casler. "That is why I asked Mr. Bardell to bring me here. I think we should attend the meeting of the Worldwide Friendship Society."

That brought an indulgent smile from Weston.

"It is more important than you think," continued Casler. "The society is composed of very wealthy people, and tonight they are subscribing to an international aviation fund for men in the services of all United Nations. Hart Ribold is the sponsor."

Weston recalled the name of Hart Ribold as that of a well-known society man. He couldn't see anything wrong about Ribold leading a drive for funds. Casler didn't agree.

"Ribold wants a quarter million," he declared. "The whole amount is to be placed in his hands in the form of certified checks. So far, there have been no objections. Now, suppose that Ribold happened to be a Hydra Head—"

"He'd clear out with the entire fund!" interrupted Weston. "You've made your point plain, Casler. It's just the subtle sort of crime that the Hydra would try, and with the organization behind him, Ribold would vanish completely.

"You're right, Casler: we must go to that meeting. At a time when men of reputed character may all be criminals, we can't afford to overlook a case like this!"

LEAVING the club in Weston's car, they drove past the International Antique Gallery, where the famous display of crown jewels was to be held. Fronting on an open square where Broadway crossed an avenue, the Antique Gallery occupied the ground floor of an early-modern office building.

Its location was convenient, for there were several subway entrances nearby, and from them branched numerous underground concourses to other lines. This was a spot where visitors could converge from all sections of the city.

An excellent place, likewise, for police precautions. From side streets as well as locations in the parklike square, detectives could command the Antique Gallery to the extent of setting up machine guns, had they so chosen. Indeed, the area was already an armed camp, the best feature being that the fact wasn't visible.

So many parking spaces were handy that patrol cars and armored trucks looked few and far apart. Uniformed police, though numerous, were too scattered to attract more than passing attention. As for the detectives, they couldn't be spotted at all. They were everywhere, by newsstands, in doorways, near subway entrances. It was a perfect setup, not for crime but against it.

The jewelry show was to open this evening, and it was already dusk. The last exhibits were arriving, but they were chiefly antiques, loaned by the directors of the gallery. Some large objects were needed to trim the exhibit room, which would look too monotonous if nothing but jewel cases were about the place.

Weston ordered his chauffeur to stop behind the gallery. There, Inspector Cardona was supervising the unloading of crates and boxes, checking on their contents. Four truckmen appeared carrying a box that measured about six by ten feet.

They paused with their burden on their shoulders, while Cardona checked the bill of lading.

The item in the packing box was an antique spinet. Looking through an antique catalogue, Cardona found the number of the exhibit and learned that a spinet was an early form of piano. So he waved the truckers through, and was examining a marble statue in an open crate when Weston's car pulled up beside him.

Briefly, Cardona reported that all was quite in order. Unless the Hydra had subsidized half of the headquarters force, there wouldn't be a chance for crime tonight.

After that quip, Joe added emphatically that

there wasn't a disloyal man in all the force. He'd picked men who had already tangled with the Hydra's followers, and Cardona's present contingent included a batch of the traffic squad who had mopped up at the theater following The Shadow's single-handed rout of Medor and his henchmen.

So the commissioner's car rolled along, with The Shadow peering from a window to catch signals from certain men he passed. They were his secret agents, on duty like Cardona's squad. They, too, were reporting all well to their chief.

There was only one thing unusual in the whole vicinity of the Antique Gallery. The Shadow didn't notice it, because the commissioner's car arrived by another street. Neither did Cardona nor the agents report it, because it could hardly be classed as important.

Two blocks away from the Antique Gallery were a pair of subway entrances, of the old kiosk type that looked like little houses set up on the sidewalk. These old structures were quite close together, because one was used only during the rush hours when the crowds were heavy. At present, some workmen were busy in the extra entrance. They were about to paint the interior, now that the rush hour was past. They were laying boards down the steps to the landing and beyond. While some began to prime their paint brushes, others put up a wooden barrier at the top of the steps and stenciled the word "Closed" upon it.

That done, the workmen suddenly lost interest in their job. They drifted away one by one, a fact which wasn't noticed because the barrier hid the steps where they had been. A few blocks distant and completely away from the Broadway square, the workers assembled anew, entered a truck containing more supplies, and drove off to complete another job.

They had a new trick, these. In identifying one another, they used the clenched-fist system, but each man opened his hand twice and stressed the fact that all fingers were extended. Anyone could count those fingers, thumbs included, at a glance.

The sign of the Hydra, with the number of fingers shown announcing the Head for whom this crew worked. Twice five told the fact that tonight Head No. 10 would strike.

How Head No. 10 expected to succeed in impossible crime was something that would be learned only when it happened. A crime was planned that was calculated to produce double surprise—this time to The Shadow as well as the law!

## CHAPTER XIV
## THE CHANGED TRAIL

THE Worldwide Friendship Society was throwing quite a dinner, to welcome new guests. Impounded under that clause, Commissioner Weston and his companions joined the banquet table. Over glasses of rare champagne supplied by one of their group, the members of the society heard Hart Ribold deliver his impassioned plea for funds.

He was a convincing speaker, this Ribold. His tone was a persuasive basso that he modulated to a musical pitch. Handsome in a virile way, Ribold had a bronzed complexion topped by light-blond hair, giving him the appearance of a Viking back from an adventurous voyage in tropic seas.

In dress, Ribold was different. Where others wore conventional evening clothes, he sported a plum-colored uniform jacket shaped to a Tuxedo cut, with a single epaulette upon its right shoulder. Below his other shoulder were ribbons and medals tastefully arranged upon his manly chest.

From what he knew about Ribold, The Shadow assumed that the suntan was a product of Palm Beach rather than Equatorial Africa. The uniform was that of a foreign air force that had been very free with honorary commissions. The medals were the sort that could be obtained through certain channels for a price.

Men like Ribold weren't uncommon among Manhattan's social set. As Cranston, the Shadow had met many of them and found them generally harmless. But the people present were taking this comic-opera character seriously. Precisely as claimed by Lloyd Casler, the self-flattering Mr. Ribold was seeking funds and getting them.

This affair was being held in a private dining room of the Hotel Metrolite. A connecting office had been hired for the occasion, and from it secretaries were bring sheaves of letters and impressive documents as fast as Ribold called for them.

Correspondence from high officials of exiled governments gave endorsement to Ribold's work. They backed his claim that if funds were available at the right time and place, much could be done to aid a united cause. It wasn't just a case of aiding the morale of airmen fighting in the forces of other nations.

Captain Ribold, as some of the letters addressed him, was planning the organization of new corps everywhere. He believed that he could reach men who were immobilized in occupied countries, smuggle them out and place them where they would count. Such an effort would require three things. All three were money.

Of the thirty-odd people present, all were willing to subscribe. Many had brought along certified checks and were tendering them to Ribold. The Shadow saw the look that Casler gave Weston, along with the nod that the commissioner returned. Then Weston came to his feet and asked just how Ribold intended to safeguard those funds.

It was a neat point. Subtly, Weston was expressing concern for Ribold, whereas he actually felt it toward the subscribers. The commissioner was handling that angle quite well, so The Shadow arose and strolled away among the guests who were crowding around Weston and Ribold.

Stepping into the little office, The Shadow found that the secretaries had gone, taking along Ribold's records.

Picking up a telephone, The Shadow made a call. There was something that he wanted, and when he learned that it could be delivered within ten minutes, he gave a satisfied laugh, then sat down to have a smoke while he waited.

DURING those ten minutes, Weston was making out well with Ribold, who was quite willing to accept suggestions. Ribold agreed that the funds should be safeguarded and offered to place them in the hands of certain persons present. When Weston insisted upon choosing the people in question, Ribold shrugged his epaulette and gave Weston the privilege.

Thereupon, Weston chose a retired jurist, Judge Kerland, who was the very symbol of integrity; a lawyer named Hubert Luhrig; and finally a prominent banker, James Aldan. Having thus combined honesty, legal skill and finance, Weston announced himself as an ex-officio member of the fund committee.

This was all accomplished when The Shadow reappeared. When he gave an inquiring look that suited Cranston, he was drawn aside by Bardell and Casler, who told him privately how his friend the commissioner had managed matters.

Lloyd Casler was particularly elated.

"Look at Ribold," he undertoned. "See the way he frowns. No wonder, with a fortune going right out of his clutch!"

At that moment, Ribold explained his frown. He was thinking of future problems, so he said. Ways in which to disburse the fund that he had raised, so that there would be no question about its proper use and that every dollar of the hundred and fifty thousand would be spent to best advantage.

He would report on these problems when he solved them. Meanwhile, he hoped that the fund would continue to accumulate. Ribold said he'd like to see it reach a quarter million.

"No wonder!" whispered Casler caustically. "The bigger it gets, the more for Ribold when he completes the flimflam. But the only future problem that really worries him is how he can manage that grab. I'd say that Captain Ribold is due for some headaches."

Judge, lawyer and banker were about to leave with the cash and certified checks. While shaking hands with them, Ribald took a few looks toward the connecting office. Weston noticed it when he joined Bardell and Casler. It was Casler who commented:

"That chap is plotting something."

Noting the glances he received, Ribold came over. In his smooth style, he suggested that the men with the funds might need protection on the way to the bank, that he'd thought of sending his secretaries along with them. The secretaries had left, but Ribold was sure he could reach them if he phoned to the hotel lobby.

"I'll do better than that," rejoined Weston. "Tell the committee to wait, Bardell. I want to talk to you, Ribold, and meanwhile, Cranston can phone headquarters to say that I want two men for special detail."

Turning as he gestured, Weston stared blankly when he found that Cranston was no longer present. Casler stated that the commissioner's friend had just remembered an important date and had left to keep it. Weston gave a deprecating grunt.

Those sudden dates that so often spirited Lamont Cranston away could all be blamed on a nuisance named Margo Lane. Without inquiring why Weston was so annoyed, Casler volunteered to make the call in Cranston's place.

From the moment that Lloyd Casler entered the adjoining office, his actions became peculiar. A gleam on his broad, blunt face, Casler took a quick look at his watch, then locked the door behind him. Crossing the office, he opened another door and found that it led to a back stairway.

Locking that door, Casler tried a third. It showed a closet where several coats and hats were hanging. Closing the closet, Casler went to the desk and picked up the telephone. Its cord was hooked in the crack of a top drawer, so Casler wrenched it loose, then dialed a number. When a voice responded, Casler spoke:

"This is Head No. 10—"

An amazing statement! Given in as insidious a tone as Casler could command, it revealed him as a master of subterfuge. As a Hydra Head, Casler was planning crime tonight, a thrust wherein his Teeth would act upon information supplied by Eyes and Ears, who could also have had much to do with the preliminary arrangements.

To cover his identity as a Hydra Head, Casler had picked a perfect alibi. He had arranged a side issue under the auspices of Commissioner Weston, in whose company Casler would be when crime struck elsewhere!

WHILE plotting his own crime, Casler had been looking for a man toward whom he could divert attention, and he had found one: Hart Ribold. Whatever the shortcomings of the pretentious captain, they could be no worse than Casler's own.

What Casler was now saying to the Ear at the other end of the wire proved that Head No. 10 considered his own future as assured.

"I've steered the commissioner the way I wanted," spoke Casler. "I'll hold him here so he can't make trouble. He's leaving the jewelry show to Cardona. We've fixed that angle."

There was a pause as Casler listened to something from the other end. Then:

"Well, what about The Shadow?" demanded Casler. "He hasn't shown up so far, has he? I tell you, he's an unknown element that has to be handled when and where he enters. I'd be willing to take my chances with The Shadow right now!"

That settled the Ear. He must have reverted to the matter of scheduled crime, for when Casler spoke again, the Head used a confirming tone.

"Correct," declared Casler, glancing at his watch. "The zero hour is nine o'clock. No change."

It was just ten minutes of nine. Replacing the phone with one hand, Casler was putting his watch away, when its dial seemed to cloud. Odd, the lighting in this office to dim itself so suddenly. While Casler puzzled, the phenomenon was explained.

Close to the Head's ear came a whispered laugh. Looking up, Casler saw why the light had faded. Between him and the wall bracket had stepped a figure cloaked in black, whose eyes bored from beneath the brim of a slouch hat.

The Shadow!

Mere moments ago, Casler had said that he'd like to meet this personage in black. Here was his chance to test the unknown element. As proof that The Shadow wasn't supernatural, Casler saw the open door of the closet and realized that the weird visitor had simply been in hiding behind the hanging coats.

If so, The Shadow had heard everything.

That alone was enough to make Casler turn murderer. If he could kill The Shadow, the Head would be clear. Casler could call it a mistake, claiming that he'd thought the cloaked master was a criminal teamed with Ribold. After all, Casler was supposed to be calling headquarters for the police commissioner. He'd naturally think that anyone who interfered must be tied up with crime.

Those were reasons why Casler boldly whipped a revolver from his pocket and aimed it at The Shadow. But the final and most important reason was The Shadow's pose. Arms folded calmly, the cloaked accuser didn't look prepared for the surprise attack that Casler gave.

The surprise proved Casler's.

**The Shadow's thumb and second finger snapped together. The result was a sharp explosion that sounded like a cannon shot.**

Up came The Shadow's hand, gunless and ungloved. Thumb and second finger snapped together, straight toward Casler's face. The result was a sharp explosion that sounded like a cannon shot. Two chemical pastes, meeting in the friction of thumb and finger, produced a burst of flame along with the huge report.*

The blast staggered Lloyd Casler.

Shaken, dazzled, the Hydra Head nearly lost his grip on the revolver while he tried vainly to glimpse The Shadow anew. All that Casler saw was blackness, enveloping himself and the desk against which he leaned. Living blackness that gripped Casler and delivered another of those weird laughs that came as a whisper of doom.

Blindly, Casler was reeling toward the door, the gun plucked from his hand. He thought he was getting clear of The Shadow, not realizing that he was actually being guided to further disaster.

For when Casler managed to unbolt the door, The Shadow gripped him again, sending him into a whirl that carried the Head away from the door, then back to it, into the clutch of Commissioner Weston and a pair of husky hotel detectives who had started for the office when they heard The Shadow's blast.

Before Casler could even begin to alibi himself, full attention was captured by The Shadow's laugh. The cloaked master was opening the top drawer of the desk to display a flat recording machine, which was the thing that The Shadow had ordered earlier.

Beside the device was a broken thread, which The Shadow had attached to the telephone cord. In jerking the cord from the edge of the drawer, Casler had broken the thread and started the recorder!

Now the machine was speaking back in Casler's own voice, disclosing him as the tenth Head of the Hydra and revealing that the zero hour was at hand for his thrust at the Antique Gallery. As that criminal confession ended, the laugh of The Shadow came anew.

Weston and his companions looked for the master in black. He was gone, through the outer door, which he had opened while their attention was on Casler's recorded statement. This laugh that they heard was the one that The Shadow had first given Casler. The recorder had picked up that sinister mirth.

The Shadow had left on a rapid trip to the Antique Gallery, a race against time, wherein he hoped to conquer crime at its own zero hour!

## CHAPTER XV
## WHEELS OF CRIME

ALREADY wheels of crime were on the move. Lloyd Casler, the tenth Hydra Head, had started them—human cogwheels, deft in evil. But they weren't the only wheels that were to produce results.

One wheel had already done its stint. It was the circular turntable of the recording device in the desk drawer. That wheel provided an odd aftermath, hard upon the mechanical laugh that symbolized The Shadow's recent departure.

The recorder issued a terrific bang!—a replica of the explosion with which The Shadow had startled Casler. This time the sound marked Casler's recuperation. He sprang away from the desk, shaking off the grip of the hotel detectives. Punching his way past Bardell in the doorway, Casler raced across the banquet room.

Ribold was too far away to block him. The fancy-dressed captain began barking orders, but no hands could stop Casler's frenzied surge.

Out through another door, down a stairway to the lobby, the frantic Head was off to safety.

Spurring Casler, came a mocking laugh. It was the final taunt that The Shadow had given during the office scene. Casler snarled happily as he heard it. This time, The Shadow wasn't here to back his powerful mirth. Yet the laugh still had merit.

Though Lloyd Casler didn't realize it, The Shadow was no longer lopping Hydra heads, unless dire circumstances should compel him. Instead, he was seeking to ensnare the various leaders while breaking up their crimes. For the way in which the Hydra branched was its most insidious feature.

Wheels were whirling The Shadow to his appointment with crime—the swift wheels of Moe's cab, which had been waiting outside the Hotel Metrolite ever since The Shadow went there. But with all Moe's efforts, the cab was some blocks short of its goal when the zero hour struck.

Visitors at the jewelry show heard the nine-o'clock clang of a great clock in a tower across the square. They were giving the time little heed, for the famed crown jewels were on display.

Beside the exhibit stood Inspector Joe Cardona, somewhat annoyed by the way some people mistook him for a guide. Joe kept gesturing to a withery old gentleman who was describing the various gems.

---

*Note: Because The Shadow's explosive powder used in this instance is too dangerous for any but the most experienced to use, we do not reveal the nature of its formula, so that the inexperienced might not attempt this experiment and thereby suffer harm.
—Maxwell Grant.

These were the crown jewels of many countries, brought to America for safety, placed on display that the proceeds from their show might go to the aid of refugees from those lands. Crowns, tiaras, scepters, rings, and even sword hilts, provided a glittering array of color from the closely guarded stand on which they reposed.

Diamonds were, of course, the main attraction, though rubies, emeralds, sapphires and some rare specimens of topaz were in abundance. The lecturer was finished with the diamonds and was pointing out the rubies.

Close to the display, Clyde Burke and Harry Vincent were noting the faces around them and finding none that was suspicious. As visitors to the show, these agents of the Shadow had so far failed to scent a trace of budding crime. Nor, for that matter, had Inspector Cardona.

"This immense gem," declared the lecturer, pointing to a great red stone that studded a sword hilt, "was long regarded as the world's largest ruby. A misnomer, because in the actual sense there is no true ruby. Garnets, carbuncles, other ruddy stones, were all termed rubies by the ancients.

"The Oriental ruby, most precious of the entire category, is properly a red variety of sapphire. Being the most valued of ruddy gems, it has claimed the title of ruby. If this great stone"—he gestured to the sword hilt—"were of Oriental origin, its value would be fabulous.

"Unfortunately, it is only a spinel, identified as such in recent years. A spinel is a gemstone found in various color varieties, among them red. So you are viewing not the world's largest ruby, but a fine specimen of spinel."

The repeated term was striking home to Cardona. Half aloud, Joe muttered:

"A spinel. Where did I hear that before? Spinel... spinel! One looks like a ruby and the other a piano. Spinet—"

With that, Cardona turned to look at the antiques, hoping he'd see the spinet. But there wasn't anything resembling a piano among the ancient furniture that was ranged to cover barren spots amid the showcases. Behind the exhibit of crown jewels, Joe saw a fancy, gold-decorated screen. Past the screen, he spied a corner of the six-by-ten packing box that contained the spinet.

Before more than a flicker of suspicion could cross Joe's mind, crime crashed through.

THERE was a roar from behind the screen, muffled only for a few seconds. Then, with a splintering smash, the front of the box ripped wide. Something avalanched forth, flattening the screen, and hurtled like a miniature juggernaut toward the display of crown jewels.

All the visitors dodged, with men's shouts and women's shrieks punctuating the process. The withery lecturer went away in a hurried dive. Harry and Clyde were among those who cleared a path as they would have for a raging bull. For the thing that was hurtling at them meant business.

It was a bantam automobile, spurting with a power that threatened mayhem to anyone who blocked its course!

This was the thing that truckers had brought into the Antique Gallery. Light in weight, four men could easily carry it on their shoulders. Instead of an old-fashioned piano, Cardona was seeing the latest type of midget car, a two-passenger coupe occupied by its advertised human quota.

Two Teeth of the Hydra!

The driver of the bantam car could have cut a vicious swath right through the witnesses, but he didn't. Instead, he jammed the brakes and the midget menace shrieked to a halt beside the display of crown gems. The door on the right flipped open and the man beside the driver scooped the plush drape that covered the jewel stand.

Bundling a vast fortune of gems as a waiter would gather up silverware when removing a tablecloth, the daring thief hauled his wholesale prize into the tiny car and slammed the door.

Only Cardona could have stopped it. He'd been standing at one side of the display, hence hadn't needed to dodge along with The Shadow's agents and detectives who were in the car's path. But Joe was handicapped very unfortunately. He was on the wrong side of the car. Before he could get around to the right, the door had banged shut.

The way ahead was clear. The midget machine had transformed itself from a mechanized menace into a getaway car. Two men made a valiant effort to stop it when they grabbed for its rear bumper. Those two were Harry and Clyde. If they'd gotten their grip, they could have lifted the rear wheels of the undersized car and kept them whirling uselessly.

But the car spurted off too soon. It was roaring down an aisle between showcases, ducking antique couches and other furniture while Cardona tried to stop it in his own way, with gunfire. Other detectives joined in with their revolvers, but no shots counted.

You could armor-plate a midget car and supply it with bulletproof glass and tires, just as with a full-sized vehicle.

The Hydra had.

Deluged by bashing slugs, the peewee vehicle reached the street door, dented by impact. Like a hummingbird buzzing out through a window, it hopped the curb and spurted across the square.

Mere sight of the tiny car was enough for Cardona's outside squad. All the machinery of the law went into motion to make the escape short-lived.

Patrol cars were wheeling in from side streets. Big armored trucks were heaving up to throw a blockade. But the midget car was as difficult to catch as a greased pig. It could take to sidewalks and it did, as soon as traffic snarled about it. Cut off from a corner, it wheeled through the park, trimming benches so closely that a group of bums went diving over the bench backs to escape the half-pint menace.

What it lacked in size, the bantam made up for in speed and maneuverability. All the while, its occupants were safe from the steady hail of lead that flew about it. One car alone, of all in the vicinity, could have given the midget a hard run. That was Moe's cab, arriving with The Shadow.

Moe would have found a way to cut off the thing's escape, for he could handle his hack like a stunt driver. But there were places where the cab couldn't go, and one of them was through the mess of traffic that cluttered the avenue from curb to curb. The sidewalks, wide enough for the midget auto, were just too narrow for the cab.

Still, the crooks didn't seem to have a chance. Streets were blocked, and the sirens of motorcycles told that a new class of vehicles were in the chase. The trouble was that the cycle cops were vulnerable, which the men in the bantam weren't. A gun was chattering from the top of the small car's window when it neared the subway kiosk where workmen had begun a paint job.

With a rip like its departure from the crate, the tiny car carved through the flimsy barrier and zoomed down the steps into the subway, using lengthwise boards for a roadway, the very boards that the fake painters placed there beforehand!

MOTORCYCLES rallied to the chase. From side streets where they had dodged, they converged upon the kiosk, racing to see who could reach it first.

The cop who won wasn't happy over it. His motorcycle took a jolt and he disappeared down the opening, while others pulled up their two-wheeled steeds and tumbled to the street, in preference to a longer fall.

The men in the midget car had stopped at the bottom of the subway steps just long enough to grab the lower ends of the boards and haul them to the bottom. That done, they were on their way again, traveling underground.

Officers and plainclothes men were dashing for the various subway entrances all around the square. They still thought they had a chance to trap the midget car where it was. Sooner or later, they would hound it to a subway platform. Police were getting to those platforms to make sure the crooks didn't hop from the car and run along the tracks or board a train.

Meanwhile, The Shadow's cab was gone.

To Moe's amazement, his black-cloaked chief ordered him to wheel from the beleaguered square and drive across to the other side of town. It wasn't until the trip was underway that Moe realized what it might produce.

Never calculating that the subway could have played the part it did, the police had treated the situation as a local one. They knew that two subways crossed at the square and that both were express stops. That meant several platforms on two levels would have to be covered. But the police had just about forgotten that those subways linked to a concourse that led to another subway on the opposite side of town!

When they remembered, it would be too late. On foot, they couldn't hope to overtake the tiny automobile. By the time they hauled motorcycles down the steps, a mechanized pursuit would be useless. Of all the trickery that the Hydra's men had shown, their final stroke was best—that of leading the police underground, only to learn that they should have stayed on the street and sent cars everywhere to cut off the crooks wherever they might reappear.

That was exactly what The Shadow planned, and he wasn't trusting to mere chance. The Hydra had gauged this thing so well that there was a chance it could have been handled too well. On the barren cross street, The Shadow's cab was making as good time as the midget car in the underground concourse. Therein lay his hope that the Hydra had itself provided a clue.

The Shadow's hunch proved justified.

Reaching the far side of town, Moe was up against a tough proposition. There were subway exits here in plenty, a dozen of them, some several blocks apart. How to find the right one, was the question; but it answered itself, thanks to the Hydra.

As Moe cruised rapidly in and about this sector, still following The Shadow's order, a closed exit came in sight. The Hydra had overdone its trick, by providing the tiny getaway car with a quick way out when it finished its underground trip. The painters had come here after finishing their first job, and in preparing the last lap for the getaway they had planted a marker for The Shadow!

From within the cab, Moe heard a whispered laugh. Needing no further order from The Shadow, Moe plunged the brake pedal and brought the cab to the spot where the crooks would soon emerge.

Wheels of crime were still in motion, rolling perpetrators to a new meeting with The Shadow!

## CHAPTER XVI
## WEALTH REGAINED

LIGHTS out, Moe's cab was a lurking thing in darkness, while his chief, The Shadow, waited. The cab had come by a straight route, whereas its midget prey had veered considerably. This accounted for the difference, but during the wait it was quite evident that the Hydra's strategy had completely baffled the law.

Sounds of sirens were so distant as to be practically negligible. Only The Shadow had guessed where the trail would lead. This time, The Shadow was ahead of crime!

To Moe, the game seemed as good as won, until he heard a singular whisper close behind him. It was The Shadow's warning tone, ordering Moe to keep low, which often meant that Moe would have to claw the floorboards. Such a warning promised shooting, which made Moe think that The Shadow's keen ear had heard the underground approach of the midget getaway car.

As Moe slid down into the seat, his last glance in the mirror showed him another cab pulling up behind his own. He realized then that The Shadow had looked even farther ahead. The arriving cab belonged to the Hydra. It was here for transfer purpose when the midget car arrived.

Almost inaudible was the soft thud of the rear door in Moe's cab. Absolutely invisible was the cloaked shape that slid to the darkened sidewalk and glided under the shelter of one cab back to the other. Mobsters had extinguished their lights while coasting up to Moe's cab. Now men were creeping out to slug the unfortunate hackie who had accidentally—so they thought—chosen their rendezvous as a parking spot.

Those Teeth of the Hydra never reached Moe's cab.

Blackness whirled literally among them. It was as if night itself had solidified to strike like an invisible thunderbolt. The guns that slugged were The Shadow's. They found targets with every stroke. Three thugs literally melted with hardly an outcry. Not one even found a gun trigger, for they hadn't intended to start shooting this soon.

In the cab up front, Moe heard The Shadow's low, triumphant laugh and popped up behind the wheel. No need laying low any longer, Moe knew.

Another cabby heard that strange mirth from the darkness where figures were mysteriously thudding the curb. He reached for a gun and thrust it through the window, this man in the Hydra's cab. A Tooth like the rest, he was ready to do his bit for Head No. 10.

His bit was simply proving that he couldn't take it. In from the opposite window came a gloved hand that pressed a cold gun muzzle against the driver's neck. Wilting, the crook let his own gun clatter outside his cab. His hands were rising, when The Shadow ordered them down again.

Then, with harder pressure of his gun, The Shadow was ordering the fellow to get going, which the cabby did. How his hands managed to grip the steering wheel was something quite remarkable; but the speed with which the cab shot away was to be expected. The driver simply let his foot jam to the floor and stay there.

Back at his own cab, The Shadow found Moe climbing anxiously out. Hearing his chief's whisper, Moe subsided, to learn why The Shadow had sent the other cab away. The Shadow simply stated that since only one cab was supposed to be waiting here, he'd sent the other away. Moe began to understand.

"And say, chief," declared Moe, "can those Blue Spots travel! They're a new job, those hacks. How they'll make dough, I don't know, with so many companies already in the business. I'll bet that guy you just chased still doesn't know how lucky—"

Moe broke off at a whisper from The Shadow, who was now inside the cab. There was a muffled roar below ground, a hard rising spurt, the clatter of boards that served as tracks. Then, like a jack-in-the-box, out popped the midget car that was bringing the crown gems!

SMASHING through the thin boards of the subway exit, the mechanical jackrabbit took a bounce across the sidewalk and stopped by the curb. Its doors popped open and out sprang its two-man crew, one carrying a large suitcase in which he had packed the royal jewels.

While he was dashing to the cab with it, the other crook shoved the front of the stalled bantam and sent the tiny car backward down the subway steps.

At that moment, the cab door was opening. The crook who shoved the bag inside let go of it and snatched for a gun. He didn't reach the weapon, nor did his lips finish the savage oath they started. An interruption came in the shape of an automatic, landing hard against the skull of the astonished jewel thief.

The other thug heard nothing because of the clatter that the bantam car was making as it zigzagged, unguided, down the subway steps. When the fellow turned, he saw the cab pulling away; at the same time, the chug of a motorcycle joined the wail of a patrol-car siren from a few blocks away.

This Hydra Tooth didn't realize that he was

being given a chance for short-lived flight on foot, with peaceable surrender to the law. He thought he was being double-crossed by pals, who preferred not to wait for him, now that the police were coming to this side of town. Angrily, the crook pulled a gun and opened fire at the departing cab.

An automatic answered with a single stab. The Tooth reeled, wounded. The Shadow's shot was necessary, for with a few bullets more, his frantic foe would have found the window of the cab. Looking back, The Shadow saw his adversary sag beside the huddled figures who had been lying behind Moe's cab. The other man from the midget car was caved in the gutter.

This concluding episode had proven very rapid. The last shots came amid the echoes of the final crash from the midget car when it reached the subway platform. The wail of the approaching siren had halted just before the gunfire; hence the shots were heard.

As ill luck had it, a patrol car zoomed down the very street that Moe intended to take. When the cab veered to take a new route, the men in the patrol car saw it and the chase was on. Dodging one patrol car was a simple task for Moe, but by the time he did it, motorcycles were in the chase.

They were everywhere, those pests, passing word to each other that crooks had transferred to a cab, which didn't make it pleasant for The Shadow, considering that he didn't care to throw away a suitcase full of rare crown jewels. So he kept them, but with the knowledge that he would take the blame for the crime if found with such baubles in his possession.

Calmly, The Shadow guided Moe through devious routes that promised safety. Strange, how this cloaked fugitive could tell the exact locations of the pursuing vehicles. Time and again, Moe cut across a street thinking he was going right into a snare, only to see a motorcycle going the other way.

Usually, the cops spotted the cab, but they had to turn around to go after it, and by then, Moe was elsewhere. Cops were constantly overhauling the wrong cabs and stopping them, which helped a great deal; but there were still too many in motorcycles.

In fact, Moe felt that, for once, the game was through when The Shadow ordered him to wheel through a side street near the Times Square area. Even worse, The Shadow called for a stop midway through the block.

As Moe pressed down on the brake pedal, the cab slewed beside a limousine that was parked in front of a nightclub. Moe didn't hear what happened, nor did the drowsy chauffeur in the limousine. Out one window, in through another went a heavy suitcase of untold value. With that transfer of the crown gems from cab to limousine, The Shadow gave Moe the order for another spurt.

The motorcycle cops proved too pesky. Twenty blocks to the south, one of them overhauled the cab and inquired about its hurry. A second cop arrived and each yanked open a door. Moe gave an anxious look in back, then opened his eyes wide when he saw that his passenger was no longer The Shadow. Nor was there any suitcase.

In Cranston's guise, The Shadow was leaning back in the seat smoking a thin cigar. His cloak and hat were tucked away in a special drawer beneath the rear seat. He'd put his guns there, too, in case the cops decided to frisk him. But they weren't in a frisky mood.

"Say!" exclaimed one. "Here's the pal who handed us those tickets to the theater!"

"We want to thank you, mister," expressed the other. "What a party that turned out to be!"

The Shadow was shaking hands with both the cops. When they got around to the present question, he told them that he hadn't seen any cab that appeared to have crooks in it; at least, no such cab in flight. He'd noted a parked cab that looked suspicious, but the cops told him the one they wanted wouldn't be stopping anywhere.

"When you see the police commissioner," remarked The Shadow, "give him my regards. We're old friends, you know. In fact, I think I'll pick up my car and stop around to see him shortly. Maybe this very evening."

As the cab pulled away, the motorcycle cops went to a phone and called headquarters. They were told to report to Inspector Cardona at the Cobalt Club, where he had gone to see Commissioner Weston.

MEANWHILE, The Shadow was putting in a call around the corner. It was another of those Cranston to Cranston conversations that brought prompt results. Called to a phone booth in a nightclub, the real Cranston caught the drift of things. Margo Lane was finishing a dance with another partner when Cranston joined her and suggested that they leave.

In the limousine, Margo almost stumbled over a suitcase, which Cranston promptly lifted to the seat beside him. He was smiling somewhat cryptically when Margo asked where they were going. She learned the answer after a northward trip, when the cab pulled up in front of the Cobalt Club.

Some motorcycle cops were coming out, and others were arriving on the street. They nodded to Cranston as he went by carrying the suitcase. Inside the club, Cranston and Margo reached the grillroom which Weston had turned into his headquarters. Interrupting a report by Inspector

Cardona, Cranston planked the suitcase on the table and opened it.

Margo gasped at sight of the fabulous crown jewels, but her surprise was mild. Weston and Cardona were pawing through the gems, totally confounded, while motorcycle cops came flocking back at Weston's bellow. Then Cranston was explaining how he'd found the suitcase in his limousine, entirely by accident—a thing to which Margo could testify, and did.

There were two things that still puzzled Margo.

She couldn't understand how Lamont had turned himself into The Shadow, recovered the jewels for which the whole police force were searching, and still stayed around the nightclub as much as he had. Margo was sure she hadn't been absent from Lamont for more than a single dance. Whatever miracles he'd performed as The Shadow, he must have managed them in something less than ten minutes at a stretch.

Which would have caused Margo to decide that someone other than The Shadow had stifled crime tonight, except for the second fact that puzzled her.

That was: when Cranston found the suitcase in the limousine, he didn't open it. So how could he have known the gems were in it unless he had personally reclaimed them as The Shadow?

Again, Margo's case was mild.

As she and Lamont left the Cobalt Club to the congratulations of Cranston's friends, the traffic cops, two new officers arrived on motorcycles and alighted to learn the news. They happened to be the pair who had overhauled The Shadow's cab twenty blocks the other side of the street where the nightclub was.

They stared very hard at Lamont Cranston.

"So the guy did have the jewels!" exclaimed one. "And he brought them here!"

"That's what he meant when he said he was going to see the commissioner," put in the other. "It shows he was right all the time."

"But how did he get here ahead of us?"

"Say... now you're asking something! Don't that beat all?"

The two cops stared at the departing limousine as though they expected it to sprout wings and take off over the Empire State Building. The more they tried to explain the thing, the more it bothered them, considering that they'd lost but little time in coming to the Cobalt Club.

To those two cops, The Shadow's latest victory over the Hydra was dropping right out of mind. They knew that The Shadow could work wonders. But if they'd been asked to name the champion at such business, they'd have voiced their candidate as Lamont Cranston!

## CHAPTER XVII
### CRIME COMES C.O.D.

THE blue light glimmered in The Shadow's sanctum. Long, deft fingers were sorting through reports from agents. From one of those fingers gleamed a rare gem, a fire opal that changed from hue to hue. This stone, known as a girasol, wasn't a souvenir from the crown jewels that The Shadow had reclaimed.

Rather, this girasol that The Shadow had worn for years was the magnet that had attracted the other gems into his hands. For never did The Shadow fare forth without this strange talisman, which had carried him through threats of death that had seemingly required more than mortal effort to survive.

First of the reports were from Rutledge Mann. They went back to the death of Edmund Glencoe, a Hydra case that still was unidentified as such by the law. Mann was seeking data that would prove murder and robbery in that instance.

The evidence looked negative. The funds paid to Glencoe's estate had been used to purchase stocks in legitimate companies, as he provided. All the companies were doing well, their shares selling at a premium. Bardell and others were buying into them, and Mann's advice, as a broker, was that either The Shadow or Cranston should do the same.

Passing from that routine report, The Shadow found one from Moe. The cab had been in an accident and would need a few weeks for repairs. Substitute cabs were hard to find, so Moe was taking a job with a company for a while. He'd still be available when The Shadow needed him, but fares would count when run up on the meter.

The Shadow's low laugh was whimsical as he finished that brief report.

Clippings on The Shadow's table told of his victory over the Hydra, and described the widespread hunt that the police were making for Lloyd Casler. The Shadow had already read those, and they didn't matter much. He preferred that Casler should be alive and at large, rather than have new Hydra Heads appear.

Hunted by the law, with most of his crew eradicated, Head No. 10 was Eyeless and Toothless. At most, he could still have only a few Ears left.

One more report was needed, from Clyde Burke. It hadn't arrived, so The Shadow reached for the earphones. Before he grasped them, a tiny light blinked, announcing a call from Burbank.

The contact man stated that Lamont Cranston was on the wire. The Shadow said to put the call through.

Phoning from his home in New Jersey,

**CLYDE BURKE**

Cranston begged to be excused that evening. He felt his present popularity would handicap The Shadow. With the Hydra still a pressing menace, every motorcycle cop in Manhattan felt it a duty to convoy Cranston's limousine each time it appeared in town.

"I'm too much of a hero," complained Cranston. "I hope you settle this Hydra business promptly, so I'll be forgotten. What's more, I can't see Margo because she asks too many questions, and if I don't see her, she'll cook up more.

"I wish you'd take over a while, old man. It would be to our mutual interest. You can get around places in that cloak of yours without being recognized as me. So you won't be bothered by the motorcycle squad, and when you meet Margo you can give her a few answers which I can't."

Granting Cranston a deserved leave of absence, The Shadow resumed his chat with Burbank and inquired about Burke's report. He learned that Clyde was still at the commissioner's office and would probably be heard from shortly.

INTERWOVEN through all The Shadow's campaigns were many important twists. Clyde Burke's visit to the commissioner was one of them.

Clyde's effort to halt crime at its source during the jewel robbery had not escaped Cardona's notice. In return for services rendered, the inspector had promised Clyde an inside track on future stories.

Cardona was making good his promise, by inviting Clyde to a conference where he had a reasonable right to be, anyway, since he'd figured in one Hydra case. At Weston's office, Clyde had met Dustin Bardell, who was still at a loss regarding members for his civic committee.

"It's impossible to trust anyone!" Bardell was declaiming, with one of those hand thwacks that struck the desk resoundingly. "When Lloyd Casler turned out to be a Hydra Head, my faith in friends was utterly destroyed!"

"Why not look elsewhere than among your friends?" queried Weston. "What about Hart Ribold?"

Bardell's eyes narrowed sharply. "Can you be serious, commissioner?"

"Certainly," returned Weston. "It was Casler who threw suspicion on Ribold. That ought to prove Ribold's integrity."

"It doesn't follow, commissioner," argued Bardell. "I still don't trust Ribold. He might have made away with that fund, if you hadn't appointed trustworthy men to keep it."

"If he had," declared Weston brusquely, "he'd have done crime his own way, not the Hydra's. We are sure that Ribold isn't a Hydra Head. Mark that to his credit."

Bardell wrote Ribold's name on a sheet of paper. Weston then told him to begin another list, headed by the names of Kerland, Luhrig and Aldan—judge, lawyer, and banker—who were holding the Worldwide Friendship Society fund.

"There are three good men," asserted Weston, "but we can keep them for the future. This evening, I shall confer with them regarding the fund. After that, they may be candidates for the civic committee. And now—"

The commissioner paused in a manner so impressive that Clyde knew his story was coming up. Taking some report sheets that Cardona handed him, Weston glanced from Bardell to Clyde and asked:

"Did either of you ever hear of Ira Ilchester?"

"Why, certainly," returned Bardell promptly. "Ilchester is noted for his philanthropic achievements."

"His latest being the gift of his very valuable library," added Clyde. "He turned it over to an upstate university. Before that—"

Bardell broke in with a recitation of Ilchester's earlier endowments, since they had begun years ago, at a time that Bardell remembered but Clyde didn't. However, the reporter was able to correct Bardell as he went along. Bardell had lost track of Ilchester's later philanthropies.

"That's all I need to hear," declared Weston. "It proves that Ilchester is more interested in humanity than in wealth. Therefore, we can accept whatever he says as valid."

Thinking that he was going to obtain a committee member, Bardell started to put Ilchester's name on paper, when Weston stopped him.

"Ilchester is no longer active," stated Weston. "We cannot ask him to help us uncover Hydra Heads. We must do that for him. We must find at least one Head on his account. Ilchester has been threatened by The Hydra."

From Cardona's reports, Weston laid bare the Ilchester situation. The philanthropist had been hearing from a mysterious extortionist who liked to deal in the number twelve. Phone calls had come at noon and midnight, all bearing the same demand: that Ilchester pay the sum of fifty thousand dollars, or take unstated consequences.

True to the number twelve, the unknown persecutor had sent messages in packages delivered to Ilchester's home. Every dozen eggs included an extortion note. When Ilchester ordered new silverware, there had been a message with each twelve-piece batch. An encyclopedia which happened to come in twelve volumes contained a loose threat note in each book.

"What Ilchester fears is abduction," stated Weston. "He's been living in a bomb shelter that was dug in his cellar some months ago. He went so deep with the shelter that he struck an old water main and had to have it cemented over.

"He decided that was deep enough for a bomb shelter." With a slight smile, Weston produced a picture of the cellar. "But it wouldn't do against this terrorist whom Ilchester terms 'No. 12.' That title that Ilchester chose at random should suggest something to you."

"Another Hydra Head!" exclaimed Clyde.

"Head No. 12!" added Bardell. "The Heads have probably reached that total, since Casler's number was Ten!"

"That is my opinion," agreed Weston. "And Head Twelve has informed Ilchester that the deadline will be twelve o'clock the night of the twelfth. Which means"—the commissioner gestured to his calendar—"that Ilchester's limit will be midnight this very evening!"

CLYDE couldn't hold back his enthusiasm over such a story. Telling him he'd have to hold it for tomorrow's newspaper, Weston assigned Clyde to a meeting with Ilchester this evening.

Clyde went out to call his newspaper, the *Classic*. In the meantime Weston phoned the club to see if Cranston happened to be there.

Cranston wasn't, but before Weston could put in a call to New Jersey, his friend rang up. Needless to say, it was The Shadow, phoning after receiving a rapid report from Clyde. Repeating the details of the Ilchester case, Weston asked Cranston to visit the threatened man that evening.

The idea was this: Ilchester simply would not trust the police inside the house, fearing that No. 12 would notice their arrival and use extreme measures in retaliation. Between them, Weston and Cardona had wheedled him into inviting other guests. With people present, Ilchester's abduction would prove difficult.

Naturally, police would be on hand outdoors. Inspector Cardona was taking the assignment, with a few handpicked men, the sort who could stay undercover. As for the party, if Cranston could suggest suitable persons to attend it, Weston would be grateful.

Stating first that he'd reach Ilchester's before midnight, The Shadow suggested that Harry Vincent be invited. Weston approved the choice, since Harry rated well with Clyde Burke, the two having teamed against crime at the jewelry show.

Adding that if Vincent had a girlfriend for the evening, her presence should be suitable, too, The Shadow hung up. The conclusion of his call irked Weston immensely.

"Cranston and that Lane girl again!" snapped Weston. "She's dated him this evening, so he wants other guests to bring their girlfriends, or he won't show up at Ilchester's."

"That Lane dame!" gruffed Cardona. "She's getting to be a milestone around Cranston's neck!"

"You mean millstone," corrected Weston. "Still, it doesn't matter. Both are heavy enough. Nevertheless"—an idea struck Weston—"some feminine charm would help the occasion. It would look like a genuine party to the Hydra's spies, if ladies were present. Call up Vincent, inspector, and ask him to bring a girl along."

LEAVING the sanctum, The Shadow was enjoying a laugh at Weston's partial expense. The Shadow's suggestion had solved a pressing problem. He'd decided how to postpone Margo's questions, perhaps to sidetrack them permanently. Through Burbank, The Shadow was instructing Harry to invite Margo to Ilchester's party.

Thus Margo wouldn't meet The Shadow until nearly midnight, by which time the situation would be tense. If the Hydra should take over the party in the shape of Head No. 12, enough things would happen to make Margo forget the previous episode involving Cranston.

Darkness had already settled; hence The Shadow found his cloaked garb to his liking. Contacting Moe, The Shadow found him driving a Blue Spot cab. As they cruised along, with the meter ticking very slowly, Moe talked about the taxicab company that was employing him.

"It's like you thought, chief," informed Moe. "There's a bunch of deadpans working for this outfit. A couple of dozen hacks on the street, with a zombie back of every wheel."

"Do they know your lingo?" queried The Shadow.

"How can I tell?" demanded Moe. "They don't open their faces except to eat. Take tonight, for instance. I never saw so many rush jobs. While we were in the one-arm lunch joint across from the garage, the checker pops in and orders five guys onto the street all at once. I was the only Blue Spot driver left in the hash house."

The Shadow was keeping a strict lookout for other Blue Spot cabs. He noted one parked in front of a pretentious apartment house on the avenue that Moe was following. Telling Moe to pull up beside the company cab, The Shadow added a question for his own driver to ask.

Moe piped it from alongside.

"Hey, Blue Boy! Seen any coolie cabs around?"

"How would I know?" retorted the deadpan in the other Blue Spot. "I ain't been down to Chinatown!"

Wheeling along, Moe spoke eagerly to The Shadow.

"That did it, chief!" declaimed Moe. "One crack at your suggestion and I found out what I couldn't get for three days! That guy isn't even imitation McCoy! If he was—"

"He wouldn't have confused a coolie cab with Chinatown," put in The Shadow. "He would have found out that the coolies are the drivers who are stationed at the ferries, so-called because they work long shifts."

Moe nodded. He was particularly pleased when The Shadow told him to keep cruising this area. Moe sensed from his chief's tone that The Shadow's keen brain was thinking in terms of crime. Oddly, though, the evening was yet young, and this wasn't Ilchester's neighborhood.

Therefore, other crime must be brewing, though The Shadow had sound reasons for linking it with the Hydra. Considering the unique methods used by Hydra Heads, as displayed by Mance, Medor and Casler, The Shadow was again expecting something startling or novel.

Nor would The Shadow be disappointed on that score, should he manage to witness the scheduled events of evil. Tonight, crime was operating on a sound merchandising system. It was coming C.O.D.

Cash on delivery to the Hydra!

## CHAPTER XVIII
## HEADS OFF AND ON

A CAB was rolling slowly along a side street, its driver acting as if he'd lost his way. An impatient man in cape and high silk hat wagged a cane through the window to the driver's seat and snapped testily:

"Come, my man! Make up your mind, or I'll be late to the opera!"

The cab stopped under a light, while the driver thumbed a street guide. The blue spot on the door was quite conspicuous. At last the driver started again, remarking to his passenger:

"I'm headed the wrong way. I'll cut through this alley to the next street. That will fix us."

It fixed them, right enough. The alley widened into a courtyard, where lights were glowing. A man stepped up and opened the door, to press a gun against the passenger's chest. Coming out with raised hands, the man with the high hat gave a hopeful look back to the street from which they had come.

Therewith, the victim's hope became despair. There wasn't any street, nothing but a solid wall of brick! Then, still gasping with amazement, the silk-hatted man was piloted around the corner of the courtyard, to find other rueful prisoners like himself.

**HARRY VINCENT**

They were seated under a low roof fitted with large panes of frosted glass that covered the entire courtyard. All had come in Blue Spot cabs, for others of these vehicles were parked across the court. The cab drivers, men with hardened faces, were keeping guard with guns.

Tables were spread for a buffet supper, with thuggish waiters presiding, but none of the guests was inclined to eat. They knew one another, for they were all members of the Worldwide Friendship Society. As for their host, he was the fanciful Captain Ribold, wearing his honorary uniform with its customary display of medals.

"Relax, everybody," suggested Ribold, in his eager tone. "You are all worth more alive than dead. I am not treating you like goods delivered C.O.D., though in fact you are. I hired this forgotten dining garden for your benefit, so you may as well enjoy it."

A buzzer sounded and Ribold stepped to a deep wall to press a switch. Those near enough to the corner saw an amazing happening in the alley. The front wall rose inward on hinges to admit a Blue Spot cab. Once the vehicle was past, the baffler dropped again. Another piece of human baggage was delivered when the cab stopped.

Another cab was approaching along the street out front. This one contained a very observant passenger in the person of Hubert Luhrig.

The lawyer was shrewd enough to suspect that something was wrong. His driver had been acting queerly ever since leaving Luhrig's apartment house for the Cobalt Club.

Temporarily ignoring the driver, Luhrig reached for a revolver that he carried under special permit, and looked to see who might be lurking on the street. All appeared serene, particularly in front of a two-story brick house that was wedged between two other buildings. The only peculiar thing about the house was its lack of front steps. Its closed door was on the sidewalk level; the windows above showed drawn shades.

Just when Luhrig was beginning to relax, he saw the housefront rising inward. A dummy housefront, its wall of canvas painted to resemble brick, with door and windows!

Before Luhrig could shake off his surprise, the cab was wheeling into the alley that the dummy front had hidden. By the time the lawyer could haul his gun from his pocket, he had no chance to use it.

His cab was in a courtyard, where someone opening the door was displaying a gun of his own. Letting his revolver slide back in his pocket, Luhrig came out with hands raised. He was marched to the group over which Ribold presided.

"The visitor we have awaited," announced Ribold with a smile. "If others come, they will be welcome, but we can now proceed with business. My terms are simple. I want a ransom for your persons, in the form of funds already paid. I refer to the subscriptions that you so obligingly raised at my behest."

Ribold was speaking chiefly to Luhrig, who met him with an angry glare. To which Ribold responded:

"It may help matters if I introduce myself as Hydra Head Twelve. Our organization owns the Blue Spot Cab Co., whose drivers were assigned to pick you up and bring you here. My lookout is admitting only those cabs, so you have no chance of rescue.

"In fact, the police have no idea that this could even happen. I decoyed them to the home of a gentleman named Ira Ilchester. I threatened him with death at midnight unless he paid over a given sum. Whether I choose to collect from Ilchester has nothing to do with yourselves."

STEPPING to a table, Ribold picked up a telephone and handed it to Luhrig.

"Call Commissioner Weston," ordered Ribold, in a grating tone. "Tell him that you want to talk with Judge Kerland and James Aldan, the banker. State that you have checked my last report concerning disbursement of the fund; that you have contacted a majority of the society and that they agree I should receive the fund tonight. Make it impressive, Luhrig, for yours is only one of the lives at stake, should you fail!"

Luhrig made the call, while mopping perspiration from his high forehead. The lawyer had a determined jaw and he kept thrusting it as he talked. Finished, Luhrig sat down heavily, too weak to glare.

"I settled it," he declared. "Kerland and Aldan took me at my word. The commissioner would have been easy, too, if he hadn't kept talking to that fool Bardell, who shouldn't have been there anyway. Bardell kept telling him that he shouldn't accept one man's say-so, not even mine."

The Teeth who served Hydra Head Twelve were moving forward with their guns. Ribold waved them back, then stepped to the wall to press the switch in answer to another buzz from the lookout. While a gun-laden Tooth was bringing in another prisoner, Ribold demanded:

"So how did you settle it, Luhrig?"

"The commissioner asked if others would call him," replied Luhrig. "I said they would. That satisfied him, or at least it will after he hears from enough of them."

Prisoners were crowding forward frantically, each anxious to make the first call. Using a gun as a pointer, Ribold picked the ones he thought could tell the most convincing tale. He gestured his first choice to the telephone, then stepped back to press the wall switch, for the buzzer had given another summons.

"When this red tape has been unwound," stated Ribold, "I shall leave you here while I collect the fund. How long you will all remain depends on circumstance. I am sure that Aldan will give me cash for those certified checks, so I can start for Lisbon at once. Perhaps by morning, you can be released. Possibly I may demand a longer wait—"

Ribold's speculations ceased. At that moment, the last cab had stopped. Something was happening to the Tooth who opened the door.

A chunk of blackness swooped like a living arm, drove the fellow's gun straight upward, and descended with a hard thud to his skull.

As the thug collapsed, blackness materialized into a cloaked fighter who sprang from the cab and whirled like a human gun turret, blasting the fake cab drivers who served the Hydra. The Shadow was in action at his mightiest, losing no time in withering that horde of foemen.

They were far too many for any single fighter to handle, but The Shadow had a capable ally. As a whole crew of gunners swept across the courtyard to gain a sure angle of fire against The Shadow, Moe spurted his cab into their midst. Thugs went flying right and left, save for a hapless few who were bashed against the wall. With a spin of the wheel, Moe was around again, looking for more human marks.

These Blue Spot taxis were good jobs, Moe learned. They could turn on a dime, and people simply couldn't dodge them. With The Shadow knocking off Hydra followers like clay pigeons, Moe was turning the remainder into sheep, literally herding them with his cab into the hands of prisoners, who were now on the loose and showing their mettle.

Ribold was wrenching himself from half a dozen hands. The Shadow, so far, hadn't time to deal with him. It was all the better, for The Shadow wanted to keep Head Twelve alive, rather than have the Hydra sprout two others like him.

But Ribold was loose, aiming at his cloaked foe. As the Head fired, The Shadow faded, half faking a fall to make Ribold forget other foemen in his overzeal.

Luhrig saw The Shadow's falter and misunderstood it. Whipping out the gun that Ribold didn't know he had, Luhrig poured close-range shots into the murderous Head.

As Ribold struck the cement court, riddled with bullets, Luhrig gave a grateful cry to see The Shadow rising. By then, battle was ended. Dead, wounded, captured, the Hydra's men had met with complete disaster.

THE SHADOW gestured Luhrig to the phone. Pocketing his gun, the grim-jawed man put in a prompt call to the commissioner and told him the truth about Ribold, adding that Head Twelve was dead.

By then, The Shadow was placing the Hydra's followers in batches and pointing the members of the Worldwide Friendship Society to their cabs.

With former passengers as drivers, the Blue Spots wheeled out to the street, The Shadow standing with one hand on the switch, the other keeping a gun turned toward the line of huddled prisoners, whose own guns were heaped on the other side of the court.

"The commissioner is coming right over," announced Luhrig. "I told him he would find an open alley when he arrived. He is bringing men to take away the prisoners. Kerland and Aldan are coming with him."

With a low laugh of approval, The Shadow moved away, leaving the switch to Luhrig, whose eyes followed the mysterious cloaked being with an expression of full admiration. The last of the cabs was gone, with the exception of Moe's. The Shadow's driver followed his chief along the row of prisoners, awaiting new orders from him.

The telephone bell began to ring. Turning, The Shadow saw Luhrig leave the switch to answer it. Finishing his patrol, The Shadow returned to the near end of the row. Luhrig was putting down the telephone as The Shadow gave the prisoners another glance.

And then—close by The Shadow's ear came a voice, a low harsh tone that carried strange foreboding. It said:

"You did me a good turn, Shadow. I appreciated it when it happened, but matters are different now. The Hydra is too big for you to ever squelch. We both know its way: how its remaining Heads appoint new ones whenever such a member dies."

A revolver was pressing between The Shadow's shoulders to emphasize the words to come.

"I have just heard from the Hydra," the harsh voice continued. "I have been offered the post of Head Fourteen. Any man would be a fool to refuse such a proposition, especially when he is in a position to immediately dispose of the Hydra's only menace. I am no fool, Shadow!"

The speaker was Hubert Luhrig! Loyal through it all, Luhrig had accepted the insidious offer of the Hydra to become one of the replacements for the very Head that he himself had killed, Hart Ribold!

Only the Hydra could have inspired such double-dyed treachery in any human. Ready to serve his manifold master, Luhrig meant his threat of death.

Hard upon his victory over Ribold, The Shadow was on the verge of defeat and doom, both to be delivered by Hubert Luhrig, Hydra Head Fourteen!

## CHAPTER XIX
## CRIME TRIES TWICE

ONE question was pounding through The Shadow's brain: why didn't Luhrig deliver the death shot?

It was a question that must be answered instantly; yet, for once, The Shadow groped. The Hydra menace had multiplied to so incredible a degree that answers simply wouldn't seem to come. Then, like a flash, The Shadow saw the answer.

It was pacing the courtyard in the person of Moe.

Luhrig was holding The Shadow's fate in abeyance until he'd be sure of getting Shrevvy, too. As a Hydra Head, Luhrig wanted a profitable future, not quick death as vengeance for The Shadow's. Moe's handling of the juggernaut cab had given Luhrig respect for the cabby's ingenuity. He was waiting for Moe to pace to the proper angle and the right range, where a quick shot would get him after The Shadow was finished.

And Moe was on his way to the fatal spot, at this moment only a few paces short of it!

If The Shadow had whirled, he'd have done something Luhrig wanted. Cleverly, the newly appointed Head had let his gun recede, so The Shadow couldn't catch it with his shoulder blade while starting a spin.

There was only one other course. The Shadow took it on the instant, though it was something that Luhrig preferred. With a long fling, The Shadow dived to the cement courtyard ahead of Luhrig's gunshots.

Perfect for Luhrig. With three shots from his reloaded gun, he'd surely bag The Shadow and have a clear aim at Moe. The courtyard was wide open. It didn't have a single spot of shelter. At least, so Luhrig thought. In becoming an inhuman Hydra Head, he had forgotten the human element, if it could be termed such.

As Luhrig's first shot whined above The Shadow's head, the black-cloaked diver veered into the ranks of the nearest prisoners, those fake cab drivers who had served as Hydra Teeth. He was clutching two of them as Luhrig's next bullet chipped the cement, this shot grazing The Shadow's leg.

Then the cloaked fighter was up and around, two struggling men between himself and Luhrig before the Head could fire the third and fatal shot!

The Shadow didn't keep these men as human shields. They were still too active. Instead, he used them as missiles, heaving them hard at Luhrig. Then The Shadow was wheeling away, bringing his own guns into action, while Luhrig, half dragging the men who had encountered him, was making for the pile of discarded guns.

Half a dozen hitherto helpless Teeth were piling for The Shadow, clutching him frantically to destroy his aim. As The Shadow flung them off, they dived for the gun heap to become Teeth again. Servers of a man they recognized as a new Hydra Head, Hubert Luhrig!

It was battle all over again, this time with no aid for The Shadow. Whipping loose, the cloaked fighter thrust Moe into the cab, but his aide was helpless, for the vehicle was pointed out into the alley. Moe heard The Shadow's quick command, "Get started!" but he was loath to obey.

Then The Shadow was doing the amazing. He was among the tables, jabbing shots from behind them. As Luhrig dodged behind a screen of followers, The Shadow planked one table on another and sprang on both, carrying a chair to top the pyramid. He was short on bullets and men were almost at the tables, pointing guns upward to clip their black-clad foe, when The Shadow delivered a single, timely shot.

He aimed it for one of the big glass roof panes. His shot cracked the square just above the heads of aiming foemen. Down came the shattered mass of heavy frosting, its chunks felling the men who didn't dive away. Even Luhrig was forced to dodge from the spot that he had reached.

That was their last chance at The Shadow. A spring from upper table to chair; then, like a trick balancer, The Shadow was tumbling the pyramid forward. Down came the furniture at other aiming men, while The Shadow's hands, swooping upward at a forward angle, caught the edge of the empty frame from which he had shot the glass and took himself up through, and out, with a strong lift of his forearms!

A dozen feet to that roof, which seemingly could give no exit. The Shadow had cut three fourths of the distance with his improvised pyramid, and chopped an outlet which he first used as a missile. His final launch was simplicity itself. He was gone while enemies were still taking the brunt of the final missiles, in the form of tables and chairs that he had toppled at them!

And Moe was gone, too, spurting his car through the alley. There was a note close to accusation in The Shadow's parting laugh, which

Moe took as a personal rebuke for not obeying orders. Straight through the wall that looked like brick but wasn't, Moe hurled his car, to learn why The Shadow had wanted him to go.

Weston and the police cars had arrived. The barrier being shut, the fake housefront had fooled them. They didn't know how to reach the source of gunfire. Sight of Moe's cab ripping out through brick-painted canvas told the police the proper place to go.

The patrols wheeled into the courtyard. There, frantic crooks were bringing more than panic on themselves. They were shooting at the glass roof, hoping to clip The Shadow, but they were only bringing frosted glass down upon one another.

They couldn't find The Shadow, because he was using the simple system of moving to the squares that were broken by gunfire. Trying new panes all the while, crooks were forgetting the blackened blocks that were perfect blending spots for The Shadow.

Of those who wheeled to meet the arriving police, only one man was dangerous. He was Luhrig, the new Hydra Head. Spotting Weston, Luhrig aimed point-blank, but never fired. From an empty space above, The Shadow staggered Luhrig with the last shot from his otherwise empty guns. As Luhrig reeled, policemen flattened him among his sagging followers.

Better to have left him wounded from The Shadow's bullet. Two new Hydra Heads would crop up to replace dead No. 14!

DURING the progress of this second garden party, the siege had lifted at Ilchester's. Guests, among whom were Clyde Burke, Harry Vincent and Margo Lane, had been humoring old Ira Ilchester and finding him a responsive but wheedly old gentleman.

The party was being held in Ilchester's first-floor parlor when Inspector Cardona shouldered into the house. At first, Ilchester had shown panic, but when he learned that Hydra Head Twelve was dead, he became elated.

A keen old man with sharp face and bright, beady eyes, Ilchester had craned his neck forward, one hand to his ear, while Cardona related the facts concerning Hart Ribold.

Knowing nothing about the prompt way in which Hubert Luhrig had accepted appointment as another Hydra Head, Cardona bluntly announced that the menace was permanently ended. Which, in Ilchester's language, called for a celebration. He sent his butler down to the cellar for some of his best wine.

The wine had just arrived when Ilchester received a phone call. He answered it and chortled happily. Laying the phone aside, he said he'd received new word from Commissioner Weston, corroborating Cardona's tidings. But Ilchester's glee soured when he saw the bottles that the butler had brought.

"Bah! These are not the best!" snapped Ilchester. "We can choose better for ourselves. To the cellar, everyone, to take your choice of the best that we can find!"

When they reached the cellar, Ilchester smiled. He pointed to a flight of narrow steps and beckoned. They followed the sharp-faced man down into the bomb shelter that he had built. It was a square room, supplied with all the comforts for a long stay. Gesturing his guests to chairs, Ilchester paced over to the far wall.

With a smile at his own expense, Ilchester faced a square of cement which looked quite new. It was where his diggers had struck the old water main, he said. Though no longer in use, the pipe was still city property, hence it had to be covered again.

"And to think," declared Ilchester, "that I intended to stay cooped up in this horrible hole! Why, I even had these!" From a rack on the wall, he produced a pair of long-barreled revolvers. "I kept them here thinking I would need them for my self-defense.

"But that time is over. Really over." Ilchester chortled as he cocked the loaded guns. "Because now I am the hunter, not the hunted. More than that"—the old man's eyes were narrow slits, his tone a ferocious gloat—"I have already trapped my prey. Allow me to introduce myself. I am Hydra Head Fifteen!"

LISTENERS didn't believe it until they made slight motions. Then Ilchester became so threatening with the guns that they subsided.

Ilchester laughed in gritty style as he looked over his human prizes. There were four who counted: Inspector Cardona first; next Burke, the troublesome reporter; third, the chap Vincent, who had meddled with the Hydra's business, too.

Finally, Ilchester's cunning eyes settled on Margo Lane. She was a close friend of Lamont Cranston, reputed millionaire. For Margo alone, Ilchester could demand a sizeable ransom. The look that he gave the others so belittled them that they felt themselves slated for death, rather than belonging in Margo's category.

Back and forth, with short paces, Ilchester's feet clicked on the cement, but always his thin hands were steady with their guns, while he declaimed more for his own amusement than the information of his prisoners:

"I was wealthy once. Very wealthy." Ilchester's

features mingled smiles and frowns. "So wealthy that I became a philanthropist. A bad mistake, for it made me a forgotten man. I might as well have been dead, with my name engraved on a tombstone, as to have it placed on buildings which my money had endowed.

"My fortune dwindled from many causes. Where, then, was my share of wealth? Gone into things for which I had no use. My last endowment, that library of mine! Bah! I would have sold it, but the prices offered were insults. I had no room for it, having been forced to sell my country mansion. So I gave my books away."

The guns were quivering in Ilchester's hands, but not because his grip had weakened. Weapons seemed eager of their own accord, like deadly fangs of snakes about to strike.

Harry and Clyde were exchanging looks with Cardona. They were ready to rush those guns, though chances were that two men would be doomed. The third might make it before Ilchester could again cock one of the old-fashioned weapons.

"Then came the Hydra," spoke Ilchester, "as personified by Head No. 12. The Hydra, hungrily demanding what money I had left. I feared... and I admired. The Hydra was honest in its way. It didn't wheedle for funds and then forget me. It asked for them outright.

"The Hydra must have known my thoughts. When the twelfth Head was lopped tonight, the others got together. They needed new Heads and they considered me, because as a threatened man I was in the very position to turn the game about. I could turn guests into prisoners and demand a ransom by merely cocking these guns.

"That phone call I answered wasn't from Commissioner Weston. It was from the Hydra, offering me the chance that I accepted. I shall have wealth equal to my former dreams! Crime—even murder—why should I forego it? I have experienced everything else. With the Hydra there can be no penalty. Because by now the Hydra's only dangerous enemy is dead. I mean The Shadow!"

That was enough for the trapped men. Their glances said one word:

"Now." Leaving Margo by the steps, the three men charged. Clyde and Harry were ahead of Cardona, but not because Joe wanted it that way. They were simply quicker on the takeoff, that was all.

A takeoff to doom!

For with the moment of their lunge, Ilchester thrust his guns at Harry and Clyde respectively. Before they'd covered three paces, the new Hydra Head fired both weapons point-blank at his victims!

TREMENDOUS was the blast, far greater than a double discharge of revolvers could produce. Like the explosion at Glencoe's, this one rocked the premises. Only stone walls could have stood its force, which they did. But cement gave, the thin layer beneath Ilchester's feet. It sprouted upward like the mushroom puff of a fired oil well, and Ilchester went with it.

The man of intended murder seemed to fly apart. His guns were scaling to the ceiling as they flashed. Harry and Clyde were hurled to the wall, not by the impact of bullets but by the concussion from the floor. They found themselves on the floor beside Margo and Cardona, staring at the whitish smoke that issued in grotesque shape from the great gap in the cement.

The white cloud cleared. Blackness replaced it in the shape of a rising form. There stood The Shadow, up through the hole that he had blasted with a well-placed charge of explosive. He'd come to Ilchester's after his fray with Luhrig, knowing quite well what he might find there.

Instead of wasting effort upon the cellar door that Ilchester had barred above the stairs, The Shadow had remembered the old water main. He'd crawled through it, and listened to Ilchester's threats and paces while setting the charge that could alone effect the rescue of four helpless prisoners.

The way above was open, for the upper door was bolted from this side. The Shadow gestured his friends along that route, while he returned to the underground tunnel from which he had arrived. As the four ascended the steps to freedom, they heard the strains of a hollow, deep-toned laugh.

Regretful mirth, The Shadow's. Not so much for Ira Ilchester, who had voluntarily accepted his course of evil, as for Hydra Head Fifteen, which the dead man represented. For Ilchester's death would bring another duo to the many-brained monster of crime.

Tonight, in winning three triumphs over the Hydra, The Shadow had actually added four future tasks to the already formidable campaign that he had undertaken.

Without a doubt, the greatest foe that The Shadow had ever met was that one composed of many: the Hydra.

## CHAPTER XX
### THE STROKE SUPREME

LAMONT CRANSTON was reading up on mythology. He already knew that the Hydra was a many-headed monster, but he wanted to know what was done about it in ancient times. Cranston learned that a gentleman named Hercules had strangled the creature, more or less.

So Cranston went to the telephone and called Burbank, who connected him with The Shadow. In identical voices they discussed the Hydra, and Cranston learned a few things about the modern model. He had a chat on the subject later, with Richards, his valet.

"About the Hydra, Richards—"

"A horrible creature, Mr. Cranston," agreed Richards. "Such a plethora of information that one hears on the radio. Yet no one seems to know what to do about it."

"I do," asserted Cranston. "It must be strangled."

"But how, sir, with so many Heads?"

"That's just it, Richards. Those Heads have been deprived of Eyes, Ears and Teeth. Now is the time to defeat them."

"Very good, sir," Richards acknowledged. "I trust that you will voice your opinion to the civic committee."

Something other than the civic committee was at that moment busy on the Hydra situation. The Shadow was in his sanctum, studying reports from agents. To those from Clyde and Harry, The Shadow added another, the mutual report of Cliff Marsland and his sidekick, Hawkeye, who covered the underworld.

What The Shadow had told Cranston seemed definitely true. Shorn of lesser workers, the Hydra was dependent solely on its Heads. They would soon grow the needed members with which they saw, heard, and bit their way to supercrime. The time to stop the Hydra was now.

Rutledge Mann had submitted his usual report. Recommended investments were doing better than before. New stocks were being issued in all the companies that Glencoe liked. But The Shadow was interested in all reports only so far as they pertained directly to crime.

Leaving the sanctum, The Shadow paid a Cranston visit to Weston's office. Bardell was there with a list of names for his committee. He'd just about given up after Luhrig and Ilchester had swung over to the Hydra. Then, on the basis that no men were perfect, Bardell had formed his committee anyway.

"Nothing can be lost," declared Bardell, "and much can be gained. Our only danger is that the Hydra may threaten us. On that account, we have not yet decided upon a meeting place."

The Shadow pondered over that one; then, in Cranston's casual style, he stated that he could find one. Indeed, he could think of one already, the roof garden of the old Hotel Marmora. It was being remodeled into a private dining room and would probably be available whenever the committee required it.

When Weston suggested tomorrow evening, The Shadow called the Marmora and found that it could be arranged. The rest of that day he spent with his agents. There were four that he could use: Harry, Clyde, Cliff and Hawkeye.

Burbank and Moe being required for their present duties, The Shadow wanted another, because for his particular purpose he required five. So he sent for Miles Crofton, an aviator who had served him on other important occasions.

That done, The Shadow made provision for a sixth man, one whose special abilities would prove very useful.

LATE the next afternoon, The Shadow entered Moe's cab. Not the Blue Spot, but the old reliable, again in service. A week had passed since the Ribold-Luhrig fray, and out of that entire period Moe had but one thing to report to his cloaked chief. The incident had occurred today.

"Got rid of the Blue Spot this afternoon," said Moe. "Took it out for another cruise and picked up a fare who steered me to a repair shop. They were buying cabs. Paid me cash on the line, no questions asked."

Moe exhibited the cash in question, a fistful of it. Quite interesting, since Moe hadn't owned the Blue Spot cab. The Shadow's laugh anticipated further facts from Moe. They came.

"They had some other hacks there," continued Moe. "All new paint jobs. Looks like they've been calling in all that were left. They thought I was another guy named Joe who didn't get around to that big brawl where you staged the cleanup."

Modest of Moe to overlook the helpful part that he had played in the courtyard fight. But The Shadow was more interested in what had happened today. Questioning Moe, he learned that the repair shop where the Blue Spot cabs were being camouflaged occupied a portion of a warehouse belonging to the Diana Storage Co. Apparently the repair shop had served previously as a garage for the trucks that served the storage company.

But there were no trucks there any longer. Nothing but the cabs that were undergoing transformation. Again The Shadow laughed. He could deal in camouflage, too, as he intended to prove before this night was over.

Becoming Cranston, The Shadow stopped at the Cobalt Club, to find Commissioner Weston all enthused about tonight's committee meeting. When The Shadow casually stated that he wouldn't be there, Weston glared indignantly, then changed his expression when he thought he understood.

"I know you're not on the committee, Cranston," declared the commissioner. "But you will have to help me explain matters to the members. Bardell has chosen a dozen men of repute, who have heard only vaguely of the Hydra menace. Your recovery of the crown gems is something they would like to hear about, firsthand.

"Similarly, I think Miss Lane's testimony would help, since she was the target of crime in the Ilchester episode. And so"—Weston's eyes showed a twinkle—"I would appreciate it if you would bring Miss Lane to the meeting. It wouldn't chance that you have a date with her this evening?"

It chanced that Cranston had. That was all arranged, with The Shadow fishing for the very invitation that Weston extended. But it wasn't The Shadow who would take Margo to the Hotel Marmora. The assignment belonged to the real Lamont Cranston.

The Shadow notified his double in a most unusual way.

When the phone rang at Cranston's, both Richards and his master answered it, one downstairs, the other on the second floor. When he heard Richards speak, Cranston hung up, as he left most of his calls to the valet.

Strolling to the top of the stairs, Cranston saw Richards coming from the telephone. Looking upstairs, the valet inquired:

"Were you jesting, sir?"

"About what, Richards?"

"That phone call," explained Richards. "There was no one on the wire. Except you, sir, using the extension phone. I distinctly heard you say 'tallyho' before you hung up."

For a moment, Cranston's eyebrows raised. Then:

"An odd habit of mine," he said. "Acquired from my fox-hunting friends in England. Curious how it cropped up on me. By the way, Richards, tell Stanley to bring the car. I am going into town at once."

Tallyho!

The token that The Shadow had promised. The word that would bring Cranston to the kill of something more than a mere fox. In this case, it could apply to one creature only: the Hydra!

WHEN the commissioner's official car arrived at the old Hotel Marmora, it was accompanied by a flock of motorcycles, whose riders were again convoying their friend and hero, Lamont Cranston, along with the police commissioner. Margo Lane also alighted, and the trio entered the hotel.

Again, Weston thanked Cranston for selecting this meeting place. By stationing detectives in the lobby, Weston was protecting the upper floors, including the roof dining room.

Inspector Cardona joined the group and went up in the elevator, since he was to testify before the civic committee, too. At the top floor, the arrivals were received by an African attendant in a resplendent uniform. Hired specially for this occasion, he bowed them to the remodeled dining room, where Dustin Bardell and the rest of the committee awaited.

Placed beside Cranston, Margo glanced about at the decorations of the new dining room. It bore no resemblance to an old-fashioned roof garden, the sort of place that would have full-length windows opening outdoors. Instead, it was like a modern nightclub, sleek and streamlined.

An oblong room, with smooth, unbroken walls done in tasteful style, a compromise between plain papering and mural paintings. A plain pattern would have made the place boxlike, whereas murals would be too garish. So the decorator had chosen an ornamental wallpaper bearing pictures of old-time ships in New York harbor.

The same motif was repeated all about the room, there being just enough variety in the design to make it interesting. Margo was counting the masts on an old frigate, when Cranston quietly informed her that the meeting had been called to order.

Amid the dozen committee members, one man had risen: Dustin Bardell. Bluntly, he was voicing the sentiments of his companions, who listened approvingly, their faces firm with dignity. What Bardell had to say was very pointed.

"Crime has gone beyond all bounds," declared Bardell. "We concur in the opinion that the law is unable to cope with the monster known as the Hydra. For example"—he swung to Weston—"can you tell me, commissioner, how many Hydra Heads are still active?"

Weston shook his head.

"You are admitting negligence," snapped Bardell. "I have been able to compute the number. My records show that Heads Two, Three, Five and Six are men who have purposely disappeared from sight. Heads Four, Seven, Ten, Twelve, Fourteen and Fifteen have been eliminated, not by you, commissioner, but by The Shadow.

"Allowing for five Heads with numbers lower than Fourteen, six new appointments after Ribold's death; eliminating two, namely Luhrig and Ilchester, the Hydra should by now have four more. Five and four are nine in all—do you follow me, commissioner?"

Weston was using his fingers on which to count, and Joe Cardona was trying to help him, which mixed them both. Bardell gave a pleased chuckle.

"I know more about the Hydra than you do, commissioner," declared Bardell. "For instance, it has occurred to me that Head No. 1, the original Hydra, is still at large and active."

"Impossible!" exclaimed Weston. "Why, then the Hydra would actually be embodied in a single man, the rest of the so-called Heads being his lieutenants. I couldn't believe that, Bardell, not without proof!"

Hands in his pockets, Bardell bowed. As his face came up, it displayed a vicious glare, as fiendish a gloat as any that Weston and his companions had ever seen. Bardell's eyes glinted like steel, as did the object that his hand whipped from his pocket. For the object in question was steel. It was a revolver.

The gun's sparkle flashed a signal for others. The rest of the committee men were on their feet, producing guns. Those prominent persons chosen by Bardell to aid in a campaign against crime were showing their preference for evil.

Bardell was Head No. 1, the real Hydra! These others were the remaining Heads that he had appointed to replace those lopped by The Shadow. An organization by one superbrain, the Hydra, with lieutenants to whom that leader had granted title equal to his own.

Such was the Hydra, personified by Dustin Bardell & Co. Deprived of lesser workers, the Heads were taking over on their own. This was crime's stroke supreme!

## CHAPTER XXI
## TOO MANY SHADOWS

WHILE the many Hydra Heads held their prisoners helpless, Dustin Bardell explained the reason for his supreme stroke. He began with a few preliminary remarks, delivered in caustic style.

"New York needs a new police commissioner," decided Bardell. "You have been very inefficient, Weston, as we, the Hydra, are qualified to judge. As for your ace inspector, we have found Cardona stupid but troublesome. So we shall dispose of you both."

Looming gun muzzles backed the Hydra's threat, but Bardell did not give the order for slaughter. He preferred more subtle methods of delivering death to helpless victims. Besides, he had more to say.

"However, commissioner," the chief Head gloated, "you must not flatter yourself with thoughts of importance. We could put up with you and Cardona, if we chose. We staged this stroke for the prime purpose of trapping our only dangerous enemy, The Shadow!"

With that, Bardell turned his eyes directly upon Lamont Cranston!

The way Cranston took it was remarkable. Glancing toward her companion, Margo was amazed at his calmness. She'd always thought that in a pinch like this, Cranston would galvanize into The Shadow in a trice. Instead, he was blandly returning Bardell's gaze.

"Come, Cranston!" sneered Bardell. "You know that Willard Mance was Head No. 4. We finally learned that he went to your home after he had murdered Edmund Glencoe. Which proves that Mance had marked you as The Shadow!"

"So that was it!" remarked Cranston. "I wondered why Mance talked about a showdown over something that I couldn't understand."

"Therefore, you killed Mance—"

"Because I had no other choice. The elephant gun went off and that was the end of him. When I learned he was already supposed to be dead, I hushed up the matter."

Cranston's reference to an elephant gun left Bardell somewhat puzzled. Thinking in terms of .45 automatics, Bardell was finding it hard to visualize Cranston as The Shadow. Then:

"You can't deny your identity," asserted Bardell. "Your recovery of those jewels was another giveaway."

"A mere accident," insisted Cranston. "You see—"

"Your broker kept snooping into my investments," interrupted Bardell. "You should have learned enough to know that I controlled the companies in which Glencoe had promised to buy stock. I was getting mine from Glencoe while Mance was getting his!"

Cranston simply sat speechless. He hadn't an idea that any such thing was going on. The Shadow should have told him.

"I covered my trail well," continued Bardell, "until the night when Ribold died. Knowing that you were The Shadow, I tried to finish you, Cranston. I was with the commissioner when he heard of Ribold's death, and I stayed at the club when he left.

"From there I phoned Luhrig and Ilchester, appointing them Hydra Heads. One was to kill you, Cranston, the other to trap the Lane girl, in case the first missed out. You finished them both, and from that time on, you should have marked me as the Hydra. Furthermore, there are many other heads working for me, that you do not know about!"

The fact was self-evident. Only Bardell could have signed up Luhrig and Ilchester so promptly after Ribold's death. What amazed the listeners, Cranston included, was that The Shadow hadn't divined those facts himself. True, no one else had grasped them, but analyzing such matters was The Shadow's specialty.

Perhaps The Shadow did know!

If so, he had been letting Bardell live on sufferance until the present. Worried by the thought, Bardell had staged his present trick of forming a committee all of Hydra Heads. If only The Shadow could have foreseen that prospect, too!

Apparently The Shadow hadn't. There was no place for him to be concealed in this room of barren walls, with its heavy, bolted door. Hence Bardell, confident that The Shadow would not miss this meeting, was more than positive that Cranston was The Shadow.

Venom flashing from his eyes, the Hydra could wait no longer to dispose of his archfoe. With a snarl that promised death, Bardell thrust his gun toward Cranston.

FIERCE, challenging was the mighty laugh that interrupted, a mirth so unmistakable that Bardell forgot his prey for the moment. A dozen Hydra Heads were turning, all with guns, hoping to deal with a lone foe. Bardell's theory regarding Cranston was therewith rejected. The Shadow's laugh hadn't come from Cranston's lips.

A laugh from nowhere!

Such was the effect, until Bardell broke the spell by snarling across his shoulder to Cranston:

"Another trick of yours, Shadow! You can't be nowhere anymore than you can hope to be everywhere."

Bardell was wrong. Amid the snarled statement, The Shadow arrived from nowhere and appeared everywhere. The echoes of his laugh were drowned by surrounding crashes as the side walls of the room broke open, delivering six fighters cloaked in black.

Six Shadows, three to a wall, each with a brace of automatics. Twelve guns in all, to match the weapons of the Hydra. Those guns talked ahead of their rivals. Automatics were jabbing deadly tongues of flame, while revolvers were merely glinting in the light, as their owners swung them to aim.

This was The Shadow's way of strangling the Hydra. Bringing its Heads together, he was smothering them en masse with a blanket of gunfire. If the Hydra could have twelve Heads, The Shadow could supply six Selves. It stood proven.

Every revolver had been beaten to the shot. Each of six Shadows had picked a pair of Hydra Heads. Only Bardell remained unscathed, for he had dodged instead of trying to shoot. Now, Bardell was springing to the door, unbolting it under a shield of crippled lieutenants, those who had managed to detach themselves from their more seriously wounded companions.

Weston and Cardona were after the remnants of the villainous tribe. Cranston remained calmly at the table, restraining Margo. Quite foolish, Cranston thought it, to block off six avenging Shadows from their prey. Weston and Cardona were too impetuous.

Yanking the door wide, Bardell dashed through. Six other Heads were behind him, but their dash didn't last. They wagged guns back at Weston and Cardona, who ducked for cover; but the delay suited the giant African who was standing outside the door.

His name was Jericho and he worked for The Shadow. Plucking the crippled Hydra Heads in pairs, Jericho clapped their skulls together and tossed them aside, using each pair as a shield, until he thrust his massive hands for the next two comers.

The last pair offered trouble. They were aiming their guns when Jericho reached them. But by then, a flood of Shadows was upon them from the rear, snatching their weapons away from them while Jericho took the necks of his foemen and showed what should be done to Hydra Heads.

Only one Head had escaped, the one who was truly the Hydra, Dustin Bardell. He was in an elevator, going down; but in a second car, The Shadow followed. Five other Shadows were taking to a stairway, removing their cloaks and hats. They weren't the one and only Shadow; he had taken the Hydra's trail. These were The Shadow's secret agents, the five that he had chosen to aid him in a multiple appearance.

Back in the dining room, Lamont Cranston was pointing to the gaping walls. There, Margo Lane saw six deep, full-length windows, a feature of the old Marmora roof garden in the days when a sixteen-story hotel offered a good view of Manhattan.

Those deep-set spaces had been papered over. Six Shadows had reached the windows along the narrow promenade outside the garden. Screened only by wallpaper, they were ready to rip through from the moment the meeting began. They had waited only for Dustin Bardell to declare himself the supreme Hydra.

It happened that The Shadow, as Cranston, had suggested this meeting place, knowing how effective its arrangements could be. Conversely Bardell, the Hydra, had totally overlooked the purpose behind the suggestion.

RACING from the Hotel Marmora, Bardell was on his way to the Diana Storage Co. Gesturing his revolver, Bardell frightened away the cabby who had brought him and dashed into the repair shop that had once been a garage.

In answer to Bardell's bellows, men hurried down from storage rooms on the floor above.

They were the Heads that Bardell had written off. Foremost of these men who had disappeared was Lloyd Casler. Bardell had mentioned him along with lopped Heads, purely because Casler had been trapped in crime by The Shadow.

Bardell gestured his living associates to the repainted cabs. When they hesitated, the chief Hydra roared:

"Forget Glencoe's treasures stored upstairs! Let the police recover them, as they did the bank money and the crown jewels. The Hydra still lives and it yet possesses Heads! We are stronger now than when we first encountered The Shadow! But time is short and we cannot afford to waste it!"

Time was too short. As taxicabs wheeled from the garage, the whines of sirens came from all around. Scattering, the Heads drove their vehicles savagely, but to no avail. Tuned to the shrieking sirens was the laugh of the fighter who had purposely brought police cars along this trail.

Again The Shadow seemed to be nowhere, yet everywhere. He was shifting rapidly as he spurted his guns at the tires of the fugitive cabs. They weren't armored like the bantam car that had once served the Hydra. These cabs were vulnerable.

So were their occupants. Some were clipped by The Shadow's gunfire. Others wrecked their cabs when his bullets burst their tires. As they clambered out with guns, the Heads were confronted by arriving police, who gave them short shrift. The desperate criminals wanted to fight to the finish.

So they did—to their own finish.

One alone managed to offset the odds of many police guns. Out of his wrecked cab, Dustin Bardell flung himself across the hood to reach the sidewalk side. Turning spryly about, he jutted his gun across the hood, hoping to riddle three motorcycle cops who were already shooting after him.

From behind Bardell came a sinister laugh, the final warning of The Shadow. Swinging about, Bardell jabbed shots at blackness, probing for a foeman that he couldn't find. Blackness was thick and plentiful, too great an expanse for Bardell's frantic shots to cover. Besides, it was filled with shelters—doorways, house steps, and other objects that he couldn't see.

One shot answered the Hydra's frenzied volley.

Clipped by The Shadow's unerring aim, Bardell jolted high, twisting half across the hood of the cab, his gun hand going ahead of him. A hand with an empty gun that it couldn't aim; but that was something the motorcycle cops didn't know.

Three police guns spoke, completing The Shadow's work. Slumping to the gutter, Dustin Bardell emitted a rattling snarl, his last. That dying gasp had a peculiar likeness to the gargle of a strangling creature.

It represented such. With the death of Dustin Bardell, the Hydra was gone forever, strangled by that modern Hercules, The Shadow. Instead of lopping off Heads, The Shadow had choked them all at once, the final member of that cluster being the one Head that contained the real brain of the Hydra.

Strange was the laugh that faded into night, trailing into echoes that still persisted in this battle area where crime had been totally conquered.

The triumph laugh of The Shadow!

ELSEWHERE, Margo Lane was frowning in perplexity as she stared at Lamont Cranston, riding beside her in Weston's official car. Until tonight, Margo was sure that Lamont must be The Shadow.

And now—

Cranston couldn't be The Shadow, because he'd been himself when the cloaked avalanche smothered the Heads of the Hydra.

And yet—

There could only be one Shadow.

With six on the scene, five must have been mere masqueraders, enlisted to confuse the Hydra Heads. If five were spurious, why not six?

In that case, Lamont Cranston still could be The Shadow. Yes, it would be his way to guise six men in black and let them deliver an attack from ambush under conditions where they couldn't lose.

Still, the laugh that produced six Shadows couldn't possibly have come from Cranston's immobile lips. Or could it?

Strange, this riddle of The Shadow!

THE END

---

**Now on sale:**
**DOC SAVAGE—Volume 1: "Fortress of Solitude" and "The Devil Genghis"**
**DOC SAVAGE—Volume 2: "Resurrection Day" and "Repel"**
**DOC SAVAGE—Volume 3: "Death in Silver" and "The Golden Peril"**

For ordering information, contact sanctumotr@earthlink.net or visit www.nostalgiaventures.com

# INTRODUCING MARGO LANE

Fans of the Shadow radio dramas are often surprised to discover that Lamont Cranston's "friend and companion," Margo Lane, was not part of Walter Gibson's principal cast of characters for the first decade of *The Shadow Magazine*. She was created for radio, where she debuted in 1937, but wasn't featured in the pulp novels until 1941.

During the time Gibson was helping *Shadow* scriptwriter Edward Hale Bierstadt with the radio pilot, "The Death House Rescue," the first draft featured Harry Vincent as The Shadow's chief aide. However, producer/director Clark Andrews and story editor Edith Meiser determined that two male leads wouldn't work. They needed what was known in radio parlance as "vocal contrast."

What was required was a female foil. But no such suitable character had appeared in Gibson's novels. "We had a few girls that would have been all right for it," Gibson admitted, "but they said they would like to have one steady girl. You see, the radio had this limitation. It was only a half-hour show, as opposed to a full-length novel, but even worse.... you always had the limitation of the cast. They wanted to keep a few key actors, and the moment you spread out and got too many actors in a radio show it can get very confusing. So we agreed that we should keep the radio stories within one orbit, where Cranston was more or less a man about town and had a few confidantes, and it was all right to have Margot Lane serve as his principal confidante...."

Thus Vincent was replaced by the newly-minted Margot Lane, a socialite in the mold of Brenda Frazier, the most famous debuante of the late 1930s. Margot was inspired by Broadway ingenue Margot Stevenson, who was starring in the original cast of the Pulitzer Prize-winning *You Can't Take It With You*. "As a matter of fact," she explained, "the character was named after me. I had a boyfriend who was the show's producer. His name was Clark Andrews. When they decided to change The Shadow from just a shadow into a man who could make himself into a shadow or make people believe he was a shadow, they decided he should have a girlfriend. Strangely enough, I didn't get the role originally. Agnes Moorehead played the role the first season. I came in for the summer season, because Agnes wanted a vacation."

The model for the Lamont and Margo relationship was the popular *Thin Man* film series featuring the husband and wife detective team of Nick and Nora Charles, played by William Powell and Myrna Loy. This cozy approach to The Shadow proved such a hit with listeners that radio fans picking up *The Shadow Magazine* began asking to see Margo in print too.

According to Gibson, Street & Smith "wanted a 'running' heroine in both senses of the term." Margo was perfect. "Later I put Margo into the stories judiciously.... a lot of readers began to scream. In fact, a lot of them said she was a troublemaker. That's true, that was the comic relief."

She first popped up in 1941's *The Thunder King*, which opened with Margo (Gibson dropped the 't') impatiently waiting for Cranston at the Hotel Metrolite, as if she had always been present in the series and always would be. Gibson depicted Margo as a sometimes helpful nuisance in the manner of Lois Lane (rumors that the two were sisters reverberated for years), who suspected but could not prove that Lamont was really The Shadow. On radio, of course, she was in on the secret.

Shadow readers quickly split into two camps: those who welcomed her and those who resented this pesky intrusion from the realm of radio. In the July 1st, 1942 letter column, longtime reader Robert Sherwood of Jersey City observed: "Mr. Grant has not explained how she first met The Shadow and entered his exciting service. I think he should. We old-time readers who thrilled to the rescue of Harry Vincent in *The Living Shadow,* the saving of Rutledge Mann in *The Romanoff Jewels,* et cetera, feel that Miss Lane is, somehow, extraneous. This can be easily remedied, you know, so get busy and introduce The Shadow's feminine agent like all the others have been."

In *The Hydra,* Walter Gibson acceded to that request. As he later explained, "She initially met ... Lamont Cranston on a cruise ship, and she looked him up when she got back to New York. She found The Shadow instead. She never knew the difference. So that satisfied readers."

From that point on, just as on radio, there was hardly a Shadow adventure in which Margo Lane did not participate. Although initially reluctant to use her, Gibson ultimately reconciled himself to the value of this Shadow outsider.

"As soon as the war hit," he said, "I couldn't have any of those fantastic spy rings....because they were in reality. And we went into whodunits. Whodunits were fitted perfectly for Cranston around the Cobalt Club and having some peculiar crime in New York. And we wanted to use Margo Lane occasionally because of the radio tie-in, and she fitted into stories as long as Cranston played the debonaire part." The Shadow ultimately promoted Margo to full agent, employing her when he needed a spy in the social world of the cafe set.

Margo Lane was also the punchline of a joke often told around the Street & Smith offices. It went: "Who knows what evil lurks in the hearts of men? *Margo* knows!"

—Will Murray

# A TALE OF TWO CRANSTONS

"The Shadow is in reality Lamont Cranston, wealthy young man about town, who years ago in the Orient learned a strange and mysterious secret—the hypnotic power to cloud men's minds so they cannot see him." The Mutual Broadcasting System introduction was one of the most famous in radio, but fans of Walter Gibson's original pulp novels knew that The Shadow was in reality aviator Kent Allard, and that there was a real Lamont Cranston who permitted the Knight of Darkness to borrow his identity.

Gibson introduced the Cranston identity in his second novel *The Eyes of The Shadow,* which he believed "provided so many details about The Shadow that readers would be apt to think that they had learned practically all there was to know about him." This was corrected in his third novel *The Shadow Laughs.* Returning from a trip to South America, the real Lamont Cranston, begins to doubt his own identity and even his sanity. During his absence, various acquaintances were certain that they had seen him at his New Jersey mansion.

Things were seldom as they appeared in Gibson's stories, and the master of misdirection quickly revealed that Lamont Cranston was but one of many identities assumed by the Dark Avenger. In a chapter titled "Lamont Cranston Talks to Himself," the millionaire awakens to discover a mysterious visitor wearing his own hawklike visage, who demands that Cranston depart immediately on an ocean voyage: "Some people call me The Shadow," explains the man in black. "That is but one identity. I have other personalities that I assume, as easily as I don my black cloak and hat. One of my personalities is that of Lamont Cranston. In the past, I have used it while you were away. At present, I choose to use it now."

**Cranston meets Cranston in *Crime Over Miami.***

When the real Cranston objects, the Master of Darkness warns:

You have been very lax in handling the affairs of Lamont Cranston. There are many matters which you have forgotten. There are many securities, in safe-deposit vaults. You do not know the exact amounts. I do. You have some knowledge of Lamont Cranston's family history. I doubt that you could recall the maiden names of both his grandmothers. I know them. Stay if you wish. Try to denounce me. But remember that I have established the personality of Lamont Cranston. Assuming that you are Lamont Cranston, I know more about you than you know about yourself! So use your own judgment. But I warn you in advance. If you are here when I come tomorrow, there will be but one result. You will be arrested as the impersonator of Lamont Cranston.

Lamont Cranston eventually became an active supporter of The Shadow's war against crime. The real Cranston was prominently featured in *The Black Falcon* (coming up in *The Shadow Volume 5), Atoms of Death* and *Crime Over Miami.* However, Cranston's finest hour occurred in *The Hydra,* a tale that was used as a model for countless comic book stories after a Golden Age editor identified it as the perfect model for a comic book plot.

In the 131st Shadow novel, *The Shadow Unmasks* (August 1, 1937), Walter Gibson finally revealed The Shadow's true identity. "It turned out that he was a famous aviator named Kent Allard who had flown down to the Yucatan to visit some Mayan ruins and had never come back, and they had been searching for him for all these years," Gibson explained at the 1975 New York Comic Art Convention. "But actually he had landed with an Indian tribe and then come back secretly, because he knew that nobody in the underworld would find out who he really was if he was supposed to be buried down in Yucatan." Gibson had based Allard on Colonel Percy Harrison Fawcett, a real-life explorer who had disappeared in 1925 searching for an ancient lost city in the jungles of Brazil.

A more dynamic persona than the languid Cranston, Kent Allard was prominently featured in Gibson's Shadow stories for more than a year, appearing in half the novels published between August 1937 and January 1939 including *The Murder Master,* in which he totally supplanted Cranston. However, the mushrooming popularity of the revamped MBS radio series would firmly establish Lamont Cranston as The Shadow in the minds of radio listeners, resulting in the eventual disappearance of the Kent Allard identity from the pages of *The Shadow Magazine.* —Anthony Tollin